After New Formalism

After New Formalism

POETS ON FORM, NARRATIVE, AND TRADITION

EDITED BY
ANNIE FINCH

STORY LINE PRESS
1999

Published by Story Line Press, Inc.
Three Oaks Farm
P.O. Box 1240
Ashland, OR 97520-0055

This publication was made possible thanks in part to the generous support of the
Andrew W. Mellon Foundation, the Charles Schwab Corporation Foundation, the
Nicholas Roerich Museum, The Oregon Arts Commission, The San Francisco
Foundation and our individual contributors.

Cover design and book design by Paul Moxon
Cover art: Odilon Redon, French (1840–1916), *Mythological Fantasy*, 1905, oil on
canvas. Corporate Art Collection, The Reader's Digest Association, Inc.

Library of Congress Cataloging-in-Publication Data

After New Formalism : poets on form, narrative, and tradition / edited by Annie Finch.
  p. cm.
  ISBN 1-885266-68-5 (alk. paper)
  1. American poetry—20th century—History and criticism—Theory, etc. 2.
Influence
  (literary, artistic, etc.) I. Finch, Annie, 1956–.
  PS325.A28 1999
  808.1—dc21
99-13414

CIP

ACKNOWLEDGMENTS

Elizabeth Alexander, "A Multiplicity of Forms." Originally published in *A Formal Feeling Comes: Poems in Form by Contemporary Women*, ed. Annie Finch, Story Line Press, 1993. **James Cummins**, "Calliope Music: Notes on the Sestina," first appeared in The Antioch Review 55:2 (Spring 1997). **Annie Finch**, "Metrical Diversity." Adapted from "Metrical Diversity," Meter in English, ed. David Baker, University of Arkansas Press, 1997. **Dana Gioia**, "The Poet in an Age of Prose," reprinted from *Can Poetry Matter*, Graywolf Press, 1994. **Daniel Hoffman**, excerpt from "Wings of a Phoenix: Rebellion and Resuscitation in Postmodern American Poetry" reprinted from *Words to Create a World* by Daniel Hoffman, by permission of the author and the University of Michigan Press. **Lynn Keller**, "Measured Feet in Gender-Bender Shoes: The Politics of Poetic Form in a Contemporary Sonnet Sequence." Excerpt from the longer version originally published in *Feminist Measures: Soundings in Poetry and Theory*, ed. Lynn Keller and Cristanne Miller, U. of Michigan Press, 1995, reprinted by permission of the author and the University of Michigan Press. **Paul Lake**, "Verse That Print Bred." Originally published in *Sewanee Review*, Fall 1991. **David Mason**, "Other Voices, Other Lives." Originally published in *Verse*, Winter 1990, pp. 16-21. **Marilyn Nelson**, "Owning the Masters." Originally published under the name Marilyn Nelson Waniek in *Gettysburgh Review*. **Robert McPhillips**, "The New Formalism and The Revival of the Love Lyric." Originally published in *Verse* 7.3 Fall 1990. **Molly Peacock**, "From Gilded Cage to Rib Cage." This essay is adapted and expanded from an essay titled, "One Green, One Blue: One Point About Formal Verse Writing and Another About Women Writing Formal Verse," in *A Formal Feeling Comes: Poems in Form by Contemporary Women*, ed. Annie Finch, Story Line Press, 1993. **Adrienne Rich**, "Format and Form," reprinted from *What is Found There: Notebooks on Poetry and Politics* by Adrienne Rich, by permission of the author and W.W. Norton & Company, Inc. Copyright 1993 by Adrienne Rich. **Anne Stevenson**, "The Trouble With a Word Like Formalism." Originally published in *New Poetry Quarterly*, 2, Winter 1994-95. **Frederick Turner**, "The Inner Meaning of Poetic Form." Originally published in *AWP Chronicle*. **Kevin Walzer**, "Expansive Poetry and Postmodernism." Originally published in *Sparrow*. **Carolyn Beard Whitlow**, "Blues in Black and White": "Verily, Verite" first appeared in *The Kenyon Review*, Vol. XVII, Nos. 3/4, Summer/Fall 1995. "The Hour of Blue" first appeared in *The Kenyon Review*, Vol. XVI, No. 3, Summer 1994. "Supermarket Blues" first appeared in *Wild Meat*, Lost Roads Publications, Providence, R.I., 1986; rpt. in *Thirteenth Moon*, Vol. IX, Nos. 1 & 2, Spring 1991. "Little Girl Blue" first appeared in *Northeast Journal*, Vol. 4, November 1984, rpt. in *Wild Meat*, Lost Roads Publications, Providence, R.I., 1986. "Rockin' a Man, Stone Blind" first appeared in *The Massachusetts Review*, Vol. XXIV, No. 2, Summer 1983; reprinted in *Wild Meat*, Lost Roads Publications, Providence, R.I., 1986, rpt. in *A Formal Feeling Comes: Poems in Form by Contemporary Women*, ed. Annie Finch, Brownsville: Story Line Press, 1994. "Local Call" forthcoming in *The Kenyon Review*, Vol. XVIII, No. 1, Winter 1996. **Christian Wiman**, "An Idea of Order" first appeared in *Poetry*, January 1999. Reprinted by permission of the editor. **Nellie Wong**, "When Form Flowers." Originally published in *A Formal Feeling Comes: Poems in Form by Contemporary Women*, ed. Annie Finch, Story Line Press, 1993.

To my son Julian

CONTENTS

Directions

Contributors   / 225

INTRODUCTION
by Annie Finch

Like many poets who love to write in form, I have nonetheless found myself uncomfortable with the images that have become associated with "new formalist" poetry. Much of the thinking about recent formal poetry has been limited to manifestoes, or appreciations of one poet by another, and the populist aspect of new formalism has led to a strong suspiciousness of "theory" that has been repaid in kind. Some view new formalism not only as insular and reactionary but also as monolithic and monotonous, a movement of predictable aesthetic consequence and little theoretical interest. These stereotypes, unfortunately, have led to the neglect of important potential avenues for the criticism of contemporary poetry.

After New Formalism is in a sense an archaeological endeavor, a cross-section of interesting thinking by poets about formalist poetry over the last decade. Over the years the mission and focus of this book changed to include thoughtful essays by poets engaging with formalism from outside its confines, as well as by younger poets who came to formalism with a more theoretical bent than their elders. While some of the essays here come much closer than others to my own vision of a "multiformalism" that truly encompasses the many formal poetic traditions, including experimental traditions, now native to the United States, this collection of thoughts on form by poets contains fresh insights about the implications of formalism for poetic history, practice, and theory.

The first section, "Traditions," concerns formal poetic traditions, particularly previously neglected traditions that preceded and developed alongside the modernist free-verse revolution. Adrienne Rich, through readings of early twentieth-century poems, rethinks the simplistic associations that often accompany the labels "formal" and "free" verse, while Daniel Hoffman locates the roots of those associations in nineteenth- and twentieth-century industrialization. Dana Gioia distinguishes the new formalist movement itself from the earlier formalist tradition of the mid-twentieth century, and Marilyn Nelson's personal essay articulates one poet's sometimes uneasy peace with traditional formal canons. Other essays in the section take fresh looks at poetic canons and their strengths, limitations, and alternatives. Paul

Lake reassesses the nature of the free verse tradition, arguing that the dominance of free verse reflects and reinforces the primacy of printed over spoken literature; Mark Jarman points out the influence of E.A. Robinson on contemporary narrative poems; and Carol E. Miller traces alternative formal poetic canons by rereading poems of the Harlem Renaissance.

At a time when the term "poetics" has been applied to fields from architecture to cooking, I have entitled the central section "Poetics" in an effort to reclaim the older, narrower sense of that term: technical aspects of poetry. While little critical writing has yet been done on the true variety of poetic forms used by contemporary poets— including oral forms such as chant; newly imported forms such as the ghazal and pantoum; and a large number of experimental forms[1] —this section reflects the renewed interest in several formal poetic techniques and traditional genres that has accompanied new formalism. Carolyn Beard Whitlow, in her memoir on writing blues, and Molly Peacock, in her consideration of the precedents set by women poets in relation to poetic conventions, both discuss the process of adapting traditional forms to contemporary uses. Robert McPhillips discusses the use of a conventional genre, the love lyric, by contemporary poets, and David Mason treats the place of narrative in contemporary poetry, while my own essay on non-iambic meters, Timothy Steele's taxonomy of iambic pentameter, and Jim Cummins' tribute to the sestina form further demonstrate the close attention some contemporary poets are paying to poetic structure.

The essays in the final section, "Directions," take up some of the problems and potential directions of new formalist theory. Kathrine Varnes engages with the vexed question of the place women have so far played in new formalism, and Kevin Walzer discusses formalism in the context of postmodern literary theory. Frederick Feirstein brings his experience as a psychoanalyst to bear on the value of poetic form and narrative, while Allison Cummings considers the relation between poetic form and the poet's subjectivity, and Frederick Turner connects poetic form and narrative to the traditional role of the shaman. Christian Wiman reexamines the late twentieth-century assumption that formal poetry ignores the chaotic and, finally,

---

[1] For a book that includes poems in all these forms and more, with discussions of them by poets, see *An Exaltation of Forms: Contemporary Poets Celebrate the Diversity of Their Art*, edited by Annie Finch and Kathrine Varnes (University of Michigan Press, 1999). For a gathering of more theoretical and scholarly essays on formalist poetics by critics and poets, see *New Formal Poetics*, edited by Annie Finch and Jena Osman (University of Michigan Press, 2000).

Anne Stevenson's pragmatic essay cautions against the whole enterprise of classifying poems in terms of form.

It is exciting to see how much the discourse about formalism changed during the years I was editing this book. I would still like to see much more critical attention to forms from other than European traditions as well as to the procedural and other forms used by "experimental" poets, but I am happy that this book includes essays on themes that were far from the consciousness of most formal poets a decade ago. I am hopeful that *After New Formalism* will play a role in the evolution of critical discussion about new formalism.

Traditions

Format and Form

Adrienne Rich

Long before the invention of the "sound byte," the anarchist poet, essayist, and activist Paul Goodman described the effects of what he called "format" on public language:

> Format.—n. 1. the shape and size of a book as determined by the number of times the original sheet has been folded to form the leaves. 2. the general physical appearance of a book, magazine, or newspaper, such as the type face, binding, quality of paper, margins, etc. 3. the organization, plan, style, or type of something: They tailored their script to a half-hour format. The format of the show allowed for topical and controversial gags. 4. Computer Technol., the organization or disposition of symbols on a magnetic tape, punch card, or the like, in accordance with the input requirement of a computer, card-sort machine, etc....
>
> Format has no literary power, and finally it destroys literary power. It is especially disastrous to the common standard style, because it co-opts it and takes the heart out of it.

Poetic forms—meters, rhyming patterns, the shaping of poems into symmetrical blocks of lines called couplets or stanzas—have existed since poetry was an oral activity. Such forms can easily become format, of course, where the dynamics of experience and desire are forced to fit a pattern to which they have no organic relationship. People are often taught in school to confuse closed poetic forms (or formulas) with poetry itself, the lifeblood of the poem. Or, that a poem consists merely in a series of sentences broken (formatted) into short lines called "free verse." But a closed form like the sestina, the sonnet, and villanelle remains inert formula or format unless the "triggering subject," as Richard Hugo called it, acts on the imagination to make the form evolve, become responsive, or works almost in resistance to the form. It's a struggle not to let the form take over, lapse into format, assimilate the poetry; and that very struggle can produce a movement, a music, of its own.

I think of Gerard Manley Hopkins's "sprung" sonnets, his wrestling not just with diction and grammar, end rhymes and meters, but with his own rebellious heart:

> No worst, there is none. Pitched past pitch of grief,
> More pangs will, schooled at forepangs, wilder wring.
> Comforter, where, where is your comforting:
> Mary, mother of us, where is your relief?

My cries heave, heards-long; huddle in a main, a chief
Woe, world-sorrow; on an age-old anvil wince and sing—
Then lull, then leave off. Fury had shrieked 'No long-
ering! Let me be fell: force I must be fried'.
        O the mind, mind has mountains; cliffs of fall
Frightful, sheer, no-man-fathomed. Hold them cheap
May who ne'er hung there. Nor does long our small
durance deal with that steep or deep. Here! creep,
Wretch, under a comfort served in a whirlwind: all
Life death does end and each day dies with sleep.

And I think of the Jamaican poet Claude McKay, writing, in more traditional meter and diction, of the 1919 "Red Summer" of Black urban uprisings across the United States:

If we must die, let it not be like hogs
Hunted and penned in an inglorious spot,
While round us bark the mad and hungry dogs,
Making their mock at our accursed lot.
If we must die, O let us nobly die,
So that our precious blood may not be shed
In vain; then even the monsters we defy
Shall be constrained to honor us though dead!
O kinsmen! we must meet the common foe!
Though far outnumbered let us show us brave,
And for their thousand blows deal one deathblow!
What though before us lies the open grave?
Like men we'll face the murderous, cowardly pack,
Pressed to the wall, dying, but fighting back!

McKay's likes hearken back to Shakespeare—not, however, to the sonnets, but to the battle speech from Henry V and with a difference: McKay takes the traditional poetic form of the colonizer and turns it into a rebellion cry, takes the poetics of war and turns it into a poetics of resistance.

More than sixty years later, St. Lucian poet Derek Walcott bursts the sonnet while keeping (and adding to) its resonance, breaks it open to his own purposes, a Caribbean poet's confrontation with the contradictions of his middle-class Anglo-Europeanized education, the barbarisms of that civilization as revealed in the slave trade and the Holocaust:

The camps hold their distance—brown chestnuts and gray smoke
that coils like barbed wire. The profit in guilt continues.
Brown pigeons goose-step, squirrels pile up acorns like little shoes,
and most, voiceless as smoke, hushes the peeled bodies
like abandoned kindling. In the clear pools, fat
trout rising to lures bubble in umlauts.
Forty years gone, in my island childhood, I felt that

the gift of poetry had made me one of the chosen,
that all experience was kindling to the fire of the Muse.
Now I see her in autumn on that pine bench where she sits,
their nut-brown ideal, in gold plaits and lederhosen,
the blood drops of poppies embroidered on her white bodice,
the spirit of autumn to ever Hans and Fritz
whose gaze raked the stubble fields when the smoky cries
of rooks were nearly human. They placed their cause in
her cornsilk crown, her cornflower iris,
winnower of chaff for whom the swastikas flash
in skeletal harvests. But had I known then
that the fronds of my island were harrows, its sand the ash
of the distant camps, would I have broken my pen
because this century's pastorals were being written
by the chimneys of Dachau, of Auschwitz, of Sachsenhausen?

In the early 1940s, even as the child Walcott was feeling "the fire of the Muse" on his island, the young woman Muriel Rukeyser was writing her own contradictions as an American Jew into a long sequence exploring war, womanhood, and politics: "Letter to the Front." The first draft of one section was written in the open, long-lined form of most of the other sections of "Letter to the Front." It reads like a working through of the poet's ideas—loose and sometimes explanatory ("[and] in America, we Jews are hostages / in a nation of hostages; we vouch for freedom, / if we are free, all may be free"). The final version is crystalized into fourteen lines, a sonnet that is a kind of prophesying:

To be a Jew in the twentieth century
Is to be offered a gift. If you refuse,
Wishing to be invisible, you choose
Death of the spirit, the stone insanity.
Accepting, take full life. Full agonies:
Your evening deep in labyrinthine blood
Of those who resist, fail, and resist; and God
Reduced to a hostage among hostages.

The gift is torment. Not alone the still
Torture, isolation; or torture of the flesh.
That may come also. But the accepting wish,
The whole and fertile spirit as guarantee
For every human freedom, suffering to be free,
Daring to live for the impossible.

June Jordan has an essay called "The Difficult Miracle of Black Poetry in America: Something of a Sonnet for Phillis Wheatley." (This is the single most cogent, eloquent, compressed piece of writing about the conditions of North American poetry that I know.) Poetic, not pedantic, it talks about the African cultural world Wheatley lost at the age of seven, and the Western literary tradition to which she was introduced via the auction block, as an African child bought in the whim of pity by a liberal Boston couple on a shopping trip for slaves and early recognized as a precocious, a "special" child.

Jordan talks about a vocabulary and imagery of the poet's situation ("It was written, this white man's literature of England, while someone else did the things that have to be done.") What happens when this is the only poetic language available to a slave? Phillis Wheatley was forcibly turned — and then, in frustrated desire, turned herself — to a formulaic language and poetics in which she acquitted herself so well that she is now known as the first African-American poet. Even in so doing, Jordan shows, she kept alive the subversive pulse in her work.

Jordan then writes a sonnet for Wheatley, a sonnet in ringing and relentless dactylic meter, a sonnet impeccably end-rhymed, that says of Wheatley all she could not have said with hope for publication:

> Girl from the realm of birds florid and fleet
> Flying full feather in far or near weather
> Who fell to a dollar lust coffled like meat
> Captured by avarice and hate spit together
> Trembling asthmatic alone on the slave block
> Built by a savagery travelling by carriage
> Viewed like a species of flaw in the livestock
> A child without safety of mother or marriage.
>
> Chosen by whimsy but born to surprise
> They taught you to read but you learned how to write
> Begging the universe into your eyes:
> They dressed you in light but you dreamed with the night.
> From Africa singing of justice and grace,
> Your early verse sweetens the fame of our Race.

Francis X. Alarcon writes his political love sonnets (De Amor Oscuro/ Of Dark Love) to a young farm worker, using fourteen lines without end-rhymes though with the inherent internal rhyming of Spanish, impossible to capture in English translation:

IV

tus manos son dos martillos que clavan
y desclavan alegres la manana,
tiernos punos desdoblados de tierra,
dulces pencas de platanos pequenos
tus manos huelen a las zarzamoras
que cosechas en los campos que roban
tu sudor a dos dolares el bote,
son duras, tibias, jovenes y sabias
azadones que traen pan a las mesas,
oscuras piedras que al chocar dan luz
gozo, sosten, ancla del mundo entero
yo las venero como relicarios
porque como gaviotas anidadas,
me consuelan, me alagran, me defienden

IV

your hands are two hammers that joyfully
nail down and dry up the morning,
tender fists that unfold from earth,
sweet bunches of small bananas
your hands smell of the blackberries
your harvest in the fields that steal
your sweat at two dollars a bucket,
they are hard, warm, young and wise
hoes that bring bread to the tables,
dark stones that give light when struck,
pleasure, support, anchor of the world
I worship them a reliquaries
because like nesting sea gulls,
they console, delight, defend me

XIV

como consolar al hombre mas solo
de la tierra? como aliviar su pena?
como llamar a su puerta atrancada
y decirle al oido embocado de alma:
"hermano, la guerra ya ha terminado:
todos, por fin, salimos vencedores:
sal, goza los campos liberados:
la eaxplotacion es cosa del pasado"?
que hacer cuando regrese malherido
con alambre de puas entre las piernas?
como encarar sus ojos que denuncian:
"hermano, el mundo sigue igual:
los pobres todavia somos presa facil:
el amor, si no es do todos, no basta"?

XIV

how to console the loneliest man
on earth? how to relieve his pain?
how to call through his bolted door
and have one's soul speak to his ear:
"brother, the war is now over:
all of us in the end emerged victors:
go forth and enjoy the liberated fields:
exploitation is a thing of the past"?
what to do when he returns, wounded
with barbed wire between his legs?
how to face his eyes accusing:
"brother, the world goes on the same:
we the poor are still easy prey: love,
if it isn't from all, is just not enough"?

Here, too, the "high" European form is turned to the purposes of anew poetry: "dark" in the sense of hidden, forbidden, homosexual; "dark" in the sense of the love between dark people.

In all of these examples, variations on form may be greater or less, but what really matters is not line lengths or the way meter is handled, but the poet's voice and concerns refusing to be circumscribed or colonized by the tradition, the tradition being just a point of takeoff. In each case the poet refuses to let form become format, pushes at it, stretches the web, rejects imposed materials, claims a personal space and time and voice. Format remains flat, rigid, its concerns not language, but quantifiable organization, containment, preordained limits: control.

Goodman writes:

The deliberate response to format is avant garde—writing which devotes itself, at least in part, to flouting the standard style, to offending the audience.... If a work is felt to be "experimental," it is not that the writer is doing something new but that he [sic] is making an effort to be different, to be not traditional.

In any period, powerful artists are likely to go way out and become incomprehensible. They abide by the artistic imperative to make it as clear as possible, but they are not deterred by the fact that the audience doesn't catch on. . . . On hindsight, the incomprehensibility of genius almost always turns out to be in the mainstream of tradition, because the artist took the current style for granted, he [sic] worked on the boundary of what he knew, and he did something just more than he knew.

Avant garde artists do not take the current style for granted; it disgusts them. They do not care about the present audience; they want to upset it. . . . Avant garde tends to be capricious, impatient, fragmentary, ill-tempered. Yet, except by raging and denying, a writer might not be able to stay alive at all as a writer. As a style, avante garde is an hypothesis that something is very wrong in society. . . .

An ultimate step is always Dada, the use of art to deny the existence of meaning. A step after the last is to puff up examples of format itself to giant size, Pop.

But in a confused society, avant garde does not flourish very well. What is done in order to be idiotic can easily be co-opted as the idiotic standard.

"Avant-garde" may well be a declaration that "something is very wrong in society." It may be a true "Howl" against a pervasively square, exclusive, dominant art allied with sexual, economic, racial repression. But, as Goodman saw well, in an age of disinformation and co-optation, "avant-garde" may become merely one dish on a buffet table of "entertainment" so arranged that no one item can dominate. It may be drafted into the service of TV commercials, or videos for executives on retreat. Its attempts to shatter structures of meaning may very well be complicit with a system that depends on our viewing our lives as random and meaningless or, at best, unserious.

"Avant-garde," anyway, is a style and movement that depends on the existence of a powerful, if dessicated, and entrenched art world, where grants are awarded, paintings selected for museum purchase, reputations polished. What is its significance in a society of immigrants and survivors of genocide, the meeting place of many colonized cultures, whose emerging artists, far from being disgusted with their peoples' traditions and styles, are trying to repossess and revalue them? "Avant-garde" has historically meant the rebellions of new groups of younger white men (and a few women) against the complacencies and sterilities of older men of their own culture. It was a powerful energy in Western Europe, the United States, and, for a while, in Russia, at the turn of this century. But among poets, at least, many or most of the early twentieth-century avant-garde, the "great modernists," were privileged by gender and class and were defenders of privilege.

The poetry of emerging groups—women, people of color, working-class radicals, lesbians and gay men—poetry that is nonassimilationist, difficult to co-opt, draws on many formal sources (ballad, blues, corrido, reggae, sonnet, chant, cuentos, sestina, sermon, calypso, for a few). But it doesn't pretend to abandon meaning or what Goodman calls "the artistic imperative to make it as clear as possible." As possible. Those poetries can be highly complex, layered with tones and allusions, but they are also concerned with making it "as clear as possible" because too much already has been buried, mystified, or written of necessity in code

Owning the Masters

Marilyn Nelson

I came of age as a reader of poetry during the early Sixties; the first contemporary poet I really read was LeRoi Jones. I was terribly moved by his public declaration, made in the middle of that tumultuous decade, of his decision to write against the white literary tradition, which he so clearly loved. Jones was a melancholy confessional Negro aesthete, confused in his identity, part of a new lost generation which called itself "Beat." He made a sudden about-face in about 1964, and changed his name and his style to become the poet of black nationalist rage, demanding

> ...poems
> like fists beating niggers out of Jocks
> or dagger poems in the slimy bellies
> of the owner-jews. Black poems to
> smear on girdlemamma mulatto bitches
> whose brains are red jelly stuck
> between 'lizabeth taylor's toes ...
> ..."poems that kill."
> Assassin poems. Poems that shoot
> guns. Poems that wrestle cops into alleys
> and take their weapons leaving them dead
> with tongues pulled out and sent to Ireland. Knockoff
> poems for dope selling wops or slick halfwhite
> politicians Airplane poems, rrrrrrrr
> rrrrrrrrr...tuhtuhtuhtuhtuhtuhtuhtuh
> ...rrrrr...Setting fire and death to
> whities ass. Look at the Liberal
> Spokesman for the jews clutch his throat
> & puke himself into eternity...rrrrr
> There's a negroleader pinned to
> a bar stool in Sardi's eyeballs melting
> in hot flame. Another negroleader
> on the steps of the white house one
> kneeling between the sheriff's thighs'
> negotiating cooly for his people.
>
> Aggggh ... stumbles across the room ...
> Put it on him, poem. Strip him naked
> to the world!
>
> ("Black Art")

As Baraka he gave up on the Angloamerican (or "white") literary tradition because, as he explains, for instance, in a poem called "Jitterbugs":

> The imperfection of the world
> is a burden. If you know it, think
> about it, at all. Look up in the sky
> wishing you were free, placed so terribly
> in time, mind out among new stars, working
> propositions, and not this planet where you
> can't go anywhere without an awareness of the hurt
> the white man has put on the people. Any people. You
> can't escape, there's nowhere to go. They have made
> this star unsafe and this age, primitive, though your mind
> is somewhere else, your ass ain't.

Though I was too timid and too thoroughly assimilated to follow Jones and other writers of the late Negro period into the literary separatism they called the Black Aesthetic, my heart went out to this struggling generation, and I think I felt my own perhaps toned-down version of the pain of their self-seeking. But Baraka's generation threw out the baby with the bathwater. In their single-minded quest for a revolutionary poetry they paid a great personal and artistic cost. Jones/Baraka confessed his loss in a 1964 poem, "I Substitute For The Dead Lecturer," explaining that his symbolic suicide was a response to the need of the poor. He asks,

> What kindness
> What wealth
> can I offer? Except
> what is, for me,
> ugliest. What is
> for me, shadows, shrieking
> phantoms.

He explains his sense of pained responsibility:

> The Lord has saved me
> to do this. The Lord
> has made me strong. I
> am as I must have
> myself. Against all
> thought, all music, all
> my soft loves.

The poem ends with his statement of fear that this decision may drive him mad. What a deep wrenching. How can a poet survive such a radical self-amputation? How can a poet survive without tradition?

In his famous essay, "Tradition and the Individual Talent," T.S. Eliot writes of an innovative male poet that "...we shall often find that not only the best, but the most individual parts of his work may be those in which the dead poets, his ancestors, assert their immortality most vigorously." Etheridge Knight, when asked which were his favorite poets, used to ask in reply: "You mean my favorite dead white poets?" Then he'd answer the question. Though I'm embarrassed to ally myself with the forces of white old-dead-boyism, I must confess that the title which came to me for this paper led me immediately to remember some MFA students I've had, who knew every poem in every book by whoever was pictured on the front page of the latest issue of a big-time little magazine, but drew a blank when I mentioned Matthew Arnold. Maybe they read "Dover Beach" in a class once? Oh, yeah: that Matthew Arnold. Student poets whose entire sense of the tradition was drawn from The Norton Anthology, shorter edition. Student poets who were never curious, or empassioned, or even angry enough to study the corpus of a dead white male poet. Student poets who measure themselves against each other and the pages of the latest issues of one or two literary journals, instead of against the old masters of our tradition.

Our tradition. I say this feeling like a woman wearing an ivory neck-lace and a mink coat at a national convention of Humans for Ethical Treatment of Animals. I know, I know: The tradition is the oppressor. The tradition doesn't include me because I'm black and a woman. If we had a time-machine which could whisk us backwards, where in the world, and to what time would the black woman choose to go? Our history has been excruciating, from enduring genital mutilation to being forced to give birth to a brutal master's pale new slaves. The history that created the traditional canon has systematically excluded blacks and women from just about every other hierarchy of honor; and there are a whole lot of other groups systematically excluded by that history, too. Its code of compulsory heterosexuality disempowers lesbians and gays; et cetera, et cetera. All those dead white guys in the tradition: When they were alive, their people were the masters, my people were the slaves. How can I read Blake without an awareness of the black-white symbolism by which Eighteenth Century Europe justified the hurt it was putting on African and American people? I knew, even as an undergraduate, that my professor was rationalizing when he explained away my question about Blake's little black boy's saying "...I am black, but O! my soul is white." He said something like, "Oh, no, Marilyn, Blake wasn't an unconscious racist. Great poets rise above the limitations of their times." Male-cow-poop. Like everyone else, poets live first in time, heirs to the racist, sexist, ageist, homophobic, war-mongering, meat-eating, environment-destroying, whale-slaughtering, ivory-coveting, seal-pup bashing, glorious long-gone and just yesterday past. I can't overlook these things when I read one of those dead white guys. Sometimes one or another of them makes me so mad I want to reach into the page like an arm coming out of a looking-glass, grab one of those old farts by the shirt-front, and shake the bejesus out of him. Okay, Andrew Marvell: Let's say your mistress has fainted three mornings in a row. Who's going to foot the emotional bills? I'm sorry you had to wait for your turn, Mr. Milton.

But my people—blacks and women—have been standing there waiting for generation upon generation upon generation. How can I read Wallace Stevens without remembering that he asked, when Gwendolyn Brooks became the first Aframerican poet to be awarded the Pulitzer Prize, "Why did they let the coon in?" What about Ezra Pound? What about Philip Larkin?

Minority students enrolled in or graduated from MFA programs at historically white institutions have begun to speak out, to let the academy know of their experiences. At a session at this year's AWP convention, for example, several minority MFA students described being pushed by white teachers to "show us your rage." Cornelius Eady writes in a poem called "Why Do So Few Blacks Study Creative Writing?" of the black student (the only one) in a creative writing course he is teaching, who comes to his office in tears after class one day, asking why "this poem of hers / Needed a passport, a glossary, // A disclaimer." Eady inwardly responds,

> ... Really, what
> Can I say? That if she chooses
> To remain here the term
> Neighborhood will always have
> A foreign stress, that there
> Will always be the moment
>
> The small, hard details
> Of your life will be made
> To circle their wagons?

No writer wants to be treated as if she had grown up in an intellectual ghetto. But the fact is that Aframerican writers do grow up in a double tradition, savoring the words of Dunbar, Cullen, Johnson, McKay, Hughes, Brown, Hayden, and Brooks as well as those of the old dead white guys who've looked down on us from a tradition our old dead brown guys weren't allowed to enter for a long, long time. We are heirs of an alternate tradition, heirs of slave narratives, spirituals, great orators, jazz and blues. Yet the once enslaved are heirs to the masters, too.

Take Phillis Wheatley, a poet who owned nothing, least of all herself. Her very name is symbolic of her condition: She was named for the ship which stole her from Africa and bore her into slavery, and for the family which the white man's law said owned her, her labor, and all of her future generations. Her language was the language spoken from the auction-block and the pulpit, the only poetry she knew that found in the holy book which allowed even religious Christians like the Wheatleys to believe they could own other people with moral impunity, and in the other books the Wheatleys made available to her: principally the works of Alexander Pope. And Phillis Wheatley, like a junkyard artist, created herself and her poetry out of the materials that came to hand. In 1767, at the age of 14, she addressed "The Atheist" with this pious, brilliant, misspelled argument:

> Muse! where shall I begin the spacious feild
> To tell what curses unbeleif doth yeild?
> Thou who dost daily feel his hand, and rod
> Darest thou deny the Essence of a God! —
> If there's no heav'n, ah! whither wilt thou go
> Make thy Ilysium in the shades below?
> If there's no God from whom did all things Spring
> He made the greatest and minutest Thing
> Angelic ranks no less his Power display
> Than the least mite scarce visible to Day.

Remember: This child was a slave. Think about what atheism would have meant to a slave: The complete meaninglessness of creation and of existence. Nihilism. The Great Nada. How differently the slave must have felt God's hand every day than the smug, blind white atheist whom Phillis addressed. Easy for the pampered master to believe there's no better existence than this one. If the slave has no heaven to hope for, what's the use of going on? The Negro spirituals express not naive, but desperate faith. Though Phillis Wheatley's poems have not yet been read subtly enough, they have outlived their frail, unhappy creator by some 200 years. This, I think, is what it means to own the master. The Wheatleys "owned" Phillis, but the Wheatley name lives now only because Phillis owns it. The classical allusions, the formal distance, the form itself which she uses come from the culture which held her and our people for ransom. Yet she was born a poet: She found her voice within the oppressor's tradition because she had to sing.

Singing seems to me to be very much to the point here. Though we still describe it as singing, most modern white poetry emulates speech, not song. Some poets do it very well: So well, in fact, that the speech of their poems lifts on its own music. Seldom, however, does a modern poem achieve the transparency available to traditional prosody, a transparency reached by the reader when words on a page, read silently, become sub-vocalized song. I hesitate to become involved in the current debate between the so-called new formalists (the singers) and the organic poets (the conversationalists). I cannot in good conscience take either side. Certainly free-verse poems can sing. Yet I hear the music more clearly, more compellingly, when I write with an ear to tradition: Hearing either the music of my people, or the rhyme and meter of the master's tradition.

Many of my people—blacks, women—argue that we have no place in the tradition, because it excludes us. One of their problems with tradition is that they believe we're born into tradition the way we're born into gender and race. If your parents were Serbs, you're a Serb, and Serbs hate Croats. If you're a Hutu, you hate the Tutsi. It's one warlord against another out there, folks, and some of us want to play Hatfields and McCoys in the literary world, too. If you're a new formalist, you don't read free verse. If you're an Aframerican woman, you don't read Paul Celan. Elizabeth Barrett Browning says nothing to you about love if you're gay; Paradise Lost is an offense to womyn. Each group wants to redefine the tradition in its own image. They think tradition is tribal and exclusive. But Zora Neale Hurston describes as a high point of her youth her enraptured reading of Paradise Lost; Maya Angelou claims that "...Shakespeare wrote for me, a poor black girl on the dirt roads of Arkansas." And Maya is right: Shakespeare did write for her. Just as I write for a 51-year-old white Oklahoma farmer.

Eliot was right, tradition "...cannot be inherited, and if you want it you must obtain it by great labour." Eliot, of course, meant by "great labour" the labor of serious, scholarly reading. We now know that the labor necessary to obtain the tradition has been greater for such differently-gifted groups as blacks and women. For us the labor is two-fold: There's the labor of studying the literature, then there's the additional labor of rising above its time-bound limitations. As Toni Morrison points out in Playing in the Dark: Whiteness and the Literary Imagination, we live, read, and write in a genderized, racialized world. If reading well means reading politically, conscious of the social considerations which inform any text, those of us who come from traditions of oppression find ourselves estranged from canonical texts, and must fight—against them and our arguments with them—to own them.

Eliot writes that obtaining the tradition "… involves, in the first place, the historical sense, which we may call nearly indispensable to anyone who would continue to be a poet beyond his 25th year; and the historical sense involves a perception, not only of the pastness of the past, but of its presence…." He saw the past as "…altered by the present as much as the present is directed by the past." The names of poets included in the canon are engraved on alabaster, but there's lots of empty space on those tablets. The canon is steadily undergoing formation, both vertically and—more recently— horizontally. The future will applaud our generation's widening of the stream. We must not, however, as we widen the course of the canon, make its bed shallow. Despite the labor necessary to recognize the wisdom which made generations consider those dead white guys great, they are great. Sometimes in spite of themselves. Sometimes, I suspect, not even knowing before they wrote the work the truth the work reveals.

Too often we ignore the fact that tradition is process. Believing that tradition is created in retrospect, we turn over boulders, stones, and pebbles in tireless quest of, for example, the unknown, unpublished great black lesbian poet of the Seventeenth Century. No doubt someday someone will find her, and that discovery will force us to make new maps of the literary landscape. But it will change not the landscape of the Seventeenth Century, but that of the generation which discovers her. For tradition, as process, is formed as we go forward. There is no doubling back, no taking that other fork in the road, no rewinding the tape. Some politically correct textbook editors have wanted to rewind and edit the tape, banning, for instance, the use of the word "slave," preferring instead the term "enslaved person." But no amount of politically correct sensitivity to potentially hurt feelings will erase the fact that African slavery played an essential role in the history and psychology of the New World. As, we must also admit, did the genocidal wars against Red injuns, or Indians, or American Indians, or Native Americans, or natives. As did the white man's war against the natural world. It has to do with time: Our tradition is what we inherit, not what we create. Perhaps the tradition we pass on will be superior to the one that got dumped into our laps. Though I doubt it. One thing we can be sure of: It will be different. Our tradition is our shared understanding of encoded meanings, the history of our words. I am reminded of a poem by Galway Kinnell, in which he drives home past landmarks, one of which is the place where he once saw a fox. Words have histories, like Kinnell's landmark, like the farm I drive past regularly, where I once saw a fox years ago and thought of Kinnell's poem. I think of the fox and of Kinnell's poem every time I drive by the place. Words have histories like that. Our understanding of figurative language has a great deal to do with our sense of word-history. You have to know what a bull is, and be familiar with the saying, "a bull in a china shop," to understand this simple metaphorical insult: "Well, I wouldn't want him in my china shop." I recently read that in one Chinese dialect, the word for "so-so" means literally "horse-horse, tiger-tiger." There must be word-histories echoing there which native speakers understand. Words mean in echoes which are derived from both their synchronic and their diachronic references, both their horizontal and their vertical connotations, both their present and their past meanings. Tradition is the living O.E.D. from which we derive our ability to receive a metaphor or decode a symbol. From which we derive many of the pleasures of poetry.

I don't believe the pleasures of poetry can be dissected and explained. But one of the pleasures of poetry must surely be its ability to give us a sense of community: We think along with someone else; the boundaries between two minds come down. And form itself is communal; it is, as Thomas Byers writes, "...one of the ways in which the poem participates in poetic, social, and historical dialogue" ("The Closing of the American Line: Expansive Poetry and Ideology." Contemporary Literature 33.2: Summer, 1992, p. 399). So a poem written with an ear to tradition enables us to think and sing along with many other minds: to join a sort of intergenerational silent interior Mormon Tabernacle Choir.

I'm convinced our inclination to create race-, gender- and ethnic-specific literary enclaves is dangerous; that it disinvites us from community. The Angloamerican tradition belongs to all of us, or should. As does the community into which the tradition invites us. That means the metrical tradition, too.

For many of today's poets the metrical tradition is a prison, and writing in verse a drudgery, like extra homework. For them, form is a strait-jacket and metrical language as stiff as starch. Most of us have lost what Alan Shapiro calls "...an instinctive sense of the delicate and subtle tensions between stress and accent, rhythm and meter, repetition and surprise, which the best poems in the tradition illustrate" ("The New Formalism," Critical Inquiry 14, Autumn, 1987, p. 213). Yes, writing in traditional form is tax-ing. But it is also liberating. To describe the freedom it bestows, I will jump to another art, music, and a long passage about musical composition, writ-ten by Igor Stravinsky. Stravinsky writes:

> The more art is controlled, limited, worked over, the more it is free. As for myself, I experience a sort of terror when, at the moment of setting to work and finding myself before the infinitude of possibilities that present themselves, I have the feeling that everything is permissible to me....Will I then have to lose myself in this abyss of freedom? To what shall I cling in order to escape the dizziness that seizes me before the virtuality of this infinitude? However, I shall not succumb. I shall overcome my terror and shall be reassured by the thought that I have the seven notes of the scale and its chromatic intervals at my disposal, that strong and weak accents are within my reach, and that in all of these I possess solid and concrete elements which offer me a field of experi-ence just as vast as the upsetting and dizzy infinitude that had just frightened me.... My freedom thus consists in my moving about within the narrow frame that I have assigned myself for each one of my undertakings. I shall go even farther: my freedom will be so much the greater and more meaningful the more narrowly I limit my field of action and the more I surround myself with obstacles.... The more constraints one imposes, the more one frees one's self of the chains that shackle the spirit. (Poetics of Music: pp. 66-68)

"The master's tools will never dismantle the master's house," writes Audre Lorde in Sister Outsider. But why should we dismantle the house? Why toss the baby over the porch railing, with its bassinetteful of soapy water? Why don't we instead take possession of, why don't we own, the tradition? Own the masters, all of them. Wordsworth and Wheatley, Hughes, Auden. As we own the masters and learn to use more and more levels of this language we love, for whose continued evolution we share responsibility, the signifiers become ours. We must not stand, like trembling slaves, at the back door of the master's house. We must recognize, as Cornelius Eady does in a poem called "Gratitude," that "I am a brick in a house/that is being built/around your house."

One of my colleagues, Herbert Lederer, retired from the German Department of the University of Connecticut a few years ago. I went to his retirement party, not because I knew him well, but because we'd been saying hello to each other in the hall every day for years, and he seemed nice. I learned from the testimonial speeches that Herr Lederer, who organized a German language choir every Christmas, who staged his own adaptations of German classics, who spearheaded the annual Kristkindlmarkt in the Student Union Ballroom (modeled after those which take place in the center squares of many German cities during the Christmas season), that this Herr Lederer, rosy-cheeked and jolly as a Bavarian baker, was a German-born Jew. I learned that he had escaped from Nazi Germany as a university student, and that he had resolved, as news of the Holocaust leaked out, not to give up his study of German literature. To give it up, he reasoned, would have been to give in to the Nazis who declared Jews unworthy of it. To study it, to teach it, to love it, was to keep it out of Nazi hands. It was to own it.

Other writers make our work possible; we write someone else's words. Which is exactly what T.S. Eliot was talking about in his famous essay about tradition and individual talent. In a book called *The Signifying Monkey* Henry Louis Gates, Jr., describes this layering of meaning upon meaning as it appears in the Aframerican tradition as "signifying." In signifying, a word becomes "double-voiced," "decolonized." Signifying, argues Gates, fundamentally alters our reading of the tradition. Owning the masters of our tradition, "signifying," paying due homage, gives us a way to escape the merely personal, puts us in dialogue with great thoughts of the past, and teaches us transparency. For the greatest masters of our tradition sought not to see their own eyes, but to see through them.

Wings of a Phoenix?
Rebellion and Resuscitation in
Postmodernist American Poetry

Daniel Hoffman

Thirty years ago, when I published an anthology, American Poetry and Poetics, Ben Shahn designed for its cover an impressively commanding bird, part eagle, part phoenix, with a shield on its breast and a gleam in its eye. Ever since, I've thought of American poetry as both an eagle soaring and a phoenix springing up anew from its own ashes. Well, the old bird, American poetry, has yet again been declared moribund, decadent, and dead by at least two rival conclaves of doctors: practical poet-diagnosticians, each would arise on their own wing from the cinders of the exhausted period style of confessional free verse to reincarnate the true spirit of inspired versing in these states. Thereby would they recover for poetry its lost audience.

But how can the phoenix fly with its two wings fanning the air in mutually opposed directions? One movement, legislating the abandonment of free verse in discipline and chaotic formlessness, would impose a return to familiar meters, forms, and the narrative mode. If these poets would seem to be turning the clock back, the others, gathered under the banner of LANGUAGE Poets, tear the hands right off its face, leaping ahead, as they think, of petrified modernism to a postmodern poetics for America based on theoretical premises imported, mostly, from France.

What is there in the recent and present situation to inspire such vehement responses? Dana Gioia, prominent in the first group I've just described, puts it this way:

> By 1980 there had been such a decisive break with the literary past that in America for the first time in the history of modern English most published poets could not write with minimal competence in traditional meters ... most of the craft of traditional English versification has been forgotten.... These young poets have grown up in a literary culture so removed from the predominantly oral tradition of metrical verse that they can no longer hear it accurately.... For them the poem exists as words on the page rather than sounds in the mouth and ear. While they have often analyzed poems, they have rarely memorized and recited. . . . [T]his very lack of training makes them deaf to their own ineptitude. (???)

Gioia makes these remarks in an article entitled "Notes on the New Formalism," one of the names by which the young poets engaged in restoring the lost conventions are known; other designations of their movement are Expansive Poetry and the New Narrative. Enrolled among them, either by their own participation in symposia or group anthologies or by assignment to these ranks by critics, are Dick Allen, R. S. Gwynn, Mark Jarman, Brad Leithauser, Charles Martin, Molly Peacock, Wyatt Prunty, Mary Jo Salter, Gjertrud Schnackenberg, Vikram Seth, Robert B. Shaw, Timothy Steele, and others. Each of these poets has written poems that give me pleasure. I take as a given their technical accomplishment and individual gifts and vision. What I am concerned to consider are the doctrines or dogmas of the movement in which they have, or have been by others, enrolled.

It may well be wondered why a New Formalism when among older poets there are those—Richard Wilbur, Anthony Hecht, John Hollander, James Merrill come to mind—who have never abandoned metrical or stanzaic verse. Ah, but they have contributed to the loss of readership and the consequent marginalization of poetry by their mandarin styles and elitist views of experience. Not for the New Formalists Wilbur's aestheticism (as they see it), Hecht's proscriptive moralism, Hollander's recondite intellectualism, Merrill's autobiographical poems based on a family background of wealth and privilege. No, the New Formalists propose poems at once democratic in subject, familiar in form, accessible in both. And, after seven or eight decades of modernism's breakup of narrative and the shrinkage of poetic ambition to the brevity of lyric, they would revive the poetry that delivers the freights stolen from verse by the novel.

I defer consideration of narrative poetry till later in this essay, but as regards the N.F. prolegomenon it must be said that despite several of their books actually achieving second printings and the runaway 25,000-copy sale of Seth's novel-in-verse, *The Golden Gate*, their movement has not yet conspicuously succeeded in stirring the non-poetry-reading public out of its apathy. Perhaps, in decades to come, such books as those the New Formalists write will gradually win back for poetry a larger audience, although the sociology of reading may uncover causes more complex than the hopes of these poets can remedy. For the present, their books are read chiefly by other poets and are reviewed in magazines mainly devoted to poetry. Indeed, they, or others of like mind, have established a couple of journals of their own (*The Reaper, The Formalist, Hellas*), and their readings, like those of all American poets who give them, are attended for the most part by students. (Who has measured the effect upon our spoken poetry of its being directed so exclusively at 18- to 22-year-olds?) Poetry in the US., of whatever ideological complexion, is assuredly a minority subculture in a mainstream environment virtually unaware of the poets, their ambitions, their books, their feuds.

How did it come to pass that most American poets and readers are metrical illiterates? Forty years ago the reverse was true — most poets wrote in meters, used received formal conventions, and could expect a readership that assumed what they assumed. Poets and readers alike, returning from the Second World War, found awaiting them a literary curriculum that followed the table of contents of T. S. Eliot's *Selected Essays*. Not for a couple of decades did American poetry (and eventually its study) change course, following now in the name of freedom Ezra Pound, who, in matters metrical, structural, and ideological, blasted apart the canon his friend Eliot had proclaimed as central to both Christianity and Western culture. Pound's countercultural tradition rested, he advised young poets in his essays, on knowing a dozen books — different books from those in the canon. And once the *Cantos* got going, verse traced the wayward courses of feeling; from imagism onward, practitioners and theorists of free verse have maintained that the true courses of feeling must be falsified by a poet's subjection to meters, rhyme, or stanzaic form.

Pound's own poetry, though constructed irrationally, is in fact very learned and even more allusive than Eliot's. But the free verse movement of which he was the major promoter and publicist engendered generations who seemed to write without reading. The suffering self in *The Pisan Cantos* is a much more complex and knowledge-freighted persona than the selves who revealed their intimate secrets in the confessional poems of the fifties and sixties and since.

Many of these later poets were taught as schoolchildren, and in their turn went on to teach, the writing of poems according to the playful formulas in Kenneth Koch's *Wishes, Lies and Dreams* (1971). This work, designed to rescue poetry from pedantry by emphasizing pleasure, offered wordgames and free association to liberate young poets from the chains of meter. Koch's book was a needed corrective, but among the freedoms it offered one does not find the freedom that comes with mastery of form. And the method, applied by others lacking its originator's gifts, quickly became a set of free verse conventions. Add to this the influx of poets so reared into teaching positions in college and university writing programs, and one readily sees the decline of free verse from the adventurousness of its first practitioners to a set of mannerisms. It is against this institutionalism of stale free verse, especially of the confessional sort, that both New Formalism and LANGUAGE poetry have arisen to save the day.

Among the defenders of free verse, the New Formalists have generated some singularly ill-tempered resistance. In view of this movement's call for democratic subject matter it is ironic to find exponents of the prevailing free verse style attacking them as cultural fascists because they favor meters and forms. For instance, Ira Sadoff, blasting the premises of Robert Richman's formalist anthology, *The Direction of Poetry*, indicts the chosen poets for promoting "a social as well as a linguistic agenda" in their "hierarchical privileging of meter over other decorations in poetry." That he considers meter as mere decoration, unable to recognize its uses as a tensor of meaning, suggests which open field in the forest Sadoff is coming from. As for the "social agenda" implicit in formal versing, how would he account for the conservative or reactionary political ideas of those who invented free verse in the first place—T. E. Hulme, D. H. Lawrence, Eliot, or Pound? Although phrased in quasi-Marxist vocables, his argument in effect revives Walt Whitman's view that American poetry must abandon the forms and meters developed through centuries of practice in king-ridden Britain.

Thus it is that those who, like William Carlos Williams, son of an English father, would banish the iamb are rejecting the patrimony of American speech from British English, of American versification from that of the English and Anglo-American tradition. Yet the alternation of accented with unaccented syllables characterizes the English language wherever spoken; the iambic line, dominant since Chaucer and the emergence of Middle English, represents a minimal organization of this alternation. The favored line-length is pentameter since it affords greater variety in the placement of caesuras than would a briefer line and avoids the monotony and tendency to fracture in lines of greater length. What free verse dogmatists abjure, along with their rejection of rhythms inherent in the pronunciation, syntax, and structure of the language, is the notion that a line of verse, or a poem, exists apart from the rest of the universe. Rhythm and form are among the poet's means of differentiating his verbal constructs from other uses of language as a made thing. Many exponents of free verse are under the illusion that by avoiding meters, rhymes, and stanzas they have produced verbal constructs self-generated by nature.

To write in measures does not signify that the poet belongs to, or longs to belong to, the class of oppressors in society. Anyone who so desires can learn to write in meters and forms; I myself have instructed immigrants and children of immigrants and of unempowered families to write formal verses. The class to which they belonged was English 113. Those with imaginative talent as well as linguistic facility used what they had learned there to write poems.

A recent book, *Missing Measures*, by Timothy Steele—himself one of the New Formalist poets—explores the historical background of free verse. Steele surveys the history of stylistic revolutions in verse, going back to the ancient Greeks. Comparing the modernist dismissal of meters to Dryden's reaction against Renaissance ornamentation and Wordsworth's opposition to the artificiality of Augustan poetic diction, Steele maintains that it is only in the modernist revolt that metrical writing itself was subverted. In their assaults on slack Victorian style, Steele finds, Pound and Eliot made the error of identifying the faults they would correct with writing in meters. Thus they perpetrated a rejection no earlier stylistic revolt had committed. Now, because of the dominance of the novel in nineteenth-century literature, poets imitated prose. Pound said of Mauberley (a mask for himself), "His true Penelope was Flaubert," and demanded that poetry be as well written as prose. Further damage was done by the aestheticism of the turn of the century, the doctrine that required poetry to be musically expressive and to have organic form. Musical expressiveness militated against the presence of thought in the poem, and organic form required that each experience reveal its unprecedented shape which the verse, in its irregularity, would replicate.

In Pound's and Eliot's critical writings Steele points to their enthusiasm for the French *vers libristes* and—without contradiction—their adoption of scientific terms. He relates this vocabulary to their notion that in poetry new techniques must be developed as they were in science. The indeterminacy of modern poetry becomes identified with that of quantum mechanics. Poets and poetry should emulate the detachment of science and of scientists, thus introducing into poetry depersonalization, difficulty, abstruseness. It was the announced intention of these pioneers of *vers libre* to usher in a new metric, an aim, as Steele says, in which they have been unsuccessful.

Missing Measures is a thorough exploration of the intellectual background of the free verse movement, yet it does not tell the whole story. In proposing the French *vers libristes* — because they were so influential on Eliot and Pound — as the chief forebears of contemporary American free verse, Steele quite overlooks the monumental presence, for most others, of Whitman. Magnanimous old Walt, in fact, is the tutelary spirit, who at many a remove and having suffered much dilution, is the principal begetter of the flatlining free verse whose emergence Steele is concerned with and the New Formalists would disestablish. There are attitudinal consequences to Whitman's great revolutionary bursting of the bonds of tradition. Whitman programmatically overthrows all restraints — not metrical rules alone — and, with his democratic sensibility he proclaims the equality of all peoples, that his body is as holy as his soul, his soul is in his sex, and every pebble, weed, leaf of grass, person, and bodily part is beautiful. Free verse comes down to us with this set of dispensations. Whitman and most of his followers lighten the burden of their imaginations by casting out the past and all its pains and anxieties. Thus are they free to follow the light of their new dawns in poems unshackled by bondage to iamb or trochee.

I would add that the twentieth century's avoidance of meters is not fully explained by intellectual antecedents alone. Rhythm in poetry, if at all effective, is expressive, emotive. Poetic rhythm is the evocation or replication of emotion by motion, the movement of the sounds and syllables of language in a physical representation of the courses of feeling. Poetry historically began in association with ritual, with dance, with song. If such associations now seem vestigial (if at all visible), it is nonetheless true that poetic rhythm, whatever it be, whether metrical or free or quasi-one or the other, should correspond to the flow, the leaps of illumination, the development of the fusion of thought and feeling which is the reason for the existence of the poem. Why, then, have so many poets in our century, in England as well as in English, found the avoidance of strict metrical writing so attractive?

The reason for this that Steele's intellectual-historical scholarship does not uncover is the omnipresence in the daily life in industrial societies of the numbing mechanical repetitiveness of machines, of work, of processes of every description. For most twentieth-century men and women these mechanical rhythms have displaced the more benign repetitions of the natural world that dominated human experience until man became separated from nature. At the same time, the Romantic movement redefined the role of the poet as that of the man of feeling, of sensitivity, the perceiver of truths hidden from those beaten into dull conformity by the abhuman lockstep, the mechanical repetitions of modern life.

The resultant confusion of poetic meters with the repressive mechanization of experience has been widespread. It appears based on the association of poetic meter with the inflexibility of a metronome—the very figure Pound used in his early advice to young poets, "A Few Don'ts," where he proposed organic rhythms in its stead. But this is to set up a false dichotomy. Verse written in mechanical meter would by definition be doggerel; verse offered in complete rhythmic "freedom" would be shapeless, diffuse, dull. In fact good metrical writing depends on variations from its underlying grid to achieve emphasis and intensity. Verse in organic rhythms achieves these qualities nonmetrically. Three-quarters of a century after Pound's essay we may ask, is it really a liberating response for poetry to avoid mechanical repetition by abandoning meters altogether, as Pound advised? Or is such a renunciation as much a restrictive gesture as a liberating one?

WORKS CITED

Gioia, Dana. "Notes on the New Formalism." *Expansive Poetry: Essays on the New Narrative & the New Formalism*, Ed. Frederick Feirstein. Santa Cruz: Story Line Press, 1989. pp. 165, 173.

Sadoff, Ira. "Neo-Formalism: A Dangerous Nostalgia," *American Poetry Review* (Jan.-Feb. 1990): 7.

Steele, Timothy. *Missing Measures: Modern Poetry and the Revolt against Meter*. Fayetteville: University of Arkansas Press, 1990.

Verse That Print Bred

Paul Lake

Although free verse had a forceful and vigorous life in America before World War II, not until the postwar period did it become the dominant form one now encounters everywhere in magazines, in books, and at readings. Not until after midcentury did William Carlos Williams emerge from the shadow of Eliot and Pound to become the predominant influence on younger American poets. Williams, in association with a younger group of Americans, the Black Mountain poets, set the terms of discussion and shaped the course of modern poetry for the next few decades. Charles Olson, who was the central figure of the Black Mountain group, also produced the document that probably had the greatest influence of any single literary manifesto published in the postwar period—his now famous essay "Projective Verse," which appeared originally in 1950 in *Poetry New York* but received much wider attention in Donald Allen's anthology *The New American Poetry* (1960). Williams greeted the essay's appearance with enthusiasm, seeing it as a forceful declaration of something very like his own poetic principles; and he helped champion both the essay and its author. The essay itself has proved to be hugely influential, amounting to something like a theoretical cornerstone to the Black Mountain poets, as well as to later writers of free verse; and today it continues to influence strongly even poets who have never read it. Terms and phrases from the essay—"open form," "closed form," "composition by field"—continue to be repeated in essays and writing workshops, and the suppositions and theoretical conclusions of the essay are today rarely questioned.

Despite its fame and influence, however, much about Olson's essay is questionable. Olson makes two fundamental errors, one of fact and one of logic; and since both entail points central to his argument, they should be reconsidered and the conclusions that depend on them re-examined. Although many regard the essay as a rhetorical tour de force and Olson's premises as unshakeable, let us look at what he actually says, for we will see that both the essay itself and much of the poetry that has been constructed on its foundation must be reevaluated.

The first and most profound of Olson's errors lies in his assertion that poetry that uses "inherited line, stanza, over-all form"—what he elsewhere calls "nonprojective" or "closed" verse—is "that *verse which print bred*" (italics mine).

That this statement, which is fundamental to his argument, has rarely been challenged despite its obvious inaccuracy, is astonishing. What Olson calls "closed verse" is not the product of print technology but a preliterate tradition extending back into prehistory. Print did not *breed* such elements as meter, rhyme, and stanza: it merely recorded and repeated them. But, since Olson has raised the point, let's explore the idea with someone who has dealt with the subject of print and its influence on literature and society more systematically, Marshall McLuhan.

McLuhan, in *The Medium is the Massage,* reminds us that "Homer's *Iliad* was the cultural encyclopedia of pre-literate Greece," and that "these Bardic songs were rhythmically organized with great formal mastery into metrical patterns which insured that every one was psychologically attuned to memorization and easy recall." McLuhan also reminds us of the communal basis of this highly patterned poetry: "What the Greeks meant by 'poetry' was radically different from what we mean by poetry. Their 'poetic' expression was a product of a collective psyche and mind. The mimetic form, a technique that exploited rhythm, meter, and music, achieved the desired psychological response in the listener. Listeners could memorize with greater ease what was sung than what was said."

These preliterate people, like all such people, lived in what McLuhan calls "acoustic space," which he describes as "boundless, directionless, horizonless." McLuhan argues that in such preliterate societies the ear dominates, and that only with the invention of a phonetic alphabet—with the subsequent need to string its sonic bits together into logical sequences—do the eye and visual space begin to dominate our perception and thought. "The alphabet is a construct of fragmented bits and parts which have no semantic meaning in themselves and which must be strung bead-like, and in a prescribed order. Its use fostered and encouraged the habit of perceiving all environment in visual and spatial terms."

Yet Charles Olson—not the writers of formal poetry—conceives of his poetry strictly in terms of visual space. The metaphors he uses to describe his new method are all drawn from the language of spatial relations, of geometry. According to Olson, a poet will work in a "field"; he can "go by no track" other than the one the poem he is working on dictates; a poem must give off energy at all "points"; in "composition by field" all parts of speech can "spring up like unknown, unnamed vegetables in the patch." Olson's emphasis on the syllable, that smallest of phonetic units, is now understandable. If syllables are not to be arranged in patterns, as in formal poetry, what exactly is to be done with them? Olson doesn't say, but perhaps we can get an idea from other instances of Olson's linear habits of mind. Think of McLuhan's phonetic units "strung bead-like" as you hear Olson declaring in bold print: **"one perception must immediately and directly lead to a further perception."** Again, as later in his essay, Olson declares that the "objects" that occur in a poem's composition "must be handled as a series of objects in a field."

Olson thinks it ironical that he will correct the errors of so-called print-bred poetry by means of a machine—the typewriter. And here lies his second fundamental error. Because, if poetry went astray some time after the Elizabethans with their tradition of linking lyric poetry with music and needed to be returned to the province of the ear and of the breath, as Olson suggests, then the logical step to take in correcting poetry's print-bred errors would be to return it to its aural and communal sources—in song. Instead Olson again shows his visual and spatial bias. Because poems in metrical rhymed stanzas *look* closed on the page (though they don't *sound* closed when given voice), Olson suggests we dispense with the last vestiges of lyric poetry's musical heritage—meter, rhyme, stanza—and instead score poems on the two-dimensional plane of a sheet of paper by means of a typewriter's mechanical spacing. Thus the omnidirectional aural space of formal poetry is replaced by the geometer's two-dimensional plane.

"What we have suffered from, is manuscript, press, the removal of verse from its producer and reproducer, the voice," he begins. Then he continues:

> The irony is, from the machine has come one gain not yet sufficiently observed or used, but which leads directly on toward projective verse and its consequences. It is the advantage of the typewriter that, due to its rigidity and its space precisions, it can, for a poet, indicate exactly the breath, the pauses, the suspensions even of syllables, the juxtaposition even of parts of phrases, which he intends. . . . For the first time he can, without the convention of rime and meter, record the listening he has done to his own speech and by that one act indicate how he would want any reader . . . to voice his work.

He goes on to describe how by leaving spaces of certain lengths a poet can indicate how long he wants his reader to pause in the reading of his poem.

The real irony involved in all of this is that while thinking he is correcting poetry's so-called print-bred errors and returning poetry to the "breath," Olson in fact is extending the mechanical domination of print technology over poetry. Projective verse is the next logical step in the abolition of poetry's communal origins. Notice that Olson says that it is by listening to and recording *his own speech* that the poet will correct the mistakes of traditional verse, with its inherited musical devices and tribal origins. Projective verse, owing its birth to the typewriter, represents the final step away from the aural space of preliterate societies to the visual space of literate, industrial man. Consider McLuhan's highly relevant comments:

> Printing, a ditto device, confirmed and extended the new visual stress. It provided the first uniformly repeatable "commodity," the first assembly line—mass production.

> It created the portable book, which men could read in privacy and in isolation from others. Man could now inspire—and conspire.

> Like easel painting, the printed book added much to the new cult of individualism. The private, fixed point of view became possible and literacy conferred the power of detachment, non-involvement.

Now look at the neglected second half of Olson's famous essay, in which the poet further expounds his new poetic, using the term *objectism* to describe the projective poet's stance toward himself, the poem, and nature. Objectism, he declares, "is the getting rid of the lyrical interference of the individual as ego, of the 'subject' and his soul, that peculiar presumption by which western man has interposed himself between what he is as a creature of nature. . . and those other creations of nature. . . . For man himself is an object, whatever he may take to be his advantages." And then Olson sums up the point of the projective poet's objectism. "It comes to this," he declares: "the use of man by himself and thus by others, lies in how he conceives his relation to nature." Thus, stripped of soul and of the lyrical interference of self as subject, the poet is free to treat even man himself as an object and to give his poetic "work" the seriousness it deserves. The individual poet in isolation, listening to the patterns of his own speech, and treating even man himself as a kind of literary commodity, replaces the bard and his communal art.

It is free verse that is print-bred, not formal verse. Formal verse retains some of its musical properties even on the printed page, divorced from musical accompaniment. Were Olson right, and rhyme, meter, and stanza were bred by print, in the new acoustic space of the electronic media, song writers of rock and pop, freed from the confines of print, would listen to their own breath patterns and write songs in free verse. Of course they don't. And a further irony is that while poets of my generation came home from poetry readings by free-verse poets such as Olson, Creeley, Bly, Levertov, and Merwin in the sixties and seventies when it was unhip to write formal poetry, they would then turn on their stereos and listen to songs by Lennon and McCartney, Bob Dylan, and Joni Mitchell, the hippest of the hip; and together with millions of others they would respond to the insistent dactylic beat of a song such as "Lucy in the Sky with Diamonds" or the trochaic pulse of "I Am the Walrus" without any apparent sense of loss or irony.

I remember my own surprise as an undergraduate one afternoon in the early seventies while browsing through my anthology of Tudor poetry and prose when I discovered these lines:

> Golden slumbers kiss your eyes,
> Smiles awake you when you rise;
> Sleep, pretty wantons, do not cry,
> And I will sing a lullaby. . . .

I recognized them immediately—not as the lines of a song from Thomas Dekker's play *Pleasant Comedy of Patient Grissill*, published in 1603—as part of the musical collage of the Beatles' *Abbey Road* album. Lennon and McCartney had appropriated the little verse and woven it seamlessly into the fabric of their own lyrical medley, and no one was the wiser. Though they only changed *wantons to darlings*, their little borrowing went undetected. Though it would be extravagant to claim from this one example that there is a tradition of English language lyric that can embrace without difficulty song lyrics and poems from the earliest anonymous balladeers to the latest rock group, from Wyatt to Frost, from Auden to Elton John, this case does show the ability of certain stanza patterns and rhythms and rhymes to bridge the centuries, of certain poetic forms to endure and remain vital to the art of lyric poetry. In free verse as it is generally practiced, the poetic line, determined as it is primarily by topography and habit, represents little more than the geometer's one-dimensional Euclidean object. A line in a formal poem, however, is not merely a breath unit signalled by a black line of print and connected to other breath units on a two-dimensional plane but is part of a nexus of sound, part of a web or net. Rhyme, for instance, is often misunderstood because of its paradoxical nature. End rhyme, for example, while it emphasizes and makes one aware of a line ending, also in a sense abolishes the line as a separate unit by linking it with earlier rhymes and setting up expectations for future rhymes. With assonance, alliteration, and internal rhyme added to end rhyme and meter, a poem can become an aural web rather than a two-dimensional grid in visual space.

Writing about Bob Dylan's lyrics in a recent issue of *Threepenny Review*, Christopher Ricks quotes Tennyson's friend Arthur Hallam on the subject of rhyme and then himself makes these germane comments on the subject:

> "Rhyme has been said to contain in itself a constant appeal to memory and hope." Rhyme contains this because when you have the first rhyme you hope for the later one, and when you have the later one you remember the previous one. So rhyme is intimately involved with lyric, and there are particularly few good unrhymed lyrics of any kind because of the relationship between lyricism and memory and hope.

Formal poetry is not an elitist but a popular art form. Urban African-American rap musicians don't use couplets in their songs so often because they have read their Dryden and Pope; nor do they use an emphatic meter because they have read Eliot's "Tradition and the Individual Talent." Like all writers of popular songs they use those devices because they give pleasure, bound as they are to the lyricism of memory and hope. Any formal resource that can exist in the work of artists as diverse as Eliot, John Lennon, and the Fat Boys has roots that are both thick and deep. Perhaps we should spend more time cultivating them instead of plowing them over in the name of progress.

The Poet in an Age of Prose
Dana Gioia

If poetry represents, as Ezra Pound maintained, "the most concentrated form of verbal expression," it achieves its characteristic concision and intensity by acknowledging how words have been used before. Poems do not exist in isolation but share and exploit the history and literature of the language in which they are written. Although each new poem seeks to create a kind of temporary perfection in and of itself, it accomplishes this goal by recognizing the reader's lifelong experience with words, images, symbols, stories, sounds, and ideas outside of its own text. By successfully employing the word or image that triggers a particular set of associations, a poem can condense immense amounts of intellectual, sensual, and emotional meaning into a single line or phrase.

When R.P. Blackmur noted that "when a word is used in a poem it should be the sum of all its appropriate history made concrete and particular in the individual context," he may have sounded abstract and coldly analytical. But Blackmur was a poet as well as a critic, and his observation reflects the practical problems of writing genuine poetry. A poet knows that a reader will bring the sum of his or her experience in both life and literature to the poem, and the text must bear the weight of that attention. Good poetry never underestimates its readers. It actively seeks their imaginative and intellectual collaboration by assuming and exploiting a common frame of reference.

Judging exactly what constitutes that common framework at any given moment is part of the poet's task, since any living literary tradition constantly changes. Defining the tradition becomes—implicitly or explicitly—part of the creative act. Composed from that portion of the reader's cultural experience that a poet can use assumptively as a foundation for new work, this framework constitutes an era's available tradition.

One always risks being misunderstood when using the word *tradition*. Even in 1917 T.S. Eliot observed that the term was seldom employed "except in a phrase of censure." To speak of tradition summons images of old books in musty libraries or rows of marble busts gathering dust along a wall. But in speaking of "available tradition" I intend something less grand and more practical—namely that small portion of the past a poet finds usable at a particular moment in history. The available tradition is not a fixed entity but a dynamic concept. It changes—and indeed must change—not only from generation to generation but also from audience to audience.

The composition of a poem requires—either consciously or unconsciously—the notion of an audience. To create language of requisite precision and intensity, the writer must assume a reader's specific response to every word, idea, or image. Some authors, like Shakespeare, knew their audience directly. Others, like Wallace Stevens, simply supposed an invisible reader of deeply sympathetic intelligence. Still others, like Pound in his *Cantos*, sought to invent, through the poem itself, an ideal reader who did not yet exist. Whatever the case, the author's idea of an audience helps shape the poems he or she creates. In the past the relationship between the poet and the public did not seem especially problematic. Societies were more compact and homogenous. Cultural traditions changed very slowly, and readers shared a common fund of knowledge and concerns. Writers—even innovative ones like William Blake or Walt Whitman—were usually able to choose an audience whose sensibilities they understood (if not entirely endorsed) and whose general cultural assumptions they shared.

Today poets face a practical problem in trying to define a common cultural tradition available to both them and their readers. The difficulty originates in contemporary society, where the continuous proliferation of information has increasingly fragmented audiences into specialized subcultures that share no common frame of reference. The situation is further aggravated by the culture's shift away from the printed word as its primary source of information and entertainment. Although this problem is not specifically literary, it does affect poets more severely than other artists because it destroys the referential framework that gives poetry its particular concentration and intensity. How does an intertextual art like poetry sustain its force in a culture that no longer studies and esteems the written text? And how, if poets limit their audiences to people for whom the written word maintains its importance, do they write for readers who have lost touch with verse as a serious artistic medium?

Merely to mention the atomization of American cultural life is guaranteed to set off alarms in every ideological camp. But—for the space of this essay—I ask the reader to put aside not only all theories of why this fragmentation has occurred but also whether the change was a positive or negative event. The relevant factor here is only that the notion of tradition a serious poet entertained in 1940 no longer exists. We live in a country where the average college freshman doesn't know in what century the Civil War was fought, cannot identify the language spoken in ancient Rome, and cannot name a single Romantic poet. Not only have these students never read a single page of Milton, they probably could not understand it if they did. The epigraph to a recent Edgar Bowers poem aptly summarizes the situation. Quoting a student, it reads, "Who's Apollo?" Students, of course, do not fully represent the American reader, but they do serve, to borrow a phrase from economics, as a reliable leading indicator of general cultural trends.

Since the poet can no longer write assumptively to a diverse audience using a common framework of history, literature, science, myth, and religion, he or she faces a series of distressing compromises. The poet can strip his or her language free of most references and create a kind of minimalist verse that achieves clarity at the expense of comprehensiveness and intensity. Or the poet can substitute a private frame of reference (which in our narcissistic society is almost inevitably autobiographical) for the lost public tradition. This confessional method gains immediacy at the price of breadth and relevance. Or the poet can adopt a public ideology (usually a particular poltical or religious creed) to provide a predetermined framework. This method gains accessibility and depth but usually at the cost of immediacy and independence. Or, finally, the poet can limit his or her audience to an educated coterie that still understands the traditional literary codes—a decision that maintains the art's intensity but risks its vitality and general relevance.

One might easily view the history of recent American poetry as a series of rebellions against and reconciliations to the writer's cultural predicament. Most major innovations have originated in the frustration generated by poetry's sequestration in the academy. Each significant new movement has attempted to form some meaningful coalition outside the university—both to link its poetry to a living cultural tradition and to revitalize it with genuine social purpose. The Beats, for example, linked their literary vision to the nonconformist attitudes of the countercultural Left. Black poets sought to become the voice of their own disenfranchised race. Protest poets in the late sixties mythologized the political framework of the Vietnam era into a publicly accessible literary tradition. Women writers adopted the ideological structure of feminism to give their poetry great social relevance. Whatever one thinks of the artistic success of these movements, one must recognize the initial jolt of energy each delivered by reestablishing poetry's link with the broader culture. (But, ironically, each rebellion from the academy was almost immediately calmed by assimilating its ringleaders into the university, and the impact on the general culture ultimately proved limited.)

New Formalism represents the latest in a series of rebellions against poetry's cultural marginality. The generational change in literary sensibility, which would eventually be called New Formalism, began 20 years ago when a group of young writers created—admittedly, only in their own minds—a new audience for poetry. Alienated from the kind of verse being praised and promulgated in the university, these young poets—like every new generation of writers—sought to define their own emerging art in relation to an imaginary audience. Their ideal readers were not the poetry professionals of the Creative Writing Department who had quite explicitly rejected formal metrics and narrative verse. Nor were they the contemporary literature experts of the English Department who often prized difficulty for its own sake.

At odds with the small but established institutional audience for new poetry, these young writers imagined instead readers who loved literature and the arts but had either rejected or never studied contemporary poetry. This was not the mass audience of television or radio, for whom the written word was not a primary means of information. It was an audience of prose readers—intelligent, educated, and sophisticated individuals who, while no longer reading poetry, enjoyed serious novels, film, drama, jazz, dance, classical music, painting, and the other modern arts. While those prose readers had limited experience with contemporary poetry, they also displayed few preconceptions about what it should or should not be. For them, formal and narrative verse did not violate any preordained theoretical taboos, since they unself-consciously enjoyed rhyme, meter, and storytelling as natural elements of the popular arts like rock, musical theater, and motion pictures. In writing for a general audience that poetry had long ago lost, the New Formalists chose to embrace rather than repudiate the broader cultural trends of their era. Rather than be bards for the poetry subculture, they aspired to become the poets for an age of prose.

Whether or not the New Formalists have actually ever reached this large audience is immaterial here. The crucial consideration is that—like the Beats and the black power poets before them—they tried to break the cultural deadlock strangling their art. In the New Formalists' case, the attempt involved the creation of an idealized common reader to define the cultural traditions available to them as poets. They took the risk of courting a prose audience generally indifferent to serious verse rather than addressing the existing academic coterie. In doing so, they openly broke ranks with the prevailing models of contemporary poetry, rejecting the hyper-sophisticated or highly intellectualized aesthetics of academically fashionable writers like Ashbery, Olson, Creeley, or Merwin whose work seemed targeted primarily at an elite readership of critics and fellow artists.

Less obvious, at least initially, was the fact that the young poets also departed from the example of the most influential formalists of the older generation (such as Merrill, Hecht, or Hollander), who saw themselves as guardians of the imperiled traditions of European high culture. The first break was announced with fierce rhetoric by the poets of the new movement, since most of them felt little sympathy with the academic mainstream. The second break, however, was not so clearly articulated, since the young writers generally admired the older formal poets and looked on them as literary allies. The subsequent direction of New Formalist poetry, however, indicates that the aesthetics of the older and younger schools are in many respects irreconcilable.

Since there was no open conflict between the older and younger generations, some critics have conflated the two schools. There has been a common criticism by detractors that the New Formalists are doing nothing new. These young poets, the complaint goes, are epigones not innovators, since they represent merely a continuation of the American formalist tradition of the 1940s and 1950s. This line of reasoning has the virtue of simplicity, but, unfortunately, it betrays little familiarity with what the young poets have actually written. One need only compare a poem by Merrill or Hollander with one by Tom Disch or Molly Peacock to see how radically they differ in terms of audience, genre, tone, cultural heritage, and even prosody. The confusion between these two related but divergent generations originates, one suspects, in the term *New Formalism* itself, which is misleadingly reductive. One need not subscribe to the philosophical tradition of nominalism to appreciate that anyone hoping to understand an artistic movement—be it New Formalism, Modernism, or Romanticism—must make a distinction between the name itself and the phenomena it tried to describe. Responsible investigation begins with the actual works of art the movement produces, not uniformed generalizations about the name literary journalists first applied dismissively to its earliest manifestations.

By focusing attention solely on the revival of formal metrics, the term *New Formalism* has obscured the broader change in sensibility that these young poets represent. The use of rhyme and meter is only one aspect of a deeper aesthetic shift away from the coterie culture of the universities. The new sensibility also has led to the return of verse narrative, the exploration of popular culture for both forms and subjects, the rejection of avant-garde posturing, the distrust of narrowly autobiographical thematics, the unembarrassed employment of heightened popular speech, and the restoration of direct, unironic emotion. Seen from this perspective, the movement might be more accurately described by the alternate term *Expansive* poetry. This expression captures the eclectic interests and broad cultural ambitions of the movement. While it is possible to focus profitably on the revival of formal metrics, such a narrow perspective risks missing the broader cultural issues at stake. It also distorts the relationship between the young formal and narrative poets and their predecessors.

There are some continuities between the New Formalist and New Critical poets. Both groups endorse rhyme and meter as legitimate and "organic" modes of literary composition. They also consider the finished poem a consciously crafted artifact rather than a spontaneous or aleatory creation. And both schools believe that poetry is an essentially intertextual art. They maintain, in other words, that poetry refers to life only through the intricately self-referential prism of language and that the individual poem discloses its full meaning only in relation to its broader literary context.

In other respects, however, the aesthetics of the New Formalist and New Critical poets stand in radical disagreement. If they share a belief in the necessity of placing new poems in relation to a tradition, they differ irreconcilably in terms of defining what traditions are available to them as contemporary artists. If both recognize the importance of the idea of an audience in shaping a poem, each group has chosen different audiences. That choice, in turn, has indeed taken the tone, style, and subject of their work in fundamentally different directions despite the occasional similarity of their prosody. And, finally, their divergent sense of available tradition and intended audience has led them to pursue different modes and genres of literary expression. That these two literary schools differ so substantially is not surprising, however, since each emerged in a different historical moment.

The older generation of formalists came to maturity during World War II, and their emergence as writers coincided with the postwar period of American cultural ascendency. The intellectual assumptions behind their work reflect the ebullient confidence of America's new international dominance. Touring Europe as soldiers or Fulbright scholars (or both), they were determined to meet the Old World on equal terms by demonstrating their mastery of its traditional modes of discourse. Likewise, these older writers were the first generation of poets in the history of American literature to move *en masse* into the university—an environment they found intellectually and artistically congenial. Here, too, they resolved to address their scholarly colleagues on equal footing. They wrote poems that displayed their full command of the traditions of English literature, informed and energized by international Modernism. Having, in many cases, risked their lives to defend (and later staked their careers to teach) Western Culture, they assumed—as a central ideological foundation—the reader's deep familiarity with traditional literature. Their work was designed to bear the full weight of tradition and withstand the scrutiny of critical examination. Their work was intellectually demanding, aesthetically self-conscious, emotionally detached, and intricately constructed. Their audience was, by definition, limited to fellow members of the academy's intellectual and artistic elite.

The New Formalists emerged in less optimistic and assumptive times. They came to maturity in the cultural disintegration of the Vietnam era, when a series of ideological revolutions challenged the conventional notions of literary value and intellectual objectivity that had shaped the older generation's aesthetic. The idea of tradition—even including its corollary principles of genre, diction, prosody, and form—was rejected. The notion of a common canon of universally acknowledged masterpieces was exploded into splinters of competing traditions, each grounded in its own exclusionary aesthetic. Art was divorced from pleasure and bound to ideology—especially to the reductive notion of the perpetual avant-garde, which proclaimed that literary styles, like the blueprints for microchip hardware, constantly evolved only to become immediately outmoded by the next innovation.

Having found high culture in shambles, the New Formalists looked to popular culture for perspective. In film, rock music, science fiction, and the other popular arts, they found the traditional forms and genres, which the academy had discredited for ideological reasons in high art, still being actively used. Innocent of theory, the general public had somehow failed to appreciate that rhyme and meter, genre and narrative were elitist modes of discourse designed to subjugate their individuality. The poor fools actually found such outmoded artistic technology interesting and enjoyable. The gap between what the academy declared represented democratic art and what the *demos* itself actually preferred was imaginatively provocative. The young writers realized that, while after the revolution the public might clamor for the projectivist verse and neodadaist mime shows, in the corrupt present a more accessible kind of art was called for.

What the New Formalists — and their counterparts in music, art, sculpture, and theater — imagined was a new imaginative mode that took the materials of popular art — the accessible genres, the genuinely emotional subject matter, the irreverent humor, the narrative vitality, and the linguistic authenticity — and combined it with the precision, compression, and ambition of high art. They remained committed to the standards of excellence embodied in high culture but recognized that the serious arts had grown remote and inbred. Just as the English and German Romantic poets had sought to reform eighteenth-century Neoclassicism by the adaption of idealized folk song, legend, and colloquial language, the New Formalists undertook the reclamation of contemporary poetry by mixing democratic and elitist models into a new synthesis.

The imaginative enterprise of combining high and popular culture has resulted in the confusion of most academic critics who have tried to examine New Formalism according to the orthodox conventions of their discipline. Since the movement makes no sense in the progressive Modernist framework commonly used in the university to discuss contemporary poetry, it can be viewed only as some recidivist manifestation, a throwback to the generation of Wilbur and Nemerov. Likewise, since the forms and subject matter drawn from popular culture lie outside the university's canonic modes of contemporary literature, those clarifying precedents remain either invisible or puzzling to most critics. While many influential literary theorists passionately discuss popular culture in general terms, they rarely show much enthusiasm about its gaudy particulars. Since their interest is primarily ideological, politics not pleasure becomes their governing principle. Unlike the actual audiences for popular art, they view it generically in abstract terms — often with an unconscious element of professorial condescension. Although they aspire to a classless political consciousness, they cannot escape the social conditioning of their elitist university caste. When discussing popular art, they instinctively feel obliged to signal their Brahmin taste by demonstrating a sophisticated detachment from and intellectual superiority to the lowbrow material under review. Consequently, the notion that serious artists would employ popular forms in an unironic, undetached, and apolitical manner leaves these au courant theorists not merely dumbfounded but embarrassed.

Few early critics, for instance, understood the centrality of narrative poetry to the New Formalist enterprise. Although superficially unrelated to the use of rhyme and meter, the revival of narrative verse allowed the young writers to address several of the same broad cultural problems that had initially led them back to formal poetry. First, it gave them an inclusive literary mode that, however out of favor with academic theorists, nonetheless had immediate appeal to the non-specialist reader of novels and short stories. Second, narrative provided young poets with a genre that avoided the excessive narcissism of the confessional style (which had often vitiated the work of the older generation) and yet allowed them to write directly about highly emotional situations. Third, it gave them the opportunity for innovation because narrative poetry had not been actively explored by American writers since the days of Frost and Jeffers. Finally—and most subtly—narrative poetry helped fill the void left by the diminishment of the common cultural context. A story, by definition, creates its own context as it progresses. The self-contained psychological, social, and cultural contexts that fiction constructs in the reader's mind allow the narrative to tighten at certain moments and achieve powerfully lyric moments—"epiphanies," as a Joycean might call them—that represent the quintessential poetic effect. The impoverishment of public culture made it difficult to achieve these allusive connections in lyric poetry without limiting one's audience to the elite. But by creating their own *ad hoc* context within a narrative poem, the New Formalists pursued such imaginative epiphanies in a broadly accessible mode.

The new mode, however, did not prove especially accessible to the academy, which had set notions of what contemporary poems should or should not be. Frederick Turner's epic science fiction poem, *The New World*, for instance, was met with bewilderment or abuse by academic commentators, even while it earned high praise in nonacademic journals. Likewise, Vikram Seth's novel in verse (patterned in some ways after a soap opera), *The Golden Gate*, was dismissed by a neo-avant-garde apologist like Marjorie Perloff but was greeted enthusiastically by thousands of sophisticated fiction readers. Many critics have not understood the obvious point that writers in the movement—like Timothy Steele or R.S. Gwynn—have revitalized love poetry, satire, and verse narratives, not out of literary antiquarianism but because both the authors and their nonacademic readers actually enjoy these genres. It is not coincidental, I think, that the critics most committed to the "new" are often the ones who miss what is most original in New Formalism. Nor is it an accident that so many of the leading New Formalist writers either work outside the university or, if they are teachers, often did graduate work in literature rather than creative writing. As Perloff and other critics have noted, the movement is both a generational and contrarian response to the torpor of mainstream American academic poetry.

The generational and contrarian nature of New Formalism is ultimately the source of both its strengths and weaknesses. If the new movement has the vitality and confidence of youth, it often also displays the naivete and recklessness of inexperience. It also has the toughness of a group that defined itself in opposition to mainstream practice. But if that genesis endowed the poets with a feisty independence and healthy disregard for the critical fashions and professional protocol that enervated much current poetry, it also encouraged a certain narrow self-righteousness. One sees this parochialism most clearly among a hard-core faction of young formalists who are essentially anti-modernists. As critics, they are more apt to fight than explore new ideas, and, as poets, they are more likely to imitate than innovate. The ardent traditionalists, however, represent only a small part of a large, heterogeneous movement.

New Formalism remains a young movement still in the process of development and self-definition. Despite the active opposition of the middle-aged generation that dominates the poetry establishment, the new movement has not only gained notoriety but has changed the agenda of contemporary American poetry in several important ways. First, it has shifted the concerns of contemporary poetics by bringing serious attention to considerations of form, meter, mode, and genre after decades of neglect. Second, New Formalist poetry and criticism have democratized literary discourse. The poetry is accessible to nonspecialist readers. Likewise, whatever their limitations as critics, the New Formalists have written about poetry in a public idiom and thereby both enlivened and demystified critical discourse. Finally, the return to form, narrative, and traditional genres has changed the notion of the usable past by reviving dormant possibilities in twentieth-century American poetry. Previously peripheral narrative masters like Frost, Jeffers, and Robinson now seem central to contemporary poetic practice. At the moment the changes wrought by New Formalism are still coming too rapidly, and the amount of new poetry appearing is too overwhelming, to make any cogent judgments about its long-term place, but there is no question that the movement has both transformed and expanded the possibilities of American poetry.

Aspects of Robinson

Mark Jarman

Edwin Arlington Robinson, Robert Frost, and Robinson Jeffers represent the three r's of American narrative poetry in this century. Anyone writing or reading narrative poetry needs to come to terms with all of them.

Robinson shows us how narrative works in the small, elegant space of the lyric. By contrast, Robert Frost's narratives, usually written in blank verse, and often more like dramatic monologues than narratives, are open-ended. Robinson Jeffers' narratives while varying in length tend toward the loose, baggy monster of the novel.

While Robinson, Frost, and Jeffers together are the masters of narrative in modern American poetry, it is Robinson who managed best to wed the lyric with the story, especially as he took one lyric form—the sonnet—and turned it into a narrative vehicle. We remember the stories of Reuben Bright, the butcher who, after his wife died, "tore down the slaughterhouse," of Cliff Klingenhagen, who baffled his friend by drinking a glass of wormwood at dinner, and of Amaryllis, the beauty buried in a shallow grave in the woods. All of these are Italian sonnets. They share with Robinson's famous short narratives in quatrains, like "Richard Corey" and "The Mill," a sense that an entire life has been elegantly, faithfully, and sympathetically rendered.

Those characteristics are related not only to Robinson's artistry, but to his humanity. The American poets who have worked in the short narrative like Robinson, sometimes in the sonnet, sometimes in quatrains, sometimes in forms reminiscent of these Robinson favorites, have succeeded most when they have shown an elegance, faithfulness, and sympathy, like his.

The Robinson poem that might serve best as a model for his short narratives is the sonnet "Reuben Bright."

> Because he was a butcher and thereby
> Did earn an honest living (and did right),
> I would not have you think that Reuben Bright
> Was any more a brute than you or I;
> For when they told him that his wife must die,
> He stared at them, and shook with grief and fright,
> And cried like a great baby half that night,
> And made the women cry to see him cry.

And after she was dead, and he had paid
The singers and the sexton and the rest,
He packed a lot of things that she had made
Most mournfully away in an old chest
Of hers, and put some chopped-up cedar boughs
In with them, and tore down the slaughter-house.

Reuben Bright is summed up in the first four lines as an honest man with a profession associated with brutality (cutting up carcasses), yet the poet assures us that his profession has not coarsened him anymore than yours or mine. The signal event that shows us Reuben Bright's humanity (which is always the point in a poem by Robinson) is his wife's death and his response to it. Big Reuben the butcher is weaker than the women, perhaps members of an extended family. They may be the ones who have given him the news that his wife is dying, and now they are overcome by his response. Like a Greek chorus they reflect the communal sense of tragedy. The Robinsonian touch is first to depict this devastation in a man who deals with dead bodies every day, then to dramatize the extremity of his response. Though he has assured us that Reuben Bright was not a brute (no more than anyone who earns an honest living), still Reuben feels compelled to prove it himself by destroying the brutalizing way he made his living. It should not be necessary to emphasize the poignancy of the "chopped-up cedar boughs" he puts in the "old chest" with the things his wife had made. Still, his final act of grief is, indeed, violent, if not brutal.

All of this occurs in 14 lines, an octave and a sestet. The rhymes of the octave are the most intense, the highest pitched, in English poetry (they were Emily Dickinson's favorites, too). In the sestet only one rhyming pair ("rest / chest") eases up on the length of the vowel. The b-alliteration of the octave reinforces the insistence that Reuben Bright is no more brutal than the poet or the reader and at the same time undermines it. The iambic pentameter is straightforward in the octave, and all of its lines are endstopped except line three. In the sestet the meter is not as straightforward. There are enjambments in every line but the second, and two of them, in lines 12 and 13, are wrenching. Line 12 pushes the stresses to either side with a Tennysonian emphasis on assonance and alliteration.

And yet Robinson manipulates all of these effects so that they seem secondary. We discover them when we go back to understand the poem's technique. First it is Reuben Bright's humanity and the exactitude of his story that strike the reader—not like an ax-blow, but like watching a man wield an ax or, better yet, work with a carving knife.

Among Robinson's descendants who show his humane and artistic way with narrative within the confines of the lyric, the first to come to mind is James Wright. His sonnet "Saint Judas" is indeed a Robinsonian narrative and transforms the Robinsonian narrator in an utterly original way. Usually Robinson's narrators speak for a community (true of "Reuben Bright" but also of "Richard Corey"). Occasionally the narrator is a single witness to an event and a character's fate (as in "Cliff Klingenhagen" or "Amaryllis"). Always there is a sense, and this is Robinson's form of sympathy, that the narrator is implicated in his subject's tragedy.

James Wright makes his narrator the ultimate criminal in Christian mythology, doomed despite an ultimate act of humanity, which is all the more saintly because it will not benefit him in eternity. Like Robinson's, Wright's language in this poem is straightforward, and like Robinson at the moment of most intense mystery Wright puns on a large abstraction. "Flayed without hope," says Saint Judas who has rescued the victim of a beating, "I held the man for nothing in my arms." The relative values of "nothing" and "something" are central in Robinson's work. They are the poles of his pragmatic metaphysics, in which his characters have either made something or nothing of their lives. So it is in James Wright's poem.

When Wright turned from the kind of traditional verse that Robinson wrote, he did not abandon the way he employed narrative. The late poem "Hook" in which the speaker begins, "I was only a young man / In those days," includes the same kind of encounter between a witnessing, sympathetic "I" and a lost or baffled soul as we often find in Robinson. The stanzas of various lengths in free verse lines of various lengths should not deflect our understanding that the story is told in the same small space, the same confines, that Robinson employed, and with the same fullness. In "Hook" the young Sioux with the prosthetic hand, standing with the speaker on a bitterly cold street corner one night in Minneapolis, decides that the speaker needs 65 cents for bus money. The mysterious act of kindness, in which he places the coins in the speaker's cold hand with his hook, is narrated with Robinson's economy and his sense of completion.

It is hard to find a poet writing today who combines not only the Robinsonian technique of telling a story in a short lyric, but also Robinson's temperament. Still, when a short lyric, like the sonnet, is employed to tell a story, Robinson's influence is brought to bear.

Two recent poems, neither of them a sonnet nor a formal lyric, that seem to show both how the witnessing "I" is implicated as the story is told and how brevity gives the story shape—both aspects of Robinson—are Chase Twichell's "Silver Slur" from her book *The Ghost of Eden* and Kate Daniels' "Sorrow Figure" from *The Niobe Poems*.

In Twichell's poem compression has much to do with the duration of the event, a desolate, urban scene she has glimpsed from the train. But this is not merely an impressionistic anecdote. The poem is fraught with the desire to understand, to comprehend, even as the speaker insists that she cannot understand or comprehend.

Silver Slur

Nothing stays attached to what I saw,

what I glimpsed from a train.
It has no magnet for meaning.

Four men sat on a wall shooting up,

companionable. One waved at me.
Waved the needle. Ten feet away,

a man was fucking a woman from behind,
controlling her with her heavy necklace,

a bicycle chain. The budding sapling
shook as she clung to it,

her orange dress hitched up in back.
People there throw garbage out of windows.

Who cares? Four arms, four rolled-up sleeves.

The silver slur of light along the tracks.
Four arms, four rolled-up sleeves.

The orange dress hitched up in back.

Something does stay attached to what the speaker saw, and that is the sardonic, "companionable" wave one of the men gives her. It invites her to be more than a spectator, but a witness, a sympathizing witness, too, for the drug addicts and for the pair copulating out in the open. "Who cares?" the speaker asks, and as if to show her answer, the poem ends with an echo of the formal closure we would have in a Robinson lyric, accomplished by the repeated line, "Four arms, four rolled-up sleeves" and the rhyme of "tracks" and "back." The story itself is the magnet of meaning, and this poem clings to it with the symmetry of iron filings.

Where Robinson at the grave of Amaryllis states, "It made me lonely and it made me sad / To think that Amaryllis had grown old," Twichell repeats the bleak detail of "the orange dress hitched up in back." To deny comprehension, as she does, is not to deny empathy. And the poem's very first word, "Nothing," carries the moral weight Robinson himself attached to it.

Kate Daniels' "Sorrow Figure," a poem in prose, is shaped by an encounter between the speaker and a child who owns a set of toys she has studied. When the child addresses her, it is like the moment in a Robinson poem when a character, by thrusting himself into the speaker's consciousness, insists on being recognized and given his due.

Sorrow Figure

The toys are lying on the floor. They're some kind
of doll, plastic and bendable, blue and green, about
six inches tall. The little boy calls them his
"figures" and plays with them every day, imagining
family romances with complicated plots. One blue
figure is always placed off to the side, standing
on its feet but bent over with its hands pressed to
its face. From a distance, no one can tell what
separates this one from the rest of the group—whether
he's an expatriate, an exile, a pariah, a leper.
"Let me introduce you to the sorrow figure," the
little boy said one day. "He's so sad no one can
help him." It was then I noticed the sorrow figure
in the sunshine, glowing, a haze of blueness rising
from its bent-down body. I leaned closer. I heard
its little toy wail trapped inside the plastic body.
I heard the shudders, the sobs, the oaths. And I
heard, too, all the other toys chattering and enjoying
being played with as if nothing like this could ever
happen to them.

It is the purpose of the Robinsonian narrator to understand or to admit his inability to understand, both of which are forms of sympathy. Here the speaker has only a cursory interest in the child's toys until he makes her look closer, makes her see that for him they have a meaning more profound than she expected. She sees that the difference between innocence and experience is grief, and that a child may himself understand that difference.

Reminiscent also of Robinson is Daniels' own final figure about the toys "chattering and enjoying being played with as if nothing like this could ever happen to them." Our own humanity responds to this, since we know what causes sorrow. Yet there is that word "nothing" again. Robinson's "An Evangelist's Wife," begins "Why am I not myself these many days, / You ask? And have you nothing more to ask?'" The woman speaking in Robinson's poem is aware that her husband is unfaithful. The word "nothing" is laden with her knowledge. Daniels also employs the word to convey knowledge—the knowledge that loss ("nothing like this") can occur to anyone.

Though not a sonnet or a lyric in any traditional sense of the word, still Daniels' poem is replete with a humanity and an elegant sense of closure that recall Robinson. Both it and Twichell's "Silver Slur" confirm that today when narrative and the short lyric combine to be a study in character—both the poet's character and his or her subject's—Edwin Arlington Robinson is the presiding spirit.

Toward an Alternative Formalist Tradition: The Other Harlem Rennaissance

Carol E. Miller

It is unfortunate, but undeniable, that formalism is now most often associated with the elitism of a handful of highly influential, highly privileged artists and critics who would not acknowledge that their privilege betrayed their politics. As a result of this association, numbers of contemporary American poets for whom poetry is personal and political, politically engaged and committed do not consider writing formal verse an option. In her essay, "When We Dead Awaken: Writing as Re-Vision," first published in 1972, Adrienne Rich writes that when she began "to feel that politics was not something 'out there' but something 'in here' and of the essence of my condition," she also began to move away from formal verse, with its perceived prescription that poetry remain "universal" (44). Far from being genderless (or classless, or raceless), "universal" actually meant (white, middle- or upper-class) male; hence the desire to "[free] vision from the distorting prescription spectacles of the male 'universal,' and [let] *universal* take back its wholeness, its comprehension, without the hegemony of the defining 'the,'" as Suzanne Matson expresses it (124). Rich's investigation leads her to conclude: "We need to know the writing of the past, and know it differently than we have ever known it; not to pass on a tradition but to break its hold over us" (35). Breaking the hold of tradition has meant, in part, exposing the ideological underpinnings of its so-called universality, objectivity, and disinterestedness. It has also meant breaking from "the old political order" that tradition represents (Rich 35).

Thom Gunn believes that the "traditional poet" is one who brings "new experience to the traditional form" (224). Part of what Gunn has brought to traditional verse forms is his experience as a member of a gay community, with what he calls its "visionary carnal politics" (215). The result of this marriage between new experiences and political perspectives and traditional forms is a poetry of renewal, a poetry that is truly *new* while also being *formal.* Gunn has made it clear that he does not wish to be associated with nor encourage the new formalist school, because it draws upon "far too narrow a tradition" (227). Those who promote or claim membership in that school would do well to heed Gunn's criticism. A more comprehensive understanding of both tradition and formalism would locate new formalist poetry in the trajectory of multiple traditions rather than a single tradition. Robert McPhillips claims that new formalist poetry "transcend[s] sexual or ideological allegiances" (207). Instead of assuming that formal poetry must "transcend" such allegiances, however, it might finally be recognized for its political diversity, and as an artistic expression of multiple experiences and perspectives.

Walter Benjamin once said that remembering creates the chain of tradition. Despite current efforts to rethink canonicity and promote a more inclusive understanding of literary tradition, debates surrounding formal verse remain, in large part, enchained by selective memory. Opponents and proponents of the new formalism alike tend to "remember" formalism as a strictly New Critical phenomenon. Hence, whether they are defending or defying formal verse, these critics do so by privileging an exclusive notion of formalist tradition rather than fully considering the broad historical scope of formal verse. The danger in adopting such a myopic view of tradition, especially for those who ally themselves with new formalism, is that lines of distinction between the "new" and "old" quickly blur, and "new" formalist criticism seems merely to repeat the prejudices and privileges—and adopt the politics—of New Criticism. In "Toward a Liberal Poetics," although he cautions against polemicism, Paul Lake asserts repeatedly that "the best young poets in America" *are the best* because they have returned to "the greener pastures of formalism" (117-18). And McPhillips argues that part of what distinguishes new formalists from the "academic formalists" of the 1950s is that they are "rooted unselfconsciously in the middle class rather than in real or aspired to aristocracy," and that they "accept their own cultural tradition as firmly established" (200-201).

McPhillips not only suggests that, because the new formalists readily accept their middle class status, they don't have the "problem" with class their New Critical forebears did; he goes on to celebrate the fact that the new formalists claim both their class status and their entire cultural tradition as the norm, in precisely the same way that New Criticism assumed certain class, race, gender and cultural privileges to constitute a "firmly established" norm. These are exactly the sorts of things we can no longer afford to accept, let alone celebrate, however. As Paul Breslin writes: "If anything is clear through the murk of Bushreaganism, it's that this firmly established cultural tradition is a reactionary fantasy, papering over deep fissures of race, class, and ethnicity" (145). If the new formalist poetry is written only from the premises McPhillips delineates and only in support of Lake's claims for its superiority, then that poetry is taking "white middle-class life too readily as the universal, as 'the' established culture" (Breslin 145), and the distinction between "new" and "old" formalist ideologies collapses. As long as New Criticism remains the single historical referent in the construction of formalist tradition, selective memory will continue to bind formal verse to the politics of elitism and exclusion.

Dana Gioia positions himself, and new formalism, as challenger to what he perceives as the "ruling orthodoxy" of free verse (32), but he poses no challenge to the political orthodoxy of New Criticism. This is because, despite Gioia's and others' claims of a free verse ruling orthodoxy, those who continue to link formal verse with a particular politics do so as a result of the more trenchant orthodoxies of high modernism. Free verse may dominate the second half of this century, but the voices of critical authority that brought us the politics of disinterest in the first half are still heard today, and still exert tremendous influence. Pound's call for "[o]bjectivity and again objectivity" (48) and Eliot's claims that the "emotion of art is impersonal" and that "the poet cannot reach this impersonality without surrendering himself wholly" (59) initiated a critical practice that, in propounding an "objective" theory of art, not only privileged the formal elements of poetry, but pretended to an apolitical stance as well. As Terry Eagleton writes: "Reading poetry in the New Critical way meant committing yourself to nothing: all that poetry taught you was 'disinterestedness', a serene, speculative, impeccably even-handed rejection of anything in particular. . . . It was, in other words, a recipe for political inertia." This criticism, Eagleton continues, "displays an extraordinary lack of interest in what literary works actually *say*" as opposed to how they are *made*, while it insists that texts can and must be disengaged from any social or historical context (48-51). It is, of course, this desire to remain detached, objective and impersonal — coupled with the notion that poetry can and should be written and read in a social and historical vacuum — that renders much high modernist discourse politically suspect. For what does disinterest mask but the patent unwillingness to engage critically with the social exigencies of one's world? And what does the pretense of apoliticism communicate but willful elitism, born of the attitude that what concerns the so-called masses is of no concern to art or the artist?

In 1926, W.E.B. DuBois articulated a distinctly alternative modernist consciousness when he wrote that "all art is propaganda and ever must be, despite the wailings of the purists" (196). DuBois' aesthetic, Paul Gilroy writes, "insists (against the grain of modernity's attempts to separate truth, justice and beauty from each other and to separate them all from ethics and politics) that these three dimensions of human social practice should not, indeed cannot, be divided from each other" (161). Hence, DuBois' announcement: "I do not care a damn for any art that is not used as propaganda for gaining the right for black folk to love and enjoy. I do care when propaganda is confined to one side while the other is stripped and silent" (196). As DuBois rightly observes here, the "purists" who insist that politics only sully art are, of course, themselves propagandists, intent on silencing dissenting voices and dismissing the dissenters' art as inferior, "primitive," even (heaven forbid) "popular." Gilroy maintains that DuBois was "one of the first black Atlantic thinkers to try to theorize the relationship between modern consciousness and racial subordination," and he was clearly not wrong to do so (160). What else could explain why DuBois' pronouncement that the problem of the Twentieth Century is the problem of the color line was patently ignored by high modernists, despite its arguable accuracy? Those whom DuBois refers to as "purists" have, throughout this century, assumed that if the color line is a problem, it's not their *problem*. And it's certainly not a problem that art should address or reflect. Nor is the problem of the gender line, the class line, or other lines of discrimination drawn to protect the privilege of the few.

The fact that DuBois' politicized aesthetic was relegated to the margins of modernist discourse hardly invalidates it, however. On the contrary, it clears a space in which to locate the alternative poetic tradition I am suggesting here.[1] The work of DuBois' contemporary, the Jamaican poet Claude McKay, certainly belongs to this tradition, as does the work of other poets of the Harlem Renaissance. Certain critics, among them Nathan Huggins, J. Saunders Redding, and Maureen Honey, have faulted poets of that move-

---

[1] I do not wish to imply that this alternative tradition is a "marginal" one, however, thereby rehashing the rather tired margin/center binary. That would be counterproductive, as it would merely repeat rather than challenge the impulse to assign verse forms to discrete, easily identifiable binary categories. The point in proposing alternatives is to get beyond the either/or, to explore the interstice between the two for further possibilities.

ment for what Honey calls their "failure to challenge a literary tradition built by the very culture that oppressed them," which, she claims, "resulted in a rather awkward fusion of radical sentiment and sentimental form" (32). While this may have been the case for some poets, McKay's sonnet "If We Must Die" [discussed at length in Adrienne Rich's essay "Format and Form" in this volume] can hardly be called sentimental, nor does it fail to challenge the oppressions of the prevailing literary tradition. On the contrary, McKay's sonnet exemplifies what Rich calls a poetics of resistance: "McKay takes the traditional poetic form of the colonizer and turns it into a rebellion cry, takes the poetics of war and turns it into a poetics of resistance" ("Format" 220). Rather than fusing "radical sentiment and sentimental form" in this sonnet and many others, McKay is in fact subverting the sonnet form. McKay appropriates the form to both contest its power, its authority as part of a tradition that has excluded and silenced him, and to empower himself. Like Caliban, McKay has learned to curse, but he has learned to curse in poetry that poses a direct challenge to both the oppressor's superiority and the way he has used poetry to oppress. McKay's appropriation of the sonnet is rebellious because it subverts the ideology of apolitical formalism; it is both threatening and exhilarating because it succeeds, because the result is a powerful, important poem that cannot be dismissed.

Audre Lorde has made the cogent argument that the master's tools will not dismantle the master's house; in the case of McKay's "If We Must Die," however, one might argue that those tools, coopted and put to subversive use, will sometimes light a fire in the basement. McKay's sonnet, copied out by hand, was found by a state trooper in the aftermath of an inmate uprising at Attica in 1971. The inmates, who were protesting prison conditions, were clearly stirred by the power of McKay's sonnet, the first quatrain of which they must have felt spoke directly to their situation: "If we must die,/ let it not be like hogs/ Hunted and penned in an inglorious spot,/ While round us bark the mad and hungry dogs,/ Making their mock at our accursed lot." This sonnet was also found on the body of an African-American soldier killed in combat during World War II (Rich, "Format" n.267-8). Considering the enmity black soldiers faced from Axis and Allied troops alike, the fierce irony of McKay's second quatrain in particular could not have been lost on this soldier: "If we must die, O let us nobly die,/ So that our precious blood may not be shed/ In vain; then even the monsters we defy/ Shall be constrained to honor us though dead!" It is doubtful that this sonnet would continue to resonate so powerfully had McKay been content to merely fuse radical sentiment and sentimental form, or were he writing simply to appeal to popular sentiment, as his "purist" contemporaries might have dismissively charged.

The lesser-known work of Effie Lee Newsome, another Harlem Renaissance poet, also belongs to this alternative formalist tradition. The poetics of resistance Rich identifies in McKay's work is present in Newsome's as well, as "Exodus," a poem that uses rhyme and meter expertly to set up and subvert expectation, clearly attests. "Exodus" is a ten-line poem, divided into two stanzas of five lines each; its subject is the great migration of blacks from South to North that followed in the wake of the Civil War and continued well into this century. The poem's title also evokes the biblical exodus of the Israelites, delivered out of Egyptian slavery into the promise of their own land "flowing with milk and honey." In this respect, Newsome's poem might be read as support for Helen Vendler's claim that a poem "composed of two stanzas . . . is almost always occupied with binary terms—choice, contrast, comparison." But while "Exodus" does evoke certain comparisons between the great migration and the Israelite exodus, Newsome is clearly employing heavy irony while contesting the neat "binary terms" of the comparison. She is also contesting the "choice" those terms leave her with. Vendler concludes that "the two-stanza form insists that one must occupy one room or the other of the poem" (Introduction 8). Rather than capitulate to this either/or binary, however, "Exodus" calls it into question by suggesting that neither "room" in the poem is fit for occupancy. The North is clearly not the "promised land" it was made out to be, as Jim Crow laws, the threat of lynching, and other manifestations of extreme racism followed blacks wherever they went. What kind of "choice" is that, the poem asks, and what kind of "deliverance"?

Newsome also skillfully enlists meter to expose the inadequacies of binary terms. The poem's first stanza establishes a metrical pattern that each line strictly follows, deviating not so much as one beat. The effect of this on the reader is twofold: it sets up a predictable pattern, establishing what Shapiro calls a "norm of expectation" (205), which in turn lulls the reader into a sense of security, born of familiarity. The "pastoral" image the stanza creates only adds to this sense of predictability, comfort, familiarity: "Rank fennel and broom/ Grow wanly beside/ The cottage and room/ We once occupied,/ But sold for the snows!" True, this "garden" is untended, making it faintly sinister, but the speaker's ostensible longing for the place, and for the past, is only magnified by the final line, with its contrasting snow and cold. The metrical regularity in this stanza works in concert with the stereotypical North/South binary Newsome seems to endorse. The agrarian South here is warm, and "natural"; its cottages are quaint, the pace of life easy. In short, the poem seems to support the stereotype of the South as a paradise for black folk who just want to live close to the earth, simple creatures that they are. The industrial North, on the other hand, is snowy and cold, an "unnatural" climate for the "African." Nothing about Newsome's meter in this stanza invites the reader to challenge these fictions. On the contrary, the metrical predictability mirrors the predictable familiarity of the North/South binary, with its prescriptive racial and social norms. Nothing here disrupts the comforting image of African-Americans in their "proper place."

The only clue that stanza two will disrupt this mock-reverie comes in the last line of stanza one. The word "sold" seems a curious choice, but its effect is chilling when "blood," "crow," "grow," and "weird wastes" accumulate in the second stanza: "The dahoon berry weeps in blood,/ I know,/ Watched by the crow—/ I've seen both grow/ In those weird wastes of Dixie!" From the outset, this stanza violates the metrical pattern stanza one adhered to so strictly, only echoing that stanza in its irregularly placed anapestic feet. This abrupt metrical shift jars the reader to attention, while disquieting images displace more comfortable ones. But Newsome has not set up expectation in stanza one simply to topple it in stanza two—the stanzas don't function that independently, they are not that much at odds with one another because they are not simply binary. Stanza two sends us back to stanza one to reread its imagery—and our response to that imagery—more critically, and more realistically. Newsome shatters the veneer of tranquility by foregrounding the terror inscribed on the landscape itself, spattering the pastoral idyll with blood. She does so not to merely shatter an ideal, but to insist that *no place* is safe. The speaker in this poem is not remembering the terror of the South from the security of the North, because that "security" is a myth that she, like others, has been "sold." She may have seen the blood of her race growing on the southern landscape as densely as its rank vegetation, and the germination and rapid growth of Jim Crow there, and the weird waste of African-American lives on plantations or at the hands of lynch mobs, but that doesn't mean she escaped those terrors by migrating North. She has traded—or "sold"—one set of terrors for another.

Her forebears were sold into slavery, now she has sold the South for the North, where the legacy of slavery continues. Just as "Dixie" is exposed as a fictional construct that ignores material realities, so, too, is the "promised land" of the North, with its forbidding (and foreboding) cold, the same Jim Crow laws, and the same threat of bloodshed.

Similar to McKay's reclamation of the sonnet as a form of protest, Newsome's co-optation of this two-stanza form protests the binarisms some would have it perpetuate, binarisms that can lead to polarizing fictions of race and region which ignore the real conditions of African-American lives. Newsome's manipulation of meter in the poem is very much a part of her protest, as she creates formal tensions that force us to confront our expectations and to examine our complicity in the maintenance of essentialist constructs. Though her sentiment is radical for its time, she can hardly be accused of expressing it in merely "sentimental form."

Gwendolyn Brooks' poetry, much of which takes traditional verse forms, enacts rebellions similar to those of McKay and Newsome. Brooks' sonnet, "my dreams, my works, must wait till after hell," from *Gay Chaps at the Bar*, a collection that captures the anxieties and images of life during wartime, depicts a kind of mental preparation for combat. But the poem is also about other wars, wars waged against oppressions, including the oppressive force of literary tradition. Brooks taps the rebellious energy of those whose work and worth have been trivialized, dismissed, or sacrificed for "worthier" causes. She is well aware of this energy's potential for (self)destruction, if it is not carefully directed. Rather than striking a blow against oppression and affecting any real change, rebellion can boomerang; hence it is kept tightly in check by force of will, reserved for constructive ends. That the poem is about continuing to value oneself and one's work in the face of derision is difficult to contest. The title itself is printed in lower-case letters, suggesting the aspersions cast on the speaker's dreams and works. That it is set in a domestic space is fairly obvious as well, given Brooks' metaphors of lidded, latched, and labelled jars and cabinets. This domesticity suggests two kinds of traditionally "insignificant" and undervalued labor—that of women in their homes, and that of people of color in domestic service—both of which reflect the "insignificance" of the speaker's *other* work, the work she dreams of doing. The rebelliousness of this poem is that it promises retribution and recognition. The lines, "I am very hungry. I am incomplete./ And none can tell when I may dine again./ No man can give me any

word but Wait," encapsulate the rage of waiting and wanting, of being ig-
nored. But again, it is a rage that must be controlled and directed so as not
to consume the speaker, and Brooks' meter in these lines captures the ten-
sion between the desire to explode and the will to contain that desire. "I am
very hungry. I am incomplete," the fifth line of the poem, deliberately breaks
the strict pentameter of the first four lines, its hunger straining against the
latches and lids the form imposes. In lines six and seven, however, Brooks
reins the meter in again, as the speaker exercises her will and temporarily
succumbs to waiting. She must wait, she must endure and "keep eyes pointed
in" to keep from sacrificing her inner strength, her resilience, and her dreams.
What is external to her, what the world can currently offer is only "puny
light." The speaker knows, or hopes, however, that "when the devil days of
my hurt/ Drag out to their last dregs," what light she carries *inside* herself
will not have been extinguished by her hunger; that she will "remember to
go home," to return to herself and honor that self; that "[m]y taste will not
have turned insensitive/ To honey and bread old purity could love." When
this occurs, the subordination of her dreams and works to the "puny light"
of others will no longer be tolerated.

It is the promise that the speaker will not only *endure* the world but will
change it through her endurance—and without sacrificing herself in the pro-
cess—that makes this sonnet both hopeful and rebellious. In it, Brooks is
echoing the radical prophesy of Langston Hughes' poem "I, Too," which
envisions not only justice for African-Americans, but a sea-change in the
American aesthetic. Their patience exhausted, those consigned to the kitchen
and kept out of sight will tomorrow "be at the table/ When company comes,"
Hughes declares. Still, for Hughes, like Brooks, this is not enough. Hughes
concludes that, in addition to recognition, justice, equality, "[t]hey'll see
how beautiful I am/ and be ashamed—." In Hughes' vision for "tomorrow,"
what was considered unworthy, inferior, even repulsive will finally be rec-
ognized for its beauty, signalling a radical aesthetic shift (Vendler, "Identity
Markers" 395). In Brooks' sonnet, what comes after hell will be beautiful
too, having survived with its integrity and purity intact. The rebellious will
rise up and reclaim their voices, show themselves, their dreams, and their
works for what they are: praiseworthy, every bit as significant as the works
of those who have dismissed, ignored, or degraded them. Brooks proves, in
the very act of writing this sonnet, not only that she *can*, but that she can
descend into the hell of a literary tradition that refuses to acknowledge her

existence and emerge with her dreams, her work, her vision intact. Like McKay's sonnet, this one insists: I will not give up, give in, or disappear. Brooks uses the sonnet form to subvert it, to make it work for and with her, instead of against her. And like Newsome, Brooks responds to a literary tradition that would erase, silence, or speak for her by insisting that she speak for herself, that hers is the right to self-representation.

It is clear from each of these poems, published between 1922 and 1945, than none of the poets was willing to allow his or her imagination or artistic vision to be circumscribed by the ruling orthodoxy of the period. Nowhere in this work do we find the pretense of "objectivity," "universality" or "impersonality," nor the politics of disinterest. Rather than defer to the critical authority of those who denounced the radical politicization of formal verse, these poets, like so many others, challenged that authority, rejecting the exclusive version of literary tradition it authorized. Through them, we have access to an alternative tradition, one that grew out of the alternative modernist consciousness of those who, like DuBois, acknowledged that art is always "propagandizing" in the sense that it is always politicized. It is to this alternative tradition—which does not privilege form over content or attempt to sanitize literary works by divorcing them from their social and historical context—that much of the formal verse written this century belongs. Elizabeth Bishop's poems "Cootchie," "The Burglar of Babylon" and "Pink Dog" are excellent examples. Each one supports Rich's belief that, throughout her life, "Bishop was critically and consciously trying to explore marginality, power and powerlessness, often in poetry of great beauty and sensuousness" ("Outsider" 135). That her New Critical contemporaries were more concerned with obfuscating issues of marginality and power than exploring them apparently did not convince Bishop that this was not the stuff of "real poetry." Bishop's work reveals her world to her reader in exacting emotional and physical detail. Unable to dismiss the injustices she saw in that world, Bishop recorded them in her poetry, often in exquisitely crafted formal verse. So, too, does Derek Walcott, whose work consistently examines and questions the distributions of power that created and foster certain racial, social, and national hegemonies. His tightly wound stanzas in "The Arkansas Testament," his explosion of the sonnet form in *Midsummer*, his epic reclamation of colonial history and literary tradition in *Omeros* all belong to this alternative formalist tradition as well. So does work by Thom Gunn, Marilyn Hacker, Rita Dove and a multitude of exceptional poets too numerous to name here.

The Irish poet Eavan Boland has written widely on her discontent with and challenges to her country's poetic tradition. Because women—or the image of "Woman"—has been "allotted a place in the Irish poem ... as object, not subject," Boland realized she had been given "a place of passivity and silence in the very tradition" that gave her her poetic voice. Unwilling to sacrifice her own subjectivity in the name of tradition, she set out to alter the "powerful relations between subject and object" embodied in that tradition. Boland's desire was to see the public "joined by the private lives and solitary perspectives, including [her] own, which the Irish poetic tradition had not yet admitted to authorship." She wanted to witness "the effect of an unrecorded life—a woman in a suburban twilight under a hissing streetlight—on the prescribed themes of public importance" (183-87). Boland's critique is specific to Irish literary tradition, but it is relevant to the present discussion as well. Those poets whose work created and sustains a viable alternative formalist tradition wanted, as Boland did, to see lives and perspectives unauthorized by the existing tradition take shape and speak in poetry. They, too, wanted to see the effect of an unrecorded life, to introduce that life to formal and thematic prescriptives to see what could happen, to challenge those prescriptives. They, too, contested power relations embedded in literary tradition, its objectifications and omissions, its lapses of memory. They wanted to create something different with the tools they were told should only create a certain thing in a certain way. So they did, and still do. Boland is writing about—and fomenting—very recent changes in the Irish poetic tradition, but there is nothing "new," in a historical sense, about the alternative formalist tradition I am positing here. That tradition has been in the making at least as long as the one many poets and critics seem intent on remembering as the only formalist tradition. What would be new, however, and what would go a long way toward establishing new formalism as a truly new discipline, is a comprehensive, critical re-evaluation of formalist verse tradition, one that supports alternative formalisms and encourages poets to draw upon them.

WORKS CITED

Breslin, Paul. "Two Cheers for The New Formalism." *Kenyon Review 2* (Spring 1991): 143-148.

Boland, Eavan. *Object Lessons*. New York: Norton, 1995.

Brooks, Gwendolyn. "my dreams, my works, must wait till after hell." *Selected Poems*. New York: Harper & Row, 1963. 23.

DuBois, W.E.B. "The Criteria of Negro Art." *The Crisis 6* (October 1926): 196.

Eagleton, Terry. *Literary Theory*. Minneapolis: University of Minnesota Press, 1983.

Eliot, T.S. "Tradition and the Individual Talent." *The Sacred Wood*. London: Methuen, 1920. 48-59.

Gilroy, Paul. "Whose millennium is this?" *Small Acts*. London: Serpent's Tail, 1993. 153-165.

Gioia, Dana. "Notes on the New Formalism." *Can Poetry Matter?* St. Paul, MN: Graywolf Press, 1992. 31-46.

Gunn, Thom. *Shelf Life*. Ann Arbor: University of Michigan Press, 1993.

Honey, Maureen. Introduction. *Shadowed Dreams: Women's Poetry of the Harlem Renaissance*. Ed. Maureen Honey. New Brunswick, NJ: Rutgers UP, 1989. 1-41.

Hughes, Langston. "I, Too." *Selected Poems*. New York: Vintage, 1990. 275.

Lake, Paul. "Toward a Liberal Poetics." *Expansive Poetry: Essays on The New Narrative & The New Formalism*. Ed. Frederick Feirstein. Santa Cruz: Story Line Press, 1989. 113-123.

Matson, Suzanne. "On Reclaiming 'the Universal.'" *Where We Stand: Women Poets on Literary Tradition*. Ed. Sharon Bryan. New York: Norton, 1993. 118-124.

McKay, Claude. "If We Must Die." *Selected Poems*. San Diego: Harcourt Brace, 1981. 36.

McPhillips, Robert. "What's New About The New Formalism?" *Expansive Poetry: Essays on The New Narrative & The New Formalism*. Ed. Frederick Feirstein. Santa Cruz: Story Line Press, 1989. 195-208.

Newsome, Effie Lee. "Exodus." *Shadowed Dreams: Women's Poetry of the Harlem Renaissance*. Ed. Maureen Honey. New Brunswick, NJ: Rutgers UP, 1989. 69.

Pound, Ezra. *The Letters of Ezra Pound 1907-41*. D.D. Paige, Ed. New York: Norton, 1950.

Rich, Adrienne. "Format and Form." *What Is Found There*. New York: Norton, 1993. 217-227.

—. "The Eye of the Outsider: Elizabeth Bishop's Complete Poems." *Blood, Bread, and Poetry*. New York: Norton, 1986. 124-135.

—. "When We Dead Awaken: Writing as Re-Vision." *On Lies, Secrets, and Silence*. New York: Norton, 1979. 33-49.

Shapiro, Alan. "The New Formalism." *Critical Inquiry 1* (Autumn 1987): 200-213.

Vendler, Helen. "Rita Dove: Identity Markers." *Callaloo 2* (Summer 1994): 381-398.

—, Ed. Introduction. *The Harvard Book of Contemporary American Poetry*. Cambridge, MA: Belknap-Harvard UP, 1985. 1-17.

Poetics

Blues in Black and White

Carolyn Beard Whitlow

"Classical minus Jazz? — the Blues —"
("Verily, Vérité")

In the vernacular, Mama musta knew. Named me Carolyn, called me Carol, song. Mama, a British Isles West Indian New Yorker; Daddy, a gray collared self-employed Southern-bred gentleman, a man of property; strivers, both admired reading the classics, classical music: Mama bought season tickets each year for my brother and me to attend the Young People's Concerts conducted by Leonard Bernstein. I'd come home those Saturdays, and every other day of the week, B-lined for the radio — WJLB or WCHB — after all, I lived in the original Motown, on the lower east side, and loved to fingerpop. I could name every car eased off the GM or Ford assembly lines by make, model, year, and lip sync every song on the radio, rock 'n roll, rhythm and blues. Daddy would come home from work, tired. Not speak. Go straight to the radio. Cut it off. I'd punch it on. Off. On. Off. On. A wonder I wasn't slapped, my ear, and later my pen, stubborn; mind recalcitrant; feet hot. I learned to dance on the street corner. Ours a two-story house without stories, silent except when my mother and I tossed words over a metronome, I grudgingly fingered the piano, organ, violin. And rocked the radio like a doll.

Writing began at 30 — "nickels of daylight spent/night an empty pocket" — and won't stop. Now "eleven after thirty" (or more) "the hour of blue, monochrome/blue, mean blue, median, mode," my lyrics pluck metaphorical chords, like Lucille riffin' on B.B.'s rhythm section: lap CLAP lap CLAP-CLAP lap CLAP lap CLAP-CLAP, voice-over deep and high. I cord with language any discord with my upbringing; my personae allow me to lift the mask of shy, polite innocence, that brand of femininity defined by my parents replaced by a bragging sexuality, a ribald humor. The power in the speaker, the spoken, soup so flavorful it swells the pot; images auditory, tactile, lines that must be felt to be rendered, sung:

> Blueblack hair slicked back
> hot comb smooth, slimmer
> not slender, trunk packed,
> healthy, say she flat

chested a lie, sweet somethin'
a man wont to get a holt of,
squeeze some'nat natchel sugar, make juice,
thick nose spread to fine, sequin shimmers
stacked down to the nines,
stilettos tremblin', toes
tappin', her laugh like hand clappin', fingers
diamond ringed, eyes Rhine stoned, lashes low,
baubles lobed, spangles danglin', ruby
lipped slivers aquiver, two
teeth glinted gold behind'nat smile,
smoky spotlight pooled on a too small
stage, satin doll stylin' on the B-side,
hands hipped, beltin' out I pity
the fool leavin' south on the next train
goin' down, goin' slow slow down—
say she cry, cry, cry,
say love me, love me, say you do,
say love'll make you walk away,
lay love aside, walk away, she worry,
she worry the line, hum, scat, moan,
trumpet mumblin', backup whinin',
tenor guitar strummin'nem blues, lyin',
tryin', cryin' blues, drumbeat foot stomp,
bass taut, microphone she hold like
a telephone to her heart, say,
"I gotta sang my song..."

("Verily, Vérité")

No shuck, no jive. I don the mask of sensuality— icons of sexuality,
eroticism, freedom, power, control, choice, creativity, emotion, "masculin-
ity," nature, earthiness, fullness/roundness/plushness, give voice to women
who can sweat, haul out a song and belt it or purr it, whose hips were meant
to do more than sit, their voices instruments, their bodies the song, in lines
which call for a flat-pick guitar response; this persona just one of the folk
left by "Long Gone":

I give away my lovin' like a grocer give a sack.
Say, I give away my lovin' to anyone who ast—
Cause the one I wants to want me say he ain't comin' back.

Cause the one I wants to need me done put me on the shelf.
Say, the one I needs to need me done put me on the shelf.
Say he done foun' another, he done found somebody else.

Called me Honey Sugar Baby, said I was his Georgia peach.
Called me Sugar, Honey, Baby; called me his Sweet Georgia Peach—
Talkin' trash til I'd go crazy; Lawd that sinner man could preach.

("Supermarket Blues")

Though I must have listened (still do) to the goddesses of the godhead —Queen, Empress, Lady, Ma— these embodiments of both the serpent and Eve, they who give birth to earth, to song, women unafraid of drink, smoke, drugs, men, women, the dark, these worker/doers, these song-Smiths— the blues diva of greatest impact was and is Nina, whose renderings make every day a Billie holiday. Nina's songs epitomize the density of brain, heart, spirit, sinew, gristle and flesh (not "femininity") which is the human manifestation of the power inherent in the blend of nature/nurture, its innateness a given, not made. Nina makes black women visible through her own lens, unfiltered, natural in weakness and strength, true— "I'm a woman— can't you see what I am?" "ain't nobody's bidness what I do"; kiss "Ma Rainey's black bottom!" She commands performance. Slick, pumiced soapstone smooth, sensual, as to bathe in bubble bath ("Your lips, hands/ My many mounds—/...You turn me/Like an egg over soft/ Beat my drum slowly/ Drum song dance/ Tongue talking"), or tough, her lyrics coy, plaintive or suggestive, demanding, seductive, her piano a crescendo, but the gift the giver herself:

Sit there and count your fingers
ripple black bass blue notes—
graveled silt-throated postlude,
prelude of song,
scratchin' that old back door
where the sun gon' shine some day—
tympanic, symphonic, mechanic of grace,
major of minor chords, fortissimo, arpeggio;
trembling, hum mumbling
trumbles cleft treble; jazz razzed—

("Little Girl Blue")

Her renditions, which convey a sense of disappointment rather than bitterness, trained my ear; she makes the locus of attention listening to music that makes you remember to forget troubles; music in lowered thirds, fifths, sevenths, progressive shadings, minors, flattened notes, syncopated inflections of emotional intensity, suggestiveness, counter-rhythms and improvisations; its sweetness blends of milk chocolate, caramel, vanilla fudge, butter pecan, its tartness lemon sherbet.

Blues poetry is a poetry of SELF definition, a melodic fusion, a marriage of word and note, sound and image, a drum shout, guitar scream-hum, harmonica hollerin' a plaintive refrain, organ wail derailed, an openess, receptacle, a hole which holds, refrain standin' on the corner, just waitin' on a round:

Rockin' A Man, STone Blind

Cake in the oven, clothes out on the line,
Night wind blowin' against sweet, yellow thighs,
Two-eyed woman rockin' a man stone blind.

Man smell of honey, dark like coffee grind;
Countin' on his fingers since last July.
Cake in the oven, clothes out on the line.

Mister Jacobs say he be colorblind,
But got to tighten belts and loosen ties.
Two-eyed woman rockin' a man stone blind.

Winter becoming angry, rent behind.
Strapping spring sun needed to make mud pies.
Cake in the oven, clothes out on the line.

Looked in the mirror, Bessie's face I find.
I be so down low, my man be so high.
Two-eyed woman rockin' a man stone blind.

Policemans found him; damn near lost my mind.
Can't afford no flowers; can't even cry.
Cake in the oven, clothes out on the line.
Two-eyed woman rockin' a man stone blind.

Blues Villanelle. Blues in black and white. Touchstone of traditions, African-American and European, a fusion of form and content, embodiment of the influences of folk, blues, jazz, gospel, classical, harmonies of the musico-literary languages we speak. But this brew ain' bleach blon'. American black to its roots, even couched in a villanelle, this syncretion is poetry steeped in a folk tradition which lifts off the page in its orality. The languid eight-beat accentual-syllabic triplets with an AAa rhyme scheme in "Super-market Blues" above have been modified to fit the AbA2 structure of the standard villanelle stanza, form in both instances taking a back seat to the blusality of the content, voice dominant regardless of whether the audience —not reader, for blues is in the aural tradition— is schooled in traditional European poetic forms. In other words, as Nina Simone contrapuntally sings "Little Girl Blue" atop the tinkle of "Good King Wenceslas," so the poetic tension of blues and villanelle. The rhythm section never loses a beat, though, for fingersnaps of iambic pentameter still undergird each line, and the requisite repetitive lines come round— each propelling the narrative structure of the poem forward. Here we have a variation on expected themes and form, an anticipatory invention, as in creating an aesthetic pattern in a wall of bricks.

A blues villanelle like "Rockin' A Man," then, is musically arranged and orchestrated, as it were, by a maestro who simultaneously operates as a conductor on the historical Underground Railroad. Such a maestro knows how to lead and to follow—call and response; knows music what's good, good for what's bad, music of the good and bad; knows music levels class boundaries— the symphonic wealth in the cultures of the poor which cross boundaries of race; knows music as the truth serum of the human condition; knows ditties written in life script, the concerts of the living, the loveless, the loving and loved; hears melodies from the hearts of experience, of dreams deferred, no whitewashed soaps; dances to tunes of hip shakers, rule breakers with one life to live— the nonsynthetic chorale of straw, cotton, hemp and flax, the singing of steel and smoke and grease, the arias of brown sugar to rum, Scotch straight, Bourbon chased, "somebody give me my gin"; the unwritten book, the word wrenched from the tablet, plunked out, vocalized, hell holed up in bars and jukes:

> The whang of white-boy guitar,
> blue gums and stubble, fingers
> with bar rot, playing on my heartbeat
> a hamstrung, one-string blues—
>
> ("Verily, Vérité")

Thus, these poems pay homage to the music and its makers, the music of transcendance, liberation, which sets the imprisoned free.

Blues in black and blue. As the coalescence of form and content birth "Rockin' A Man," however, a bruising of voice occurs. Tightlipped, the persona commands her own voice only in the first two lines in the penultimate stanza and the first two in the final. Otherwise, an intimate omniscient controls the narrative in third person. First person intimacy, however, in rendering the tale is characteristic of a blues lyric. In "Local Call" below, the emotionally bruised persona owns her own tale, wrenching it out in her own voice:

Local Call

You handle me like I'm a local call.
I'm expensive. Long distance — although
having never been loved I don't know how

to tell you so. So I answer the phone
anticipate its diamond ring and let
you handle me like I'm a local call,

your line old as an old simile, stale
as a dead metaphor, you who's always had,
having. Never been loved, I don't know how

not to wish you would not stop stop not
loving me, the sidewalk running past me,
you handle me like I'm a local call,

laugh in another language, hung phone screaming,
me unsure whether my anger volcano or match —
I don't know, having never been loved, how

to love, my mind stalled with grafitti,
imagination sore, hum "don't want nobody
don't want me," accept your local call,
having never been loved, knowing I don't know how.

Caught between the need to follow "rules" as in the strict form of the villanelle — and the need for immersion in the blues-community in order to give birth to herself through the articulation of her pain, the voicing of her "I" through her eye, the persona improvises, riffs on the blues, embellishes, and emerges in a jazz-blues — Juezz — on a modified villanelle base which dances freely (Buck and Wing) into a "Winged Villanelle." Here the emphasis not the mode but the message, not the water but the water-bearer bearing. Thus in the oration of her story, the recognition of the call to "speak on it," the persona responds by aerating the form of the telling, opening the wings of the villanelle. Witness: whereas in "Local Call" only the first and last lines of the poem are end-stopped by periods, these boundaries serving as bookends, in "Rockin' A Man," the frequency of lines end-stopped with periods increases stanza by stanza such that the last three stanzas are fully end stopped— the form of the telling as roped in, corralled, constrained as the lives of which it speaks, the unyielding repetition a magnification. Instead, "Local Call," in its openness, almost freefalls with enjambment, its caesuras internalized, its repetitions liquid, self-revelatory. The syllabically-strict "Rockin'" also gives way to the full range of the pentameter-based syllable counts in "Local Call," 9-13 per line, with reason without rhyme.

"Local Call" would not exist without its precursors, "Verily, Vérité" and "Rockin' A Man." "Rockin'" written first, taught me to love the villanelle; "Verily" trumpets my tribute to blues singers and music, and is the most open in form of the three—free verse. These, together with their sister blues poems, resonate for me as a festival of sounds, carnival of voices, an instrumental picnic, a party, a lyrical celebration. Simply said, their intertextuality puts "a little sugar in my bowl."

From Gilded Cage to Rib Cage
Molly Peacock

The dazzling confusion of style and substance, like a brilliant feather which one cannot say for sure is absolutely green or absolutely blue, is what we refer to when we say that form creates content in a poem as does content create form. But this forgets the initial palette of the creator of the poem, who knows (or hopes she knows) how much green and how much blue are required for the mix. Common wisdom says that the poet must choose the suitable form for the subject, where the mind and the language are at one. Wisdom says appropriateness is all: the form must be capable of the same gesture as the feeling. Supporting this is the brilliance of finished poems, their iridescence far removed from the initial palette the poet composed, where the blue was distinctly blue, the green distinctly green, and the leap of the imagination still.

However, in examining the ways women practice traditional prosody, I have discovered that the initial choice, the conscious choice, of one traditional verse form over another *is not* always the choice to match the feeling, but rather a choice to contain, to control, or otherwise make the feeling safe to explore. Take Elizabeth Bishop's late poem "Pink Dog" for example. Here are the first four stanzas, which take place during mardi gras:

PINK DOG
(Rio de Janeiro)

The sun is blazing and the sky is blue
Umbrellas clothe the beach in every hue.
Naked, you trot across the avenue.

Oh, never have I seen a dog so bare!
Naked and pink, without a single hair . . .
Startled, the passersby draw back and stare.

Of course they're mortally afraid of rabies.
You are not mad; you have a case of scabies
but look intelligent. Where are your babies?

(A nursing mother, by those hanging teats.)
In what slum have you hidden them, poor bitch,
while you go begging, living by your wits?

Why on earth would she choose to use rhymed triplets? What a bumpy, comic way in which to lavish solicitude on a hairless bitch out without her babies during carnival in Rio. But the enormity of the subject for Bishop — a mother dog who has abandoned her children to enter the mad world of carnival just as Elizabeth Bishop's own mother abandoned her and was consigned to a mental institution — is not at all comic. The depth of feeling does not match the form; it is much larger than tercets tripping samba-like along. The feeling is the opposite of comic: it is huge, and tragically overriding; it shadowed her entire life, reaching wherever in the hemispheres she tried to escape it. The form, almost the opposite of the feeling, makes the feeling explorable; form is the anchor of the opposite which makes the feeling approachable and which allows the humor and the light touch that gives the poem its brilliance.

The tension in the lightness of the triplets, the clap-clap-clap of the rhymes, festive and absurd as mardi gras, against the depth of the poet's complex feelings about the disoriented animal, give the poem that iridescent confusion of form and content. The triple rhymes create the emotion, while the emotion creates the demand for the triple rhymes in such balance that no other choice would be right. Indeed, in final products no other choice is "right." But the initial choice, to contain, to order, to form, to combat the overwhelming darkness of that abandonment, almost opposes the very feeling it is chosen to express, and therefore it makes a safe vehicle for expression. The verse form almost becomes the arms of comfort in which to express the enormity of emotion. This is how the huge inverted world of carnival, like the huge inverted world of Bishop's mother's absence, can be both invoked and tolerated — and made to *seem* seamless.

Formal verse often makes impossible emotions possible. Look at the contrast between the children's laughter and the dark tower of night in Barbara Howes' poem "Early Supper," based on the triolet. Barbara Howes uses the highly repetitive triolet as a stanza form, building up the enormity of night in apposition to the contained repetition of the incredibly strict stanza structure. The containment of this strictness implies a terrifying chaos right from the beginning when the poem talks about children's laughter: "Laughter of children brings / The kitchen down with laughter. / While the old kettle sings / Laughter of children brings . . . ." The children's laughter exists in an atmosphere of threat, simply because the verse form that boxes the threat is so small, ornate, and delicately hinged. Thus when the children are put to bed and the dark tower of night is introduced, the threat is openly acknowledged, and finally the poem makes sense. Here is the last of its three stanzas in full:

> They trail upstairs to bed,
>   And night is a dark tower.
> The kettle calls: instead
> They trail upstairs to bed.
> Leaving warmth, the coppery-red
>   Mood of their carnival hour.
> They trail upstairs to bed,
>   And night is a dark tower.

At the opening, one almost resists it—what is this silly poem about kettles and laughter? One almost resists the Bishop poem in its opening—do we have to read about this silly dog?—because the containment has yet to reveal its purpose, or what it contains (terror, of course).

That observation could quickly lead to the fallacy of the verse form as a container or the *outside* of something, and therefore, as an outside, something superficial, not deep, merely technical. But when I speak of containment, I am speaking about not being overwhelmed; I am not speaking about tying something up in a package to be shelved. I am indicating a poetic method of coping with the vastness of emotion that makes the poem worth writing in the first place. If you think of form as the outside of an Inside, that is only half the truth. Verse form is also inside the Inside. It acts as a skeleton as well as a skin. Form is a body. Verse form literally embodies the emotion of the poem, in the sense that embodiment both *is* and *contains* the life it is the body of. The need to embody the dangerous is both a need to surround it and then to live it. Therefore the initial choice is to contain, and the subsequent writing allows the danger to live as made possible by the containment.

Jane Kenyon states this almost directly in her introductory paragraph titled "Shielding," in the anthology *A Formal Feeling Comes: Poems in Form by Contemporary Women.* She states that her poem "Travel: After a Death" was "written while I was recovering from my father's death. I don't know what made me turn to formal verse at that time, but I found that having to concentrate on the metrics I was shielded in some way from the content . . . ." Her initial choice is to shield herself, and the subsequent writing both performs the shielding task and allows her stressful mourning to go on through the distraction of counting metrical stresses. The three stanzas of "Travel: After a Death" depend on a five stress line, but the lines are only loosely iambic. The stanzas themselves are loosely the same size (11, 12, and 9 lines respectively). Rhyme is occasionally used loosely throughout. In the first stanza the poet drives through Devonshire and the occasional rhyme of the third-to-last and last lines makes a delicately good humoured connection of "perfect courtesy" and "like a maitre d'," foreshadowing the deeper activity of mourning which takes place later on in the poem:

> . . . and I watched a man
> grasping his plaid cloth cap and walking stick
> in one hand, while with perfect courtesy
> he sent his dog before him through the stile,
> bowing a little like a maitre d'.

The highly individual, slow, bumpy pentameter continues in the second stanza, where the travellers find a room "in a cold seaside hotel." End rhyme has dropped out of the poem, and the poet goes on to talk about another opening, this time not of a stile, but a door. As what the door frames becomes an image of deepening mourning, the rhyme returns.

> Why,
> I wondered, was the front door wedged open
> in January, with a raw sea wind
> blowing the woollen skirts of the townswomen,
> who passed with market baskets on their arms,
> their bodies bent forward against the chill
> and the steep angle of the cobbled hill?

Rhyme returns once more in the last stanza with an image of Donne practicing "his deathbed scene," and then is abandoned to the poet's characteristic use of ellipses and blunted vocabulary. An unrhymed, utterly human cry of a question ends the poem with a sudden raw burst of loss: "Oh, when am I going to own my mind again?" The form of the poem, which has been called upon to shield the feeling, comes to imitate a process of mourning, that process of numbing against the loss, then allowing oneself to feel a bit of it, then numbing again, then meeting the feeling in a burst just as one feels most unprepared for it, though the numbing/feeling/numbing/feeling process has perhaps prepared one for loss, even as the counting of stresses has both protected and prepared the poet for the final cry.

We see from the examples of Elizabeth Bishop and Barbara Howes, and we know directly from Jane Kenyon's statement (1) that one of the reasons women choose a traditional verse pattern is not so much to suit the outline of their subject matter, as to enable them to examine a subject while at the same time protecting themselves from the subject's explosive power. This is a bit like acquiring a thorough knowledge of all the ways of handling an unexploded bomb. There are techniques for doing so, and traditional versification offers them.

Yet why do women, in turning to traditional verse forms to contain, to control, to comfort, and even to protect, as Kenyon turns to the shield of metrics to protect her from the loss of her father, make so little effort to attain what I would call the rigor or perfection of formal verse as it has been historically practiced by men? Why, for instance, didn't Kenyon keep the poem as blank verse, which she could easily have done? Why did she interrupt the blank lines with rhyme? What made her choose to employ those crucial rhymes at turning moments? Simple instinct? Where was the instinct for "perfection," for following the prosodic rules? Why did she so readily grasp the distraction of the metrics, then just as readily sacrifice the blank endings? Was she merely not being rigorous? Of course, what she did was to choose the more effective linguistic and rhythmic heightening of those moments of loss, moments when the shield is laid down. But didn't she have a frisson of guilt and fear that the poetry police might be around the corner?

Women poets show a marked preference for an "informal" use of form. What women seem to appropriate for themselves in the realm of traditional prosody are general methods they can put to the organic purposes, or the psychological shape, of what is the attempt to convey or say or even, perhaps, be. They have not seemed to have aspired toward the perfect sonnet, the perfect villanelle, the perfect quatrain, although they have shown themselves to be linguistically virtuosic in so many ways that we must assume that they are perfectly capable of such "perfection." Poets from Emily Dickinson to Marianne Moore to Elizabeth Bishop to Mona van Duyn have appropriated formal gestures but have used these gestures inside a personally constructed poetic, eschewing that rather jesuitical idea of prosodic rigor that says, "If you're going to write a perfect x, then you ought to write one, and stop being sloppy—no lowering of sights, and certainly, no diluting of standards! After all, a sonnet is a sonnet, and that means precision of scansion, precision of rhyme scheme, and fourteen squarely rigged lines, mademoiselle, if you please."

The sensible theory of some, including the young scholar and poet Kevin Walzer, one of a new generation of men who are writing about how women practice prosody, is that as outsiders, women use formal traditions but write outside of mainstream formalism. The contemporary poet Julia Alvarez confirms this when she writes of her own use of the sonnet:

> I think of form as a territory that has been colonized, but that you can free. See, I feel subversive in formal verse. A voice is going to enter that form that was barred from entering it before! . . . In school, I was always trying to inhabit those forms as the male writers had. To pitch my voice to 'Of man's first disobedience and the fruit . . . .' What I wanted from the sonnet was the tradition that it offered as well as the structure. The sonnet tradition was one in which women were caged in golden cages of beloved, in perfumed gas chambers of stereotype. I wanted to go in that heavily mined and male labyrinth with the string of my own voice. I wanted to explore it and explode it too. I call my sonnets free verse sonnets. They have ten syllables per line, and the lines are in a loose iambic pentameter. But they are heavily enjambed and the rhymes are often slant rhymes, and the rhyme scheme is peculiar to each sonnet." (2)

Alvarez is more explicit than the more reticent poets of her own and previous generations, but her image of being in the male labyrinth of prosody with the string of her own voice easily and obviously applies to any woman poet employing formal techniques.

Look back to the example of Louise Bogan, a poet who explicitly stated about the sonnet: "Now, you great stanza, you heroic mound, / Bend to my will . . . ." She ends this poem, called "Single Sonnet," with a challenge to the form itself: "Staunch meter, great song, it is yours, at length, / To prove how stronger you are than my strength." Her contest with form, cast against the contest of the sexes, underpins much of her work. She often uses a quatrain in which only two of the lines are rhymed. At other times, she lets rhymes accumulate in the poem, as she does in "Cartography," beginning with her usual quatrain of two rhymed, two unrhymed lines, then turning to three perfectly rhymed quatrains. The first stanza reads:

> As you lay in sleep
> I saw the chart
> Of artery and vein
> running from your heart,

She certainly could have reworked it to conform to the rhyming of the next three stanzas. But Bogan fights the battle between her sensibility and the forces of form on intuitive ground: if the poem begins slowly, without full song, then the song can accumulate in fullness, which it poignantly does. The last stanza reads:

> Mapped like the great
> Rivers that rise
> Beyond our fate
> And distant from our eyes.

Not only has she tolerated imperfection; she must have felt it necessary to her art. It's as if she left grit in the oyster on purpose.

Elizabeth Bishop does this, too. Anyone familiar with her villanelle, "One Art," knows the liberties she takes with the second repeat line, modulating it to cope with the various disasters the speaker encounters. I am told that, in the manuscript drafts of the villanelle, the poem begins as personal notes, and is only later formed into the villanelle, the form that Bishop appropriated to her own purposes. (3) Throughout her work she adapts sounds to her intuitive sense of their rightness, regardless of rhyme scheme. In "First Death in Nova Scotia," Bishop works as Bogan did in "Cartography." She uses a uniform stanza and line, but begins with little rhyme, allowing the rhyme to accumulate until the final stanza, also imperfectly rhymed, but full of sound echoes: "They invited Arthur to be / the smallest page at court. / But how could Athur go, / clutching his tiny lily, / with his eyes shut up so tight / and the roads deep in snow?" The unerring steadiness of the childgaze she achieves comes in part from the odd, accumulated rhyme viscerally integral to the child's gradual comprehension of her cousin Arthur's death.

All of the poems I have discussed modify their formal apparatus to meet psychological urgencies. None of them force themselves into a so-called "right" way. Every poet appropriates verse techniques for the poet's own uses. This is not peculiar to women, but to personality. But what does belong to women poets working in verse traditions is a sense of separateness from what seems not only an imposed and perhaps haughty or unreasonable demand for perfection, but a ludicrous, inappropriate demand given the psychological urgency that necessarily tempers form in women's eyes, even in the aesthetic eyes of women who would not necessarily agree with one another about many other facets of, or sources for, poetry. Emily

Dickinson is a historical example of the break with perfectionistic form and the insistence on a personal sensibility of sound. Marilyn Hacker is an example of a heightening of virtuoso prosodic acrobatics beyond all possible demands for rigor or perfection (otherwise known as "beating them at their own game"—in her own time, Edna St. Vincent Millay occupied one of these hotseats). I hope, in looking at the techniques of both well known poets such as Bishop and Bogan, as well as poets who should be better known, such as Howes, Kenyon, and Alvarez, a new verse territory might be charted, capacious enough to include the lines of women poets appropriating forms from Marianne Moore to Sonia Sanchez, from Gertrude Stein to Carolyn Beard Whitlow, or from Amy Lowell to Leslie Simon. (Of course, I place myself in this territory. These observations began in the locus of my own work, and my own wrestling with psychological urgency and formalistic demands.)

The brilliance of a finished poem, like that iridescent feather which is both green and blue, obscures the making of it; the certain knowledge of the exact mix of the originating colors is sometimes never known. Julia Alvarez addresses the confusion of style and substance that we try to separate when we discuss content and form in her "Sonnet 42." The poem ingeniously displays a psychological process of becoming, where the activity of writing and female identity are inextricable.

> Sometimes the words are so close I am
> more who I am when I'm down on paper
> than anywhere else as if my life were
> practising for the real me I become
> unbuttoned from the anecdotal and
> unnecessary and undressed down
> to the figure of the poem, line by line,
> the real text a child could understand.
> Why do I get confused living it through?
> Those of you, lost and yearning to be free,
> who hear these words, take heart from me.
> I once was in as many drafts as you.
> But briefly, essentially, here I am . . .
> Who touches this poem touches a woman.

When Alvarez, in her essay, describes the sonnet as a cage, recalling the cliche of the bird in the gilded cage, she reminds us of a world of male perfection in which women as objects were locked away—and as artists were locked out. However, the notions of container or containment in prosody, as practised by women, so invert received ideas of poetic architecture that the cage becomes internalized, organicized, not a place to lock up emotion (as the common idea of "formally elegant, but emotionally repressed" would suggest) but a place to allow it to live, the female body of form.

WORKS CITED

1. We also know from many of the other statements which appear in the individual preface essays to the poems in *A Formal Feeling Comes: Poems in Form by Contemporary Women*. The length of this essay won't accommodate copious examples, but here is Honor Moore, explaining how she came to use the sestina to write about an incident from her childhood in which she is attacked by a male, teenage baby sitter. ". . . I had become the young woman facing her attacker, myself at five years old, powerless to protect myself. I began to write, raw in my childhood memory, and the poem came, taking dramatic, sequential shape in the sestina form. Its restraint became the walls of the room, the recurrence of end words a verbal equivalent for the relentlessness of the molester's intentions. Embraced in its sure architecture, the violated child, silenced for thirty years, is free to tell her story."

2. From Alvarez' essay, "Housekeeping Cages" in *A Formal Feeling Comes: Poems in Form by Contemporary Women*, Ed. Annie Finch, Story Line Press, 1994.

3. I learned this in conversation with Alice Quinn, Poetry Editor of *The New Yorker*, who carefully described the early drafts which have not yet been opened to the public.

The New Formalism and the Revival of the Love Lyric
Robert McPhillips

Much attention has been paid the revival of traditional forms in contemporary American poetry and of the narrative poem. "Expansive Poetry" is the phrase coined by Wade Newman to subsume the categories of the New Formalism and the New Narrative. It is the title of both a special issue of *Crosscurrents*, edited by Dick Allen, which contains both narrative and rhymed and metered poems and essays surveying the topic, and of an anthology of essays, edited by Frederick Feirstein. Both editors emphasize that if contemporary poets wish to expand their audience, they must eschew the solipsism of the typical free verse lyric. They must, that is, turn outward from the ego to tell stories about others in narrative poems, and from the subjectivity of "organic" free verse forms to the objectivity of fixed forms in the lyric. And certainly one of the delights in reading Vikram Seth's novel-in-verse, *The Golden Gate* (1986), is to see the author himself, having given center stage to the love affairs of other characters, make a mere cameo appearance in a party scene.

This argument, then, is true enough, as far as it goes. But it seems to ignore an obvious truth: that one also looks — perhaps even primarily looks — to poetry, at least to lyric poetry, to present the powerful emotions of a sympathetic persona in a voice at once alive and musical. We look to lyric poets, it might be said, to understand our own humanity in the process of reading about theirs. The first contemporary poem I remember while a student at Ossining High School, the one that started me reading contemporary poetry, was one by Anne Sexton that I came across browsing through *The New Yorker* in the public library. I immediately checked out a copy of her *Love Poems*, the contents of which were sufficiently sensational to appeal to my adolescent nature, and for a few years I became addicted to the Confessional poets, particularly Sexton and Sylvia Plath (whose posthumous reputation was then in full flower). If these poets, as well as their male contemporaries, John Berryman and Robert Lowell, seem less appealing to me now, it is probably because their lyric voices are so morbidly self-absorbed in their own neuroses. Similarly, when I read Sharon Olds's more recent free verse poems in *The Father* (1992), graphically describing her father's alcoholism and cancer as well as her own sexual exploits, I often wish that she had kept these stories to herself. Part of my resistance, I think, is because her language is so matter-of-factly prosaic. (Perhaps it is this very artlessness which has lead Helen Vendler to brand Olds's poems, only a bit hyperbolically, as pornographic.)

Conversely, what is most engaging in the personal lyrics of the New Formalists is their ability, through the restraint imposed upon them by traditional metrical and stanzaic patterns, to render their personal emotions more universally appealing. Nowhere is this more apparent than in the love lyric, a form that has undergone a renaissance in their hands. If the New Formalist movement is remarkable for focusing on formal metrics after decades of neglect, it is equally noteworthy for reviving the direct, emotional love poem long out of favor among academic poets of all schools. The love poem is unique in its attempt to present the persona's most intimate feelings while at the same time being addressed to another whose existence animates the poem: its focus is not only on the lyric "I" but on a "you" as well. The constraint in the best of the New Formalist love lyrics has the paradoxical effect of making the language (even when it is vulgar, as it occasionally is) more purified, universal, while those of rhyme make the poems at once more lively and memorable. Paradoxically too, probably because of the influence of the Confessional poets on this younger generation, the love lyrics are at once more direct and uninhibited than the ironically distanced ones of the 50s formalists or the notably genderless ones of W. H. Auden. The revival of the love lyric, then, seems among the most important contributions the New Formalists have made to contemporary poetry.

Timothy Steele and Dana Gioia's love lyrics are among the most traditional in subject matter and classically restrained in form among the New Formalists. One type of love poem that each poet excels in is the aubade, though their emphases in them are different. The speaker in Steele's "An Aubade," in *Sapphics Against Anger* (1986), lies in bed, recalling the night shared with his wife as he awaits her reappearance in the bedroom, fresh from her shower. The lovemaking that the crumpled bed recalls is evoked in beautiful detail in the second of the poem's five stanzas:

> The pillow which, in dozing, I embraced
> Retains the salty sweetness of her skin;
> I sensed her smooth back, buttocks, belly, waist,
> The leggy warmth which spread and gently laced
> Around my legs and loins, and drew me in.

Steele, a temperamentally reserved poet who is perhaps the most distinguished of his contemporaries to write almost exclusively in the plain style, has never been as concretely yet delicately erotic as in this poem which also presents a lovely image of his wife drying, after her shower, "Her fineboned ankles, and her calves and thighs, / The pink full nipples of her breasts. . . ." Steele's grounding in the plain style enables him to write intimately about eroticism without coming close to the lurid excesses of Confessionalism.

Dana Gioia establishes his own form of intimacy in his less explicit but equally sensual aubade from *Daily Horoscope* (1986), "Parts of Summer Weather." Gioia's lyric is elegiac in its juxtaposition, in its final two quatrains, of the idyllic image of the persona's shared life with his lover with one of her absence when he awakes:

> And under darkness and the breeze
> with sheets and blankets stripped away
> we lie in silence saying more
> than anything we hoped to say.
>
> And yet I wake an hour later
> reach out and find myself alone.
> No words spoken, no message left,
> the room so quiet, and you gone.

In another rueful love poem from the same volume, "The Sunday News," Gioia expresses the irrational sense of jealousy and loss he feels when coming across the wedding announcement of an old girlfriend in the newspaper. Written in a modified sapphic stanza, the poem uses its syllabically and metrically shortened final line to reflect the speaker's sense of loss, as in this concluding stanza:

> And yet I clipped it out to put away
> Inside a book like something I might use,
> A scrap I knew I wouldn't read again
> But couldn't bear to lose.

Gioia's metrical approximation of loss here is amplified by the poem's final word, "lose," which takes on a double meaning in this context, the clipping he "couldn't bear to lose" being a reminder precisely of what he has lost.

Many of the most energetic and erotic of the New Formalists' love lyrics are by women. Both Marilyn Hacker and Gjertrud Schnackenberg have written poetic sequences chronicling the arc of an affair. Hacker's *Love, Death and the Changing of the Seasons* (1986) is a book-length sonnet sequence narrating the tentative yet exciting beginning, the precarious middle, and the painful conclusion of the poet's affair with a younger woman. While overly repetitive and occasionally awkward in its metrics, the book is nonetheless dotted with pleasing linguistic moments. Hacker is best at conveying the giddiness of the onslaught of erotic love, playfully rhyming the kinds of colloquial words we don't expect to find in the ordinarily heightened diction of the sonnet, as in this sestet from an untitled poem in the book's first section:

> My eyes and groin are permanently swollen,
> I'm alternatingly brilliant and witless
> —and sleepless: bed is just a swamp to roll in.
> Although I'd cream my jeans touching your breast,
> sweetheart, it isn't lust: it's all the rest
> of what I want that scares me shitless.

Where Steele brings renewed vigor to the plain style by combining contemporary imagery with classical metrical and linguistic restraint, Hacker's ingenious use of rhyme and meter and fixed forms from the sonnet to the villanelle gives a playful spin to her low, even vulgar style, a vitality that such diction typically lacks in most contemporary poetry.

By contrast, Gjertrud Schnackenberg is most commonly given to the high style we associate with such 50s formalists as Hecht and Hollander. Her sequence of five love poems in *The Lamplit Answer* (1985), then, is more elevated and literary than Hacker's, though it is less obviously graceful than such poems about her love for her father as "Supernatural Love" in the same volume. Yet Schnackenberg's shift in voice attests to her poetic range. At times seemingly desperate, at times witty, at times meditative, she works best in this sequence when she uses meter and rhyme to restrain her expressions of loneliness and allow her to relate her more tender feelings, as in this memorable conclusion to "Love Letter," addressed to her lover travelling without her in Italy:

> Two things are clear: these quatrains should be burned,
> And love is awful, but leads us to
> Our places in the human comedy,
> Frescoes of which abound in Italy,
> And though I won't be sitting next to you,
> I'll take my seat with minimal complaints.
> May you sit in the company of saints
> And intellectuals and fabulous beauties,
> And not forget this constant love of Trude's.

As "Trude" contemplates her lover's exploits in Italy, the unusual enjambment between the poem's penultimate two lines suggests the probable envy and jealousy the speaker feels towards her lover's elegant sojourn in Italy, while the comma that precedes the letter poem's complimentary closing emphasizes the speaker's hard-won sense of both emotional and poetic control.

Other women poets have skillfully adapted traditional forms of the love poem to their own purposes, among them Mary Jo Salter, Molly Peacock, and Patricia Storace. Both Salter and Peacock have written aubades that differ in tone and content both from those by Steele and Gioia and those by each other. Salter's "Aubade for Brad," from *Unfinished Painting* (1989), addressed to her husband—poet, novelist, and critic Brad Leithauser—is as light and witty as the rhyme in the title would suggest. It amusingly describes her husband, eager to get an early start to his writing day, stumbling about in the early morning dark, trying, unsuccessfully, to dress quietly, finally prompting his wife to tempt him away from his rigorous writing schedule thus:

> Darling, if you'll untie
> your shoes again and lie
> for a moment, while the sun turns all to gold,
> I may grow very bold.

Peacock's aubade in *Take Heart* (1989), "The Surge," is an original variation on the form, a frank celebration of her lover's morning erection for which "there was nothing I did to earn its praise // but be alive next to it," but which becomes a symbol, nonetheless, of the sacred as well as the erotic "surge" which unites the lovers, spirit embodied in flesh:

> To do nothing but be, and thus be wanted:
> so, this is love. *Look what happened*, he says as he
>
> watches my hand draw out what it did not raise,
> purpled in sleep. The surge inside me must
> come from inside me, where the world lies,
>
> just as the prick stiffened to amaze us
> came from a rising inside him. The blessing
> we feel is knowing that *out there* is nothing.
> The world inside us has come to praise us.

The bluntness of Peacock's sexual language here seems both appropriate and effective because the language of the stanza is otherwise so sensually elegant, both in the alliteration and in the internal and end rhyme, and be-

cause the stunningly coarse embodies the "prick" of recognition of the shared
love that the image evokes.

The sense that the lovers' lives in Peacock's poem have been enriched is
emphasized formally as well. The final stanza of the poem swells to a rhymed
quatrain from the irregularly rhymed tercets comprising the rest of the poem,
this stanza thus reemphasizing the inward swelling of love represented by
the outward swelling of the erection. In a far more traditional version of an
epithalamium, Patricia Storace uses a similar formal innovation in "Wed-
ding Song" from *Heredity* (1987). Written in three sections each containing
three stanzas—a tercet, a quatrain, and a five-line stanza—Storace's poem
emphasizes how one's lives are made fuller through marriage. The poem
concludes thus in its third section:

> So male stars and female end their exile,
> and fuse and form in wedding life to life,
> that human constellation, man and wife.
>
> So male stars and female end their exile,
> accept the union that completes their trial,
> and fuse and form in wedding life to life,
> that human constellation, man and wife.
>
> So male stars and female end their exile,
> begin the crossing of their brilliant mile,
> accept the union that completes their trial,
> and fuse and form in wedding life to life,
> that human constellation, man and wife.

Clear and direct in diction, utterly conventional in its adaptation of the sim-
plicity of the song form with its repetition and slow accretion of new details
in each stanza, and conventional as well in its imagery—male and female
stars uniting in marriage to form "that human constellation, man and wife"—
Storace, whose book is notably feminist, demonstrates brilliantly here that
it is still possible for poets, male and female, to successfully inhabit tradi-
tional forms and imagery without ceasing to be both innovative and con-
temporary.

John Gery, by contrast, in "A Poem for Barbara," which appeared in
an issue of *Verse*, shows that it is also possible to write a love poem using
traditional form and conventional nature imagery even while questioning
the ability of such language adequately to express the love a man feels for a
woman in an era when the connection among language, power, and gender
is being critically examined by feminist and other cultural critics. Set at the

seashore where the two lovers are vacationing, the ever-shifting boundary between shore and sea representing the imprecise boundaries between the man and woman, the poem invites comparison to Spenser's famous Sonnet 75 from his *Amoretti*, "One day I wrote her name upon the strand." There, Spenser is confident of his ability to immortalize his skeptical lover by composing a sonnet about her. Gery entertains the temptation to attempt the same, "to wax sublime, / to batten down your beauty with a rhyme / or two," but he can't do that because he is aware of his lover's otherness — "You're not what I expected" — which he cannot fully comprehend. The fact that the poem is written in heroic couplets is ironic, then: the poet hardly feels "heroic" in the traditional male sense. Nor is the poem neatly and confidently logical, or, for that matter, satirical, as ones written in couplets, particularly in the eighteenth century, frequently are. Gery's triumph here is that he is able to celebrate, in traditional language and meter, the present level of his understanding of his love, an understanding he recognizes still to be evolving:

> Whatever words set sail upturn and drown
> under the waves of your otherness, while here
> in the dormant air, I stare at what is near,
> missing each arc, the muffled cry of gulls,
> the shifting tides in you, the rage, the lulls.

This is as good a love poem I know written by a man informed, at least partially, by a feminist sensibility.

In the age of AIDS, gay male poets must also confront an overwhelming challenge in determining how aesthetically to represent love, given the tragic nature and the gruesome imagery associated with the as-yet-incurable disease. Some poets, like the late Paul Monette in his sequence of poems, *Love Alone* (1988), recounting the death of his lover Rog from AIDS (as does his more effective prose memoir, *Borrowed Time*), opt to vent their rage in seemingly spontaneous lines of free verse. However psychologically therapeutic for the authors, such poems are marred aesthetically for the reader by their sentimentality and self-pity. They fail, ultimately, to give dignity to what is both a private and a public tragedy because they do not seek to find a more objective form to universalize the poet's private grief. Bruce Bawer and Vikram Seth, on the other hand, both use traditional stanzas and language to express far more eloquently than Monette different aspects of homosexual love.

Bruce Bawer, whose almost-monthly literary essays appeared for ten years in *The New Criterion* and established him as the preeminent practical critic of his generation, is quickly becoming one of the most accomplished of the younger New Formalist poets as well. In three poems from his first volume of poetry, *Coast to Coast* (1993), "Ferry," "Devotions," and "Confirmation," Bawer finds unexpected means to celebrate homosexual love when he is able to find within Christianity the possibility for celebrating his sexuality as something spiritual rather than as of a "godless virtue" to be sought merely in "rank / barrooms, staring, thirsting, standing apart" ("Devotions").

The speaker in "Ferry" is attending St. Thomas Episcopal Church in Manhattan on the feast of St. Paul's conversion with a friend who had attended this church as a child but who had felt alienated from it because of his own homosexuality. The friend is moved by Bishop Paul Moore's sermon concerning his own religious conversion during World War II. While nursing the "repulsive, shattered" bodies of wounded soldiers, he realized "that when he stared into their eyes / he'd seen the eyes of the Lord," that God resides "in the corrupt, imperfect flesh." The sermon moves the friend to tears as he realizes his own sexuality is not at odds with Christian values when the bishop uses the word "lover" instead of "spouse" as one of the possible sites to discover the divine within the flesh. He feels restored to the spiritual community of his childhood.

"Devotions," by contrast, dramatizes its persona's own embracing of Christianity coinciding with the exciting beginning of a life-altering erotic relationship when

> . . . one day in almost-winter it struck
> like thunder in his breast: not only his flesh
> was taking long-sought nourishment from flesh.
> Quietly, too, his soul had been partaking.
>
> Flesh had come accompanied by grace; the light
> in his love's eyes was the love of God.
> It was that which filled him, night after night,
> in his love's warm arms. And so he prayed.

But perhaps Bawer's lyric exploration of the bonds between erotic and Christian love achieves its finest expression in his eight-line poem, "Confirmation," from his sequence of love poems to his companion, Chris, "Sixty-Fifth Street Poems." Like Peacock's, Bawer's ultimate subject is grace:

> How is it that an old devotion calls
> across the years, and in a different key,
> discovering you in this far, foreign place,
> heart harnessed to and bedstead shared with me?
> How to discern the turnings of a grace
> that waits long years to raise a soul that falls
> out of its palm —and, in another land
> finding it, lifts with a different hand?

Bawer's lucidity and restraint render his gay, Christian love poems universal in their emotional appeal.

Vikram Seth directly confronts AIDS in his stunning poem, "Soon," from *All You Who Sleep Tonight* (1990), a poem written in the voice of a man dying of AIDS addressing his lover (and appearing in a section of Seth's book titled "In Other Voices"). Seth writes here in rhymed quatrains following a regular abab pattern in brief iambic trimeter which evokes, with shocking clarity, both the emotion experienced by the dying persona and some of the specific images we connect with AIDS. The poem opens with a blunt statement: "I shall die soon, I know," introducing a stanza whose end-stopped lines emphasize this certainty. Seth alternates this technique in other stanzas with carefully-chosen enjambment to express both the inception and growth of the disease:

> Love was the strange first cause
> That bred grief in its seed,
> And gain knew its own laws —
> To fix its place and breed.

He also uses it to convey the wellings of emotion experienced by a persona speaking to his lover from his "steel ward bed" from a "throat cased in white spawn" (Seth's chillingly objective image of thrush, a throat ailment connected with AIDS), who finally reverses the typical poetic convention of promising to immortalize one's mistress in verse. Instead, in the poem's concluding lines which both reiterate the certainty of death presented in its opening while still voicing his irrational but poignant appeal for salvation, the speaker here asks his lover who will outlive him, to immortalize him, keep him alive:

> Stay by my steel ward bed
> And hold me where I lie.
> Love me when I am dead
> And do not let me die.

In "Soon," Seth both uses and extends the metrical, aural, and imagistic conventions of the love lyric to convey the private grief of a victim of our contemporary plague on a human scale that gives it, like so many other New Formalist love lyrics covering a wide range of erotic experience, universal resonance.

Boundless Wealth from a Finite Store: Meter and Grammar

Timothy Steele

Reflecting in 1947 on his experiences as a teacher of poetry, W.H. Auden remarks:

> It's amazing how little students know about prosody. When you teach a college class, you find they read [verse] either as straight prose, or as deadly monotonous beat as in *Gorboduc*.

Auden's observation raises a crucial point. Poetry consists neither exclusively of grammatical prose-sense nor exclusively of meter, but is rather a fusion of the two. On the one hand, poets make themselves intelligible by the same means that prose writers do — by agreeably and coherently arranging words and phrases into clauses and sentences. On the other hand, poets compose according to a regular beat and recurring rhythmical pattern, a procedure not characteristic of prose-writing.

Unfortunately, this point is little appreciated. What Auden says of college students seems equally true of most other readers of poetry. Some focus on its grammatical sense at the expense of its metrical element; others concentrate on meter at the expense of meaning. Since Auden's day, the size of the former group has probably grown, whereas the latter has probably shrunk, but the division itself is much the same. In any case, neither approach serves poetry well. To neglect meter is to lose access to the music and modulation that fine metrical composition offers. By the same token, narrowly emphasizing meter can result in misunderstandings about it. Such emphasis can lead to the notion that actual metrical practice concerns merely "deadly monotonous beat." It can obscure the critical fact that though poets write according to a fixed rhythmical pattern, they do not replicate it exactly, line after line, but instead realize it in continually different ways and by means of various kinds of grammatical organization.

This essay will explore the relationship between meter and grammar, chiefly with reference to the iambic pentameter, and will discuss ways in which poets coordinate the two. I should mention at the outset that it is not my aim to challenge or discredit traditional metrical analysis and foot-scansion. Properly applied, these usefully clarify verse structure. Working poets, however, do not divide language into two- or three-syllable units and then fasten them together, one at a time, foot by foot, to form verses. Rather, they fashion their lines out of larger segments of speech. In learning their craft, they acquire a special feeling for the shapes and rhythms of words and phrases that enables them to write, simultaneously, metrically and grammatically. They learn to hear when words and phrases fit a meter, or section of it, and to make the necessary adjustments or alterations when they don't.

The elements of grammar most relevant to versification are syntax (the study of the forms of phrases and sentences) and morphology (the study of the structures and shapes of words). We can begin our discussion by examining the syntax of a common type of iambic pentameter represented by the following lines:

> My mountain belly and my rocky face
> (Ben Jonson, "My Picture Left in Scotland," 17)

> A painted meadow or a purling stream
> (Addison, "A Letter from Italy," 166)

> The smoothest numbers for the harshest prose
> (Crabbe, "The Newspaper," 32)

> The wretched refuse of your teeming shore
> (Emma Lazarus, "The New Colossus," 12)

Reading these verses aloud, we can hear their rhythmical similarity, and looking at their grammatical components, we can discover the reason for this likeness. Each line is composed of two noun-phrases connected by a monosyllabic conjunction or preposition. The first of the phrases involves a fore-stressed disyllabic adjective and a fore-stressed disyllabic noun. The second involves a fore-stressed disyllabic adjective and a monosyllabic noun. And both phrases are introduced by an article or attributive pronoun.

Overall, the lines are plainly iambic, though the rhythm is unemphatic in the middle. Neither the fifth, sixth, nor seventh syllables have much speech stress, though the sixth is a little weightier than the fifth or seventh. Putting the matter another way, we may say that the verses are pentameters with light third feet. If in scanning the lines we wish to draw attention to the light foot, we can supplement the conventional descriptive notation with the four-level stress-register that linguists sometimes employ. That is, in addition to marking the syllables as metrically unaccented or accented, we can speak of them in terms of weak stress (1), tertiary stress (2), secondary stress (3), or strong stress (4). To take the example from Jonson, we can render the line thus:

```
1   4    1    4  1 2    1   4   1   4
x   /    x    /  x /    x   /   x   /
My moun I tain bel I ly and I my roc I ky face
```

As an aside, it may be useful to remind ourselves that iambic verse requires of poets only that they adhere to the general rise-and-fall of the metrical pattern. It is not necessary that all the metrically accented syllables be equally prominent; nor do all the metrically unaccented syllables need to be equally weak. The degree of difference between the rises and falls, though affecting actual speech rhythm, is for purposes of scansion irrelevant. Analogously, an iambic foot requires only that the second syllable receive more accent than the first. Whether it receives a lot more or little more does not, in terms of metrical classification, matter. For these reasons, it is perfectly possible and commonplace for poets to write iambic pentameters with fewer or more than five notable speech stresses. Here, for example, are pentameters with two and nine:

```
1 2   1    4 1 2   1   4 1 2
x  /   x   / x /   x   / x /
In our competitive humility
        (Robinson, "Captain Craig," 169)
```

```
3   4   3   4   1 4 3   4   3   4
x   /   x   /   x / x   /   x   /
Milk hands, rose cheeks, or lips more sweet, more red
        (Sidney, Astrophel and Stella, 91.7)
```

The key thing is just to maintain the basic fluctuation. (For a detailed analysis of this and related topics, please see my "On Meter," *Hellas* 1 [Fall 1990], pp. 289-310.)

To return to Jonson's line, note what happens if we reverse the order of the noun-phrases:

My rocky face and my mountain belly.

Even though the line has the same words and the same number of syllables, its rhythmical character has changed. In particular, "my mountain belly" no longer fits into iambic measure. Whereas the shape of the phrase suits the first five positions of the pentameter, it is not well adapted to the second five. In its altered situation, it puts heavy beats on the seventh and ninth syllables, while leaving the eighth and tenth weak. Overall, the new line has a more tripping, semi-anapestic rhythm. Such a line might work in a poem in loose four-stress measure with feminine endings:

$$x \;/\;\; x\,x\;/\;\; x \;\;/\; x\,x \;\;/\;(x)$$
Behold the results of candy and jelly:

$$x \;/\; x \;/\;\; x \;\;\; x \;/\; x \;\;/\;(x)$$
My rocky face and my mountain belly

But it is not in sync with the pentametric pattern.

Turning more particularly to morphology and word-shape, we can examine another species of pentameter which we encounter fairly often and which is exemplified by the following lines:

My ship and me Charybdis wol devour
(Chaucer, *Troilus and Criseyde*, 5.644)

When I am made unhappy by my skill
(Drayton, *Sonnets to Idea*, 12.12)

To write what may securely stand the test
(Rochester, "An Allusion to Horace," 98)

And afterwards remember, do not grieve
(Christina Rossetti, "Remember," 10)

And see the great Achilles, whom we knew
(Tennyson, "Ulysses," 63)

I may have looked attentive for a while
(Wendy Cope, "So Much Depends," 6)

Though these lines are syntactically diverse (Drayton's, for instance, is a dependent clause, Tennyson's is a portion of a compound predicate, Cope's is complete sentence), their rhythmical similarity is no less hearable than was the rhythmical similarity among the earlier group of lines. In this case, the likeness seems chiefly to result from each line's having a middle-stressed trisyllabic word that runs from the fifth to seventh positions. The words themselves represent different parts of speech. We have proper nouns (Charybdis, Achilles), adjectives (unhappy, attentive), an adverb (securely), and a verb (remember). But their shape is the same. This, and perhaps the pause that generally follows the word, produce the corresponding movement.

As with the pentameters made up of noun-phrases, we can alter these verses in sundry ways without damaging their grammar, and we can in particular move the middle-stressed trisyllables to different positions. We could write, for instance,

> And remember afterwards, do not grieve
> For a while, I may have looked attentive

But metrically speaking, or at least pentametrically speaking, such changes make the verses jump the tracks. The emended lines fall into that swingy, four-beat measure that we observed a moment ago:

> x x / x / x x / x /
> And remember afterwards, do not grieve
>
> x x / x / x / x / x
> For a while, I may have looked attentive

To read these as pentameters, one would have to mispronounce some of the words and give peculiar articulation to some of the phrases:

> And remem**ber** afterwards, **do** not **grieve**
> For **a** while, **I** may **have** looked at**ten**tive

Meter and grammar are no longer in harmony, but are contradicting each other.

Beginning poets often have difficulty harmonizing meter and grammar, especially when they attempt to write in iambic pentameter. This difficulty results from the combined effect of the line's asymmetry and its extreme flexibility. As many have noted, even when a pentameter seems to fall naturally into two five-syllable sections, the first half has only two metrical beats, whereas the second has three:

> x / x / x / x / x /
> The shrieking heaven <> lifted over men
> (Louise Bogan, "Cassandra," 7)

And while the pentameter is a long line, it has no obligatory caesural division. It is not, that is, conventionally partitioned into more manageable subdivisions, as are long lines in some other poetries. In contrast to a poet working in, say, the ancient hexameter, which customarily pauses in the third foot, or the classical alexandrine, which customarily breaks after the sixth syllable, a poet writing English pentameters is free to pause (or not to pause) at any point in the line and may divide the line in any number of ways:

> A hand that taught what might be said in rhyme
> (Surrey, "Tribute to Wyatt," 13)

> The stars, I see, will kiss the valleys first
> (Shakespeare, *The Winter's Tale*, 5.1.205)

> Which only heads, refined from reason, know
> (Pope, *The Dunciad*, 3.6)

> A desolation, a simplicity
> (Wordsworth, *The Prelude*, 4.402)

> My letters! all dead paper, mute and white!
> (Elizabeth Barrett Browning, *Sonnets from the Portuguese*, 28.1)

> Good. That man goes to Rome, to death, despair
> (Hardy, "At Lulworth Cove a Century Back," 17)

Though the pentameter's flexibility makes it inexhaustibly interesting and exciting for the experienced poet, it takes a while for younger writers to develop that intuitional familiarity with it that is necessary to using it fluently. Initial attempts to write in the measure often produce verses which have ten syllables, but which are really in the loose, semi-anapestic, four-beat rhythm that characterizes the awkward emendations of Jonson's, Rossetti's, and Cope's lines. Since a good deal of popular verse and song-lyric features some sort of four-beat measure, and since such verse is very familiar to us, we perhaps naturally fall back on the measure when metrically confused. In any event, poets who wish to write pentameter must learn to distinguish between lines of this tripping four-beat sort and lines which may have only four (or three or two) strong speech stresses, but which nevertheless keep to the iambic tread or fluctuation and which merely feature a light iamb or iambs at some point:

> 1 4 1 2 1 4 1 4 1 4
> x / x / x / x / x /
> Bespotted as with shields of red and black
> (Spenser, *The Fairie Queene*, 1.9.11.5)

> 1 4 1 4 1 4 1 2 1 4
> x / x / x /x/ x /
> The clouds were low and hairy in the skies
> (Frost, "Once by the Pacific," 5)

It is not always the case that one and only one arrangement of words or phrases will prove metrically workable. In pentameters that divide into groups of four and six syllables, for instance, the phrases may sometimes be transposed, assuming no logical relationship or pattern of rhyme is violated. When Friar Lawrence advises the banished Romeo to console himself with "Adversity's sweet milk, philosophy" (Shakespeare, *Romeo and Juliet*, 3.3.55), he could just as well say, for metrical purposes, "Philosophy, adversity's sweet milk." Similarly, words in a line may sometimes be transposed with one another, especially if they are coordinate adjectives, nouns, or verbs, and have the same number of syllables and the same rhythmical contour. Indeed, on occasion a poet may artfully flipflop such transposable words, as Thomas Hood does in his rueful observation about "The Irish School-master":

> He never spoils the child and spares the rod
> But spoils the rod and never spares the child.

Though certain grammatical patterns appear relatively frequently in our verse, metrical composition is by no means limited to these. The pentameter line in particular seems capable of accommodating almost any syntactical arrangement, and the serious poet will in fact avoid relying on the more common ones. There are clichés of rhythm as well as speech, and the ear may be put off by familiar modulations no less than by stereotypical diction.

These remarks are pertinent to the line-type featuring the two noun-phrases. It has a kind of facile sweetness. What is more, it tends to feel padded, principally because of the two disyllabic adjectives and their symmetrical positioning — one in the first phrase, one in the second. A historical factor is involved as well. Eighteenth-century poets were particularly fond of this line-type and milked it to exhaustion. Perhaps because they sought to make their pentameters as smooth as possible, and because they consequently and desperately needed sources of rhythmical modulation, the line-type had a dual appeal for them. On the one hand, its paired noun-phrases made for balance. On the other hand, its light third foot made for metrical variety. Unfortunately, when one hears the line several times in close proximity — as one does, for instance, towards the close (346, 354, 361) of Goldsmith's "Deserted Village" —

> The various terrors of that horrid shore
> The rattling terrors of the vengeful snake
> The breezy covert of the warbling grove

it sets one's teeth on edge.

If the line has become something of a rhythmical cliché, its familiarity has on occasion been put to good effect by modern poets. For instance, in their memorial tributes to Arthur Henniker and John Muir respectively, Thomas Hardy and Yvor Winters seem to use the line to indicate something of the simple, old-fashioned goodness of their subjects:

> His modest spirit in his candid look
> (Hardy, "A.H., 1855-1912," 4)

> A gentle figure from a simpler age
> (Winters, "On Re-reading a Passage from John Muir," 18)

Also, if a heavy iamb appears at any point before or after the light third foot, the rhythm tilts in such a way that it loses its cloying quality and acquires (at least to our ears at this point in metrical history) a more interesting effect:

>   3 4
> A cleaving daylight, and a last great calm
> (Robinson, "Ben Jonson Entertains a Man from Stratford,")

>   3 4
> The bare man Nothing in the Beggar's Bush
> (Auden, "The Hero," 4)

It will be noted that, to produce this alteration, the poet must dispense with one of the disyllabic adjectives. Doubtless this morphological shift affects the change of rhythm.

So, too, a line of the paired-noun-phrases type may acquire rhythmical interest if it appears in the midst of enjambments. For example, when Milton writes (*PL*, 2.278-280),

>   ... All things invite
> To peaceful counsels, and the settled state
> Of order ...

even the most fastidious reader will probably not find anything trite in the movement. Admittedly, "[t]o peaceful counsels, and the settled state" might appear in isolation just another variation on a familiar rhythmical theme, in this instance the first of the noun-phrases beginning with a preposition rather than an article or attributive adjective. Yet we don't hear the noun phrases as neatly balanced. The enjambments sever the close syntactical relationship between them. Grammatically, the first noun-phrase goes with material from the line above it and the second with material from the line below.

Many other syntactical arrangements can produce lines with a sense-break after the fifth syllable, in the middle of a light third foot. Though the arrangement involving the two noun-phrases is most common, we can cite various different examples, which may give us some sense of the innumerable ways that this simple form of the pentameter may be realized:

> It frets the halter, and it chokes the child
> (Raleigh, "Sir Walter Raleigh to his Son," 12)

> The pipe, the tabor, and the trembling crowd
> (Spenser, "Epithalamion," 131)

> My sweet companion and my gentle peer
> (Cowley, "On the Death of Mr. William Hervey," 9)

> Resolved to ruin or to rule the state
> (Dryden, *Absalom and Achitophel*, 174)

> Of life reviving with reviving day
> (Scott, *The Lady of the Lake*, 2.1.4)

> There is a mountain in the distant west
> (Longfellow, "The Cross of Snow," 9)

Raleigh fills out the line with two independent clauses joined by a coordinating conjunction. Spenser uses a series of three nouns, the last modified by an adjective. Cowley deploys two noun-phrases — the first of which, however, differs from the more common pattern, by involving a monosyllabic adjective and a trisyllabic noun accented in the middle. Dryden offers a past participle followed by coordinate infinitives. In Scott's line, we see two prepositional phrases. In the Longfellow line, we have an anticipatory ("dummy") subject, followed by a verb, subject, and prepositional phrase.

A light middle foot may consist as well of a conjunction and an article:

> Of heightened wit | and of | the critic's art
> (Anne Finch, "Poem Occasioned by the Sight of the
> Fourth Epistle, Lib. Epist: 1 of Horace," 60)

Or it may entail a syllable with weak stress, followed by a syllable with tertiary (or secondary) stress, in a polysyllabic or fore-stressed trisyllabic word:

> In sad simil | itude | of griefs to mine
> (Pope, "Eloise to Abelard," 360)

> You know the moun | tainous | coiffures of Bath
> (Stevens, "Le Monocle de Mon Oncle" 29)

Let us return to word-shape and middle-stressed trisyllables. In pentametric verse, these seem most often to occupy the fifth-to-seventh positions. Or perhaps they merely have special rhythmical distinctness when so placed. Nevertheless, such words appear in all the other possible locations in the line. We frequently find them running from the first to the third position, from the third to the fifth, from the seventh to the ninth, and from the ninth to the eleventh — in this last case the final unaccented syllable of the word comprising a feminine ending:

> *Divinely* imitate the realms above
> (Sarah Fyge Egerton, "The Emulation," 35)

> The late *appearance* of the northern lights
> (R.S. Gwynn, "Horatio's Philosophy," 12)

> In marble quarried from *Carrara's* hills
> (W.H. Davies, "A Strange City," 16)

> Go, get you up; I will not be *entreated*
> (Beaumont, *The Knight of the Burning Pestle*, 4.3.3)

Moreover, two different middle-stressed trisyllables may occur at different positions in the line:

> In a *forbidden* or *forbidding* tree
> (Donne, "The Blossom," 12)

> *Adulthood's* high *romantic* citadel
> (Kingsley Amis, "Romance," 8)

Or three may appear, as in

> *Tomorrow* and *tomorrow* and *tomorrow*
> (Shakespeare, *Macbeth*, 5.1.19)

To shift morphologies, one can find as well, in the same line, a pair of trisyllables with chief stress on the first syllable and tertiary stress on the third:

> Boys seek for *images* and *melody*
> (Robert Browning, "Transcendentalism," 17)

> The *singular* idea of *loneliness*
> (Robinson, "Isaac and Archibald," 63)

And one can find the two different kinds of trisyllables mixed together in a single line, as was the case in Amis's verse cited a moment ago, and as is the case in these verses:

> *Or memorize another Golgotha*
> (Shakespeare, *Macbeth*, 1.2.41)

> *Whatever hypocrites austerely* talk
> (Milton, *PL*, 4.744)

Indeed, because most English words of more than one syllable feature alternating stress, whether rising or falling, it is easy for poets, once they get the hang of it, to fit them at any point into the line. Here, for instance, are verses that integrate, into the pentametric pattern, words of four and five syllables with rising stress:

> I saw *eternity* the other night
> (Vaughan, "The World," 1)

> *Procrastination* is the thief of time
> (Young, *Night Thoughts*, 1.393)

And here are verses that integrate words of five and six syllables with falling stress. (The first verse also features a four-syllable word with rising stress.)

> By *psychological* experiment
> (Frost, "At Woodward's Gardens," 19)

> Of all this *unintelligible* world
> (Wordsworth, "Tintern Abbey," 40)

Likewise, it is possible to integrate two four-syllable words with different stress-contours into the same pentameter:

The *reputation* of *Tiepolo*
(Anthony Hecht, *The Venetian Vespers*, 6.94)

Or two five-syllable words with different stress-contours:

Involuntary immortality
(Vikram Seth, "The North Temple Tower," 10)

Other combinations may be noted. For example, Milton gives us, in the following verse (*PL*, 3.492), four words of different length, arranged in a kind of descending succession. The first and second words have four and three syllables respectively and feature rising rhythm; the third word is a disyllable with falling rhythm, the fourth a monosyllable:

Indulgences, Dispenses, Pardons, Bulls

And in the verse below (*Troilus and Cressida*, 5.2.127), Shakespeare offers this same mix of words, but swings the polysyllable down to the end of the line and moves the tri-, di-, and monosyllable up a place:

Created only to calumniate

While the abstract norm of the pentameter has five accents, one common version of the line has only three strong speech stresses. In this type of line, which readers will recognize immediately once examples of it are given, the second and fourth feet are light, and strong beats fall on syllables two, six, and ten. Grammatically, this line most frequently involves two major fore-stressed disyllables (e.g., nouns or verbs), introduced or connected by particles (e.g., articles or monosyllabic conjunctions and prepositions). And the line customarily concludes with another major word, usually a monosyllable; however, a fore-stressed disyllable is also a possibility, in which case the word's light second syllable is a feminine ending.

This line-type appears with some frequency in Chaucer:

In Omer or in Darës or in Dytë
(Troilus and Criseyde, 1.145)

In Southwerk at the Tabard as I lay
(*CT*, Gen. Prol., 20)

Later instances include:

A kingdom, or a cottage, or a grave
        (Edward de Vere, "Epigram," 6)

The tutor and the feeder of my riots
        (Shakespeare, 2 *Henry IV*, 1.3.86)

The bosom of his Father and his God
        (Gray, "Elegy in a Country Churchyard," 128)

And listen to the flapping of the flame
        (Wordsworth, "Personal Talk," 1.13)

The glory of the beauty of the morning
        (Edward Thomas, "The Glory," 1)

As with other species of pentameter, this one can be realized in many ways. The poet can introduce, so to speak, a trisyllable for one of the disyllables and delete one of the particles:

Nor wonder at *complainings* in your streets
        (Mary Barber, "On Seeing an Officer's Widow," 30)

Or one of the disyllables may be replaced by a monosyllable and a trisyllable may make up the difference by replacing a disyllable:

As *sweet* and as *delicious* as the first
        (Ford, *'Tis Pity She's a Whore*, 5.3.9)

Or a rear-stressed disyllable can close the line, the initial unaccented syllable of this word standing, in a sense, in place of one of the particles:

The Paythan an' the Zulu an' Burmese
        (Kipling, "Fuzzy Wuzzy," 3)

Or the pattern may be accomplished by two rear-stressed disyllables flanking a polysyllable whose primarily stressed syllable occupies the sixth position in the line:

Detained for *contemplation* and *repose*
        (Wordsworth, *The Excursion*, 1.42)

Or it may involve two middle-stressed trisyllables and a rear-stressed disyllable:

Distinguished, and *familiar*, and *aloof*
        (J.V. Cunningham, *A Century of Epigrams*, 54.4)

Or a middle-stressed and a fore-stressed trisyllable and a rear-stressed disyllable:

Wherever on the *virginal frontier*
(Richard Wilbur, "John Chapman," 2)

Once readers or poets acquire a sense of rhythmico-grammatical groups, they may be able to specify other common types of this or that meter. They also may develop an ear for less common correspondences. Below, for instance, are the opening iambic tetrameters of two well-known poems. The poems are centuries apart, but the tetrameters have the same unusual rhythm. This involves an inverted (i.e., trochaic) first foot and a fore-stressed disyllabic word laid across the fourth and fifth positions of the line; the unaccented syllable of this word in turn constitutes the first syllable of a light iamb, which is followed by a heavy iamb, with the result that four degrees of stress rise over the course of two successive feet:

1 2 3 4
/ x x / x / x /
Drink to me only with thine eyes
(Ben Jonson, "Song," 1)

1 2 3 4
/ x x / x / x /
Just as my fingers on these keys
(Stevens, "Peter Quince at the Clavier," 1)

Here are two iambic pentameters that feature similarly contoured and coordinated parallel phrases:

False Friend, false Son, false Father, and false King
(Churchill, *Gotham*, 2.385)

Sans Wine, sans Song, sans Singer, and — sans End!
(Fitzgerald, Omar Khayyám's *Rubaiyat*, 23.4)

At times meter and syntax may seem to be at loggerheads, but will, upon closer examination, prove to be in lively concurrence. At times, that is, meter may seem to require an unusual reading which will turn out to be significant and appropriate for the context. A good illustration of this situation occurs towards the close of John Greenleaf Whittier's "Abraham Davenport." In this poem, an eclipse has spread darkness over the countryside, and in the Connecticut State House, most of the legislators are terrified that the Day of Judgment has arrived. Amidst a clamor for adjournment, Representative Davenport calmly rises and suggests that people cannot know the ways of divinity and that the lawmakers should therefore remain at their earthly tasks — in this case, amending an act to regulate state fisheries — until heaven explicitly orders them to do otherwise. And he concludes by saying:

> Let God do his work, we will see to ours.

Were we to encounter the first clause in isolation, we would probably read it with stresses on the two nouns. Let *God* do his *work*. However, such a reading does not fit the iambic pentameter pattern, which instead suggests that the stress should fall on "his." Though normally we do not stress an attributive adjective at the expense of its noun, rendering the line in this evidently unconventional fashion not only recovers the rhythm, but also clarifies the poem's meaning. We see that Whittier intends that the pronominal forms be emphasized right down the line and that the line itself encapsulates the poem's key juxtapositions — God/man and God's work/man's work:

> Let *God* do *his* work, *we* will see to *ours*

Generally speaking, grammatical variety is as pleasing in verse as it is in prose. In terms of morphology and word-shape, it is frequently the case that verse which naturally and unostentatiously mixes different types of words will appeal to the ear more than verse whose vocabulary is notably constrained or limited. To take an obvious case, Shakespeare time and again captivates us with the dextrous diversity of his language, often creating interesting verbal and rhythmical counterpoints simply by juxtaposing lines of short words with lines of longer ones. Consider, in this regard, that passage in *The Taming of the Shrew* (2.1.170-76) in which Petruchio announces that he will not let Kate's ill temper discourage him from wooing her. Part of the rhythmical charm of the passage results from Petruchio's hypothesizing, in verses comprised of monosyllables, ways in which Kate may insult him, and then imagining, in verses featuring di-, tri-, and polysyllabic words, complimentary replies to turn aside her rudeness:

> Say that she rail, why then I'll tell her plain
> She sings as sweetly as a nightingale.

> Say that she frown, I'll say she looks as clear
> As morning roses newly washed with dew.
> Say she be mute and will not speak a word,
> Then I'll commend her volubility
> And say she uttereth piercing eloquence.

(It may be observed that Shakespeare probably intends us to read, in the final line of this passage, the second syllable of "uttereth" as elided or syncopated away: "utt'reth." Otherwise, the line has an extra syllable. Those who, like George Saintsbury, object to resolving syllabic ambiguities by means of elision will scan the line as having an anapestic third foot.)

Another instance of this type of juxtaposition occurs towards the close of *Hamlet*. Mortally wounded, the dying prince is concerned for his posthumous reputation, and he realizes that unless he has an advocate to tell the world his side of the sad story of his family, he may be blamed for the catastrophes that have befallen the Danish court. So he begs his distraught friend Horatio, who himself wishes to commit suicide, to live at least a little longer and give a fair accounting of all that has happened. As Hamlet puts it to Horatio (5.2.349-50):

> Absent thee from felicity awhile,
> And in this harsh world draw thy breath in pain

Though it is the thought that touches us in these lines, the thought may be memorable precisely on account of the contrast between the first line's graceful paraphrasis (for "Don't die yet") and the second's clotted density. Both lines are conventional pentameters, but the first, with its disyllables and polysyllable and its alliteration, seems rhythmically to carry a sense of the happy (to Hamlet's way of thinking) realm of death, whereas the congested rhythm of the second suggests the acerbic domain of terrestrial experience.

Poems may also benefit from syntactical variety. J.V. Cunningham's epigrams and translations illustrate, in miniature, this point. For example, in Cunningham's version of Catullus's two-liner *Odi et Amo*,

> I hate and love her. If you ask me why
> I don't know. But I feel it and am torn.

we have, in two iambic pentameters, three short sentences. The first is a simple declarative sentence, with subject, (compound) verb, and object. The second sentence is complex, the dependent clause coming first, the main clause, "I don't know," following. The third sentence has yet a different structure, being introduced by a coordinating conjunction and having a compound predicate.

It is doubtful that Cunningham was solemnly deliberating about syntax when he did this translation. Like most excellent poets, once he had acquired the skills of his trade, he applied them with a natural grace and devoted most of his conscious energy to thematics or, in the case of translation, to philological and interpretive questions. (Because Latin is more highly inflected than English, and because its grammar differs from ours, the cast of Cunningham's sentences is necessarily his own as well as Catullus's.) But the quiet variety of syntax is a key aspect of the translation and significantly contributes to its success.

One needn't use fancy words and intricate grammar to write great verse. Cunningham's translation is, despite its syntactical fluidity, composed entirely of monosyllables. And many of the most memorable passages and lines in our poetry are written in simple words, with straightforward sentence structure:

> Why should a dog, a horse, a rat, have life
> And thou no breath at all? Thou'lt come no more.
> (Shakespeare, *King Lear*, 5.3.308-309)

> I must stop short of thee the whole day long
> (Alice Meynell, "Renunciation," 8)

Other things being equal, however, a poet will benefit from a good working vocabulary and a rich command of grammatical structure. They will contribute to a wider range of thought and expression than would otherwise exist.

In closing, I should like to say a few words about the advantages of considering meter in connection with grammar. The masterpieces of our poetry are an enduring resource; they have a singular power to instruct, elevate, move, console, and civilize. Yet if they are to exercise their regenerative function, we must read them not merely with the eye, but also with the ear and mind and heart. We must experience them as the integrated works they are. We must hear both their grammatical and their metrical structures, both their sense and their music. To return to Auden's comment, it is possible to read verse as pure grammar, rendering it as though it were prose, or as pure meter, simply sing-songing or intoning it forth. But the magical paradox of verse is that it joins fixed measure with fluid idiomatic speech. The better we appreciate this union, the more deeply and comprehensively we can grasp and share in the art.

Finally, the relationship between meter and grammar is worth attention, in that the two illustrate, in similar and concurrent ways, something of the nature of our being. In his stimulating study, *Grammatical Man*, Jeremy Campbell writes:

> Biologists as well as philosophers have suggested that the universe, and the living forms it contains, are based on chance, but not on accident. To put it another way, forces of chance and of antichance coexist in a complementary relationship. ... The proper metaphor for the life process may not be a pair of rolling dice or a spinning roulette wheel, but the sentences of a language, conveying information that is partly predictable and partly unpredictable. These sentences are generated by rules that make much out of little, producing a boundless wealth of meaning from a finite store of words; they enable language to be familiar yet surprising, constrained yet unpredictable within its constraints.

No less than grammar does, meter fuses and enacts those principles of constancy and of change that seem essential to life and to the world about us. Like grammar, meter involves simple structures which can nevertheless be manifested in varied and complex ways. It organizes the rhythms of speech while at the same time allowing for all sorts of modulations, shadings, and surprises. And when Campbell adds that "grammatical man inhabits a grammatical universe," poets and readers of verse might speculate that we also inhabit a metrical one.

AUTHOR'S NOTE

For this essay I have used standard editions of the poets cited, modernizing the spelling of earlier writers, so long as doing so did not obscure their metrical structures and intentions. For linguistic background, I am indebted to Otto Jespersen's "Note on Metre," (first pub. 1900), reprinted in Harvey Gross, Ed., *Structure of Verse* (New York: Ecco, 1979); to George L. Trager and Henry Lee Smith, Jr., *An Outline of English Structure*, 2nd. Ed. (Washington, D.C.: American Council of Learned Societies, 1956); to Noam Chomsky and Morris Halle, *The Sound Pattern of English* (New York: Harper and Row, 1968); and to my friend and colleague, Terry Santos. Auden's remark about the reading of verse appears in Alan Ansen, *The Table Talk of W.H. Auden*, Ed. Nicholas Jenkins (Princeton: Ontario Review Press, 1990), p. 62. Campbell's observations about grammar can be found in *Grammatical Man: Information, Entropy, Language, and Life* (New York: Simon & Schuster, 1982), pp. 11, 12. A poet and critic who has noted the possibility of discussing meter in relation to grammatical organization is J.V. Cunningham. In his "How Shall the Poem Be Written?" (*Collected Essays of J.V. Cunningham* [Chicago: Swallow, 1976], p. 266), Cunningham suggests in passing, "The descriptive problems raised by different modes of recitation can be avoided by regarding a meter, not as a schematic diagram of scansions, but as a collection of syllabic-syntactic types."

Other Voices, Other Lives
David Mason

Empathy, the act of inhabiting a stranger's experience, is a civilizing pro-
cess. It implies connection, community, releasing the poet—who otherwise
seems "[e]ncased in talent like a uniform"—from isolation. Fiction's advan-
tage has usually been considered its interest in society as well as the lives of
specific individuals, and poets can envy this, particularly when the lyric "I"
has become repetitive, nearly automatic. Tennyson and Browning began
in Romantic subjectivity, and balanced their careers on the taut line be-
tween those early impulses and an opposing impulse toward the objectivity
of storytelling. In our time the line has been stretched between similar poles;
one mode of expression loses power through overuse, and poets naturally
turn to the opposite mode to restore vital tension. Rather than leaping to
the conclusion that the subjective lyric is dead and we can only stay aloft on
the shoulders of a good story, we should admit that there are advantages
and disadvantages to every genre, and that poets are better off when they
can write more than one kind of poem.

Anthony Hecht and Louis Simpson have written about the use of nar-
rative to regain literary territory that in modern times has been lost to the
novel. More recently, a younger generation of poets, including Robert
McDowell, Mark Jarman and Dana Gioia, has argued that narrative may
be a good way to work free of the lethargy observable in many contempo-
rary poems. Recent uses of narrative are broader than this short list sug-
gests, yet poets and critics have, so far, neglected fundamental questions
about these practices. For example, is the poetic line as viable today for
characterization as it was a century (or 25 centuries) ago? What are the
objectives and difficulties of characterization in verse? If poets and their
audience can rejoin in empathy's embrace, what sort of poem will best in-
vite and challenge them?

There are at least two good reasons why contemporary poets might use
verse to create characters and tell stories. One reason is that it can rejuve-
nate their art by compelling them to reevaluate the subjects they write about,
to look more closely at lives usually deemed insufficiently flashy or spec-
tacular. By involving us in the nuances of social and individual problems,
narrative poetry can address issues beyond the narrow confines of the poet's

life, or it can focus emotions too painfully personal to be revealed directly in a lyric. It is also possible that the line has advantages lacking in prose, the chief one being that it contributes to memorability, helping to sustain a literary culture most of us would agree is in danger of extinction. The line as a unit of sound is tremendously important, but the line is also a unit of thought and feeling; it can contribute to dramatic dynamism and plot in particular ways, adding another dimension to the process of storytelling.

These advantages are found at their fullest in shorter narratives and monologues that can be read or recited in a single session. Book-length poems, even when as well-written as Vikram Seth's Byronic novel, *The Golden Gate*, and Frederick Turner's science fiction epics, The *New World* and *Genesis*, are, in our culture, too long to be experienced whole as uninterrupted aural performances, and instead we absorb them as solitary readers over a longer period of time. If the 1980s saw the publication of several book-length poems—among them James Merrill's assembly of ghosts in *The Changing Light at Sandover*, Thomas McGrath's pseudo-autobiographical *Letter to an Imaginary Friend* and Alfred Corn's *Notes from a Child of Paradise*—it was also a period that witnessed the revival of shorter narratives by poets as various as Hecht and Simpson, and younger writers like Sydney Lea, Robert McDowell, Mark Jarman, Rita Dove and Dana Gioia. Like prose short stories, these poems have to produce their impact by memorable and economical means. They can be absorbed by an audience in their entirety, rather than in fragments or highlights. Due to their relative brevity, they cannot afford a leisurely alternation of prose-like passages and lyric moments; their lines must be more consistently commanding and intense. In shorter narratives the partnership of line and narrative structure is particularly important. We can hear the adjustments of dramatic voice in relation to the line, almost a musical interplay in which the entire form of a completed story becomes audible.

Where Seth's novel owes much to Byron and Pushkin, and Turner's epics to Milton, many contemporary writers of shorter narratives look back upon Robert Frost as the most significant practitioner of their art. Frost's "Home Burial," for example, elucidates two characters and their dramatic conflict in a mere 116 lines. With economy most fiction writers would admire, Frost plunges us into the midst of marital estrangement in his first two lines:

> He saw her from the bottom of the stairs
> Before she saw him. She was starting down....

The first line is a statement of fact, but enjambment forces us into the second line; the line break itself, and the power struggle implicit in the phrase "[b]efore she saw him," creates suspense. He is at the bottom of the stairs, she at the top. But she is coming down, and already we know that their meeting will produce conflict. As the poem progresses, the suspense it achieves by line breaks and withholding exposition pulls us uncomfortably close to these two people. Frost's spare dialogue uses repetition to further suspense, while also capturing the man's alienation from his wife's grief:

> He spoke
> Advancing toward her: "What is it you see
> From up there always? —for I want to know."
> She turned and sank upon her skirts at that,
> And her face changed from terrified to dull.
> He said to gain time: "What is it you see?"

The repeated question indicates the husband's helpless frustration, even trepidation, but he speaks "[a]dvancing toward her"—his gesture is intrusive. She, who had been "[l]ooking over her shoulder at some fear," grows impassive, as if an impenetrable wall stood between them.

Both husband and wife know this wall intimately. He knows it even as he feigns ignorance of what put it there. Her angry grief and his coldness have built it, and though he insists that he will know what troubles her, she nests in her own bitterness, confident that he cannot know her secret. In the first 25 lines of the poem, Frost maps with scary accuracy the dimensions of their estrangement. Their situation is specific. Not only does their dead child's recently-filled grave, which is visible from an upstairs window, haunt her, but her pain is multiplied by the image of her husband digging—even being able to dig. When he speaks about the graves, then about their child's grave, his sensitivity is clumsy:

> "There are three stones of slate and one of marble,
> Broad-shouldered little slabs there in the sunlight
> On the sidehill. We haven't to mind those.
> But I understand: it is not the stones,
> But the child's mound—"
>
> "Don't, don't, don't,
> don't," she cried.

The verse itself, the husband's full lines wordily groping for explanation and the wife's spondaic outburst finishing a line, contributes powerfully to the scene. Details of psychological states share space in the above passage with a detail of social milieu: as in Dickens, the gravestones almost become characters, telling of the generations of broad-shouldered farmers from whom the husband is apparently descended.

This kind of specific touch is the lifeblood of any good story, but the poet balances even more precariously, dangerously, because of the added technical difficulty of versification. Mark Jarman's dramatic monologue, "The Gift," in his book *The Black Riviera* (1990), uses blank verse as strict as Frost's to limn a specific child's point of view when she is "kidnapped" for a day by her father. As her father drives them in his car, she observes,

> Outside the windshield traffic lights hung down
> From cables, and the bushy tops of palms
> Showed up at intervals that I could count.
> A pink or yellow building front skimmed past.
> But mostly I could only see the sky.

By themselves these lines are unremarkable, but in their dramatic context, given the strangeness of the event, her limited point of view and touching pride in being able to count, they carry much of the poem's disjointed mood. When the father's girlfriend shows up, Jarman's careful establishment of the speaker's voice pays off nicely:

> Then, at a stop, one of those tall palm trees
> That wears a shaggy collar of dead fronds
> Leaned down and opened up the door and got in
> Beside me. Daddy called her Charlotte dear
> And told her I was Susan.

Still, the lines themselves do not quite pay the sort of metrical dividends Frost's do. Most contemporary narrative poets are not yet adept at milking the techniques of enjambment and metrical variation for specific dramatic effects.

Despite this weakness, Jarman has made some of the most ambitious narrative forays of any poet of his generation. In "The Death of God" he experiments with the long free verse line of Robinson Jeffers, a line that enables Jarman in his next book, *Iris* (1992), the freedom and sweep of a novelist:

The woman sat on the bus, her daughter's head in her lap,
    and read a paperback of poems,
The only book from college that she'd saved, Robinson
    Jeffers, and talked back to him,
As always. He was her poet. The bus crossed the two
    lakes, and the land between them,
Like stages of warning. Glare of water, shadow of close,
    dense trees, glare again.
Then entry into the isolated flatland that she'd left,
    married, pregnant, unhurt,
Not yet in thrall to this dead stranger from California,
    who spoke of an end to the continent
She had to imagine, had to summon up even more
    strenuously while coming back
To western Kentucky, a mother, estranged, abused and
    wounded, hiding a black-eye behind dark glasses.

Jarman's protagonist, a woman torn between the decadent reality of contemporary life and the transcendent vision of Jeffers' ghost, begins a quest that Jarman the novelist cannot quite resolve; the book's lyrical resolution synthesizes sound, meaning and event as only a poet could do. Indeed, if much of *Iris* has the feel of a prose novel, its conclusion almost escapes plot altogether with its lyrical loft.

Like Jarman, Robert McDowell has brought a rugged idiom and subject matter to his poetry. His first book, *Quiet Money* (1987), works by a kind of narrative architecture as much as by the devices of a poet. In blank and free verse poems, one finds here a world akin to Raymond Carver's, in which failure predominates. The title poem, about a bootlegging pilot who has made secret transatlantic flights for years before Lindbergh's famous one, becomes one of several lovely meditations on the salvation of skill and craft. It also proves beyond any doubt that real stories have indelible structures. They are like seeds containing blueprints of complex entities, and keep growing in the mind long after one has read them. Since *Quiet Money*, McDowell has published, mostly in *The Hudson Review*, more narratives with a gritty urban vision one rarely finds in poetry, particularly "The Neighborhood," "My Corporate Life" and "All the Broken Boys and Girls." These are poems in which McDowell's blank verse technique seems increasingly assured. One of the strongest of his recent poems, "The Pact," proves a dark pastoral tale combining the narrative obsession of Jeffers with the verse technique of Frost. Its vivid opening reads as follows:

Rain bulled into the valley like a giant
Escaping from the pages of a book.
John-Allen in his garden watched it brawling
Over the coastal range. Its highest peaks
Gleamed briefly in the sun that broke above
The Cascade Mountains fifty miles to the east,
Then disappeared in swirling thunderheads.
Behind him his blue house reflected deeper blue
As all the valley darkened. He leaned the rake
Against the cockeyed table of surplus boards
And walked back to the fence to face the wind
Coming in warm gusts that flattened the grass,
Advanced on the pear tree, then on himself.
His straw hat blew off, flew crazily away,
Splitting the wicket of two apple trees
Before hanging up suddenly among the roses.
John-Allen still faced west, his hair straight back,
His eyes tearing. He knew he should go in
But tightened his grip on the fence. The storm inside
Would outlast this one, which was beautiful.
A moment's silence, then thunder came calling,
Then all the fury of the storm broke loose.

In clean, skillfully-modulated lines, McDowell establishes his setting and the ominous potential of "the storm inside." "The Pact" achieves a powerful marriage of story and line.

The saddest moment in Frost's "Home Burial" occurs when the wife, who has been almost menacingly silent, suddenly and at length describes her husband's grave-digging. Here the verse itself is compelled by the extremity of contained emotion:

"...you don't know how to speak.
If you had any feelings, you that dug
With your own hand—how could you?—his little grave;
I saw you from that very window there,
Making the gravel leap and leap in air,
Leap up, like that, like that, and land so lightly
And roll back down the mound beside the hole.
I thought, Who is that man? I didn't know you.
And I crept down the stairs and up the stairs
To look again, and still your spade kept lifting."

Now, the wife's resentment given voice, it is the husband's turn to withdraw in bitterness, his brevity proving that language cannot bridge the gulf between them: "I shall laugh the worst laugh I ever laughed./ I'm cursed. God, if I don't believe I'm cursed."

Though Frost's use of the line for dramatic effect is more successful than any of his imitators', his diction is sometimes awkward, as when the husband says, "I don't like such things 'twixt those that love." Narrative poets are caught between the lyric possibilities of the line and the necessities of storytelling, and occasionally one or the other of these elements suffers. Two of the most remarkable recent dramatic monologues, Dana Gioia's "The Room Upstairs" (from *Daily Horoscope*, 1986) and "Counting the Children" (*The Gods of Winter*, 1991), blend lyric and dramatic elements almost seamlessly. Gioia's tactic is usually to be as unobtrusive as possible, and in both of these poems he chooses speakers well-suited to his clear, meticulous voice and probing intelligence. This is particularly true of "Counting the Children," in which the speaker is, like Gioia, a businessman. Beyond that fact we know little about Mr. Choi, a Chinese-American accountant hired to audit the estate of an eccentric old woman who has recently died. We do not see him interacting with other characters, as we do the husband and wife in Frost's more dramatic poem. We hear a neighbor woman speaking as she shows Mr. Choi through the house, but he does not respond vocally to anything she says. Gioia limits the poem to the confines of Choi's mind, so it resembles a private confession to the reader. Because of this, Gioia's lines are not used dramatically in the manner of Frost; they are rarely broken out of narrative necessity, but instead retain a fluid, dream-like suppleness. Gioia's poem lacks Frost's firm grounding in a specific milieu; instead, like Poe, he emphasizes the subjective view, linking Mr. Choi's fevered vision to lyric moments in the verse.

No great drama propels this vision. Touring the house, Mr. Choi has been shown the dead woman's strange collection of dolls. His function among them is purely professional and legalistic, but the roomful of dolls on shelves startles him out of his routine:

> Where were the children who promised them love?
> The small, caressing hands, the lips which whispered
> Secrets in the dark? Once they were woken,
>
> Each by name. Now they have become each other—
> Anonymous except for injury,
> The beautiful and headless side by side.

These are well-written lines, but the image of "[t]he beautiful and headless side by side" does more to develop a mood than to illuminate Mr. Choi's character. Still, Gioia has pulled us into a mind that is recognizably individual. In the second section of "Counting the Children" Choi has a nightmare in which he cannot balance his ledger; his world has lost its customary order, and even numbers disobey him. The madness of that doll collection, of a mind that could assemble so many dead pairs of eyes, so many frozen little corpses, suggests a whole world unhinged, and when, in the third section, Choi awakes, his first thought is for his daughter's safety. He gropes down the hallway to her room, discovering her safely asleep. Gioia may have felt that the following openly emotional lines could not be written without the protective mask of a dramatic monologue:

> How delicate this vessel in our care,
> This gentle soul we summoned to the world,
> A life we treasured but could not protect.
>
> This was the terror I could not confess—
> Not even to my wife—and it was the joy
> My daughter had no words to understand.
>
> So standing at my pointless watch each night
> In the bare nursery we had improvised,
> I learned the loneliness that we call love.

Too pretty, some might say, yet in a manner that is quite unlike Frost's, Gioia has risked feelings of uncommon delicacy.

If we scarcely know Mr. Choi as a social being, it is also true that Gioia uses the man's profession, a life of columned numbers, to make specific psychological observations about dream and reality, introducing us to a world and a mind seldom seen in contemporary poetry. "And though you won't believe that an accountant/Can have a vision," he says, "I will tell you mine." The man's powerful need to shift into visionary experience, dramatized in his protective feelings for his daughter, is matched by Gioia's lyrical lines:

> We long for immortality, a soul
> To rise up flaming from the body's dust.
> I know that it exists. I felt it there,
>
> Perfect and eternal in the way
> That only numbers are, intangible but real,
> Infinitely divisible yet whole.

Here the visionary sense (a restrained and muted version of what we sometimes find in Jeffers) opens the cage of the narrative, allowing the secret it contained to fly. Frost's vision is darkly realistic, Gioia's at first more hopeful, but the last image in Gioia's poem is of the daughter's lifeless dolls, their eerie faces challenging Mr. Choi's assertions. Gioia pulls us into a dramatized epiphany that teaches us about human yearning the way Frost teaches us about grief, and he does this without seeming high-handed or condescending.

The best narrative poems instruct us about life, but also about poetic practice. There must be some reason why the story had to be told in lines, some advantage to the line as a unit that is actually used by the poet to achieve effects possible by no other means. Frost's use of line breaks is a good example of this. In some cases, the lyric qualities of the line lend the narrative cohesion; the climax or crux of the story is also a climax of sound, a moment in which saying finds an extraordinary rightness, an inevitability, as it does in Gioia's "Counting the Children." Prosaic and lyric moments will undoubtedly alternate in even the best dramatic poems, and the prosaic will leave them vulnerable to the charge that what is written is not poetry. That is why there must be, at some key point or points, a benefit from the use of lines. Good narratives have been written in free verse as well as meter, but in the best of these poems there is always a moment when we know we are hearing poetry, not prose, when the line transforms thought, feeling, plot and character into memorable speech. This needn't always be a moment of high seriousness. Frost recalls laughing with Ezra Pound over the following lines from a short poem by Edwin Arlington Robinson:

> Miniver scorned the gold he sought,
> But sore annoyed was he without it;
> Miniver thought, and thought, and thought,
> And thought about it.

As Frost points out, the final "thought," so telling of Miniver's character, achieves its charm by being placed in another line. The line break and the shift from tetrameter to dimeter verse contribute to precision of effect.

Whatever narrative voice is used—first, second or third person—the storyteller faces a dilemma of style. In dramatic poems, rhythm and diction are not wholly governed by the poet's predilections. Rather, the poet negotiates with character, and this negotiated voice must be one in which neither poet nor character is compromised. Prose stylists have the same problem, exacerbated by our modern reliance on realism. Henry James's sentences, so adept at capturing the nuances of adult minds, fail to accommodate the child's in *What Maisie Knew*. It is too easy for the stylist to condescend to his or her subject and thereby hold at a distance what ought to be intimate knowledge. The storyteller's ego must share the stage with others. Jarman and McDowell use the diction of characters from a variety of backgrounds, while Gioia chooses speakers capable of his fluid lyricism. In either approach the poet balances on a very thin line. We don't want our stories told by nonentities, but we want even less for the characters to become nonentities. We want those other lives in their particularity, otherwise we cannot believe in them as lives. At the beginning of his short story, "The Rich Boy," F. Scott Fitzgerald writes, "Begin with an individual, and before you know it you find that you have created a type; begin with a type, and you find that you have created—nothing."

Finally, dramatic poems are often at some level personal. This is the paradox of the mask, the persona: it liberates the personal by objectifying it. A male poet may write about a middle-aged woman whose father committed suicide when she was very young, and who, as a result, has never had the opportunity to feel young herself; the poet's narrative may be fueled, as it were, by his own anxieties and neuroses stemming from family problems and their effects upon children. His father has not committed suicide, but his parents were divorced and left him feeling helpless and prematurely aged. He tells her story because he can see hers clearly, his vision unclouded by self-pity. But he too is implicated; no audience would care to listen if he weren't. I have no doubt that the death of Frost's three-year-old son gave "Home Burial" some of its accuracy and power, just as the death of Gioia's infant son gave emotional truth to the meditations of "Counting the Children."

Poetic lines remain a viable medium for characterization as well as narrative, and the necessities of fiction may contribute much of value to the poet's work, making it accessible beyond a purely literary audience. At a time when so many poets work in the academy, when the very architecture of campuses sets them apart from the surrounding communities, and poets encounter an increasingly limited and specialized range of experiences, narrative poems offer the unexplored territory of other lives. Poets may write about farmers or businesspeople, children or terrorists; the point is that they look into the larger community, into the hearts of strangers, helping to restore the relation between poetry and the increasingly complicated world.

Metrical Diversity:
A Defense of the Non-Iambic Meters
Annie Finch

This essay is adapted from an essay by the same name which appeared in the book *Meter in English: A Symposium*, edited by David Baker (U. of Arkansas Press, 1997). The original essay responded to a proposal by poet Robert Wallace to revamp the prosodic system of English so that it would recognize only one meter, the iambic.

When I began work on a critical study of the changing connotations of iambic pentameter in American poetry, I didn't expect that I would devote so much attention to dactyls. In free verse from Whitman, Stephen Crane, and Eliot through Anne Sexton and Audre Lorde, I noticed the consistent presence of triple rhythms, usually falling triple rhythms. Studying these poets' prosodic practice, I found that for each of them the triple rhythm presented an aesthetic, emotional, and ideological alternative to the iambic pentameter—the standard meter for centuries by the mid-nineteenth century.

Although all but a tiny portion of poetry in English has been written so far in iambic pentameter, it is important to recognize that the iambic pentameter is not a neutral or essentially "natural" meter. Its connotations are distinct and culturally defined. Each of the non-iambic meters, also, has its own character, music, and history, however subtle or intermittent. As I notice throughout my book *The Ghost of Meter*, the dactylic rhythm carries connotations of irrationality, violent or beautiful. Trochaic poems, from MacBeth's witches to "The Tyger" to "The Raven" and even "Hiawatha," have a history of supernatural and exotic subject matter. If it is true that, as Martin Halpern posits, the non-iambic meters are a more direct legacy of Anglo-Saxon poetic rhythms than the iambic, it will be valuable to see what kind of energy a new connection with that legacy might bring into our metrical poetry and how the connotations of non-iambic meters will play out in the imagery, the mood, and the cultural role of future poems.

John Thompson establishes in *The Founding of English Meter* that the early history of the iambic pentameter in English was characterized by no substitution at all, clumsy substitution, and "forcing" the meter. As I discuss in *The Ghost of Meter*, only in the past two centuries have non-iambic meters become a barely-accepted presence in English-language written poetry. Perhaps the early history of non-iambic meters is developing analogously with the early history of the iambic pentameter. The long hegemony of free verse has finally cleared our ears of the stifling and artificial associations that haunted metrical verse, particularly non-iambic verse, at the beginning of our century. The field is, in a sense, clearer for metrical verse, especially non-iambic verse, than it has been for many generations.

Perhaps because of their roots in the rhythms of the oral verse tradition in English, non-iambic meters have been restricted to popular poetry for so long that their consignment there has become something of a self-fulfilling prophecy. The last time that non-iambic meters peered out into the world of high culture, during the late nineteenth century, the declamatory recitation style of such poets as Poe, Longfellow, and Tennyson gave anapestic, dactylic, and trochaic poetry the reputation of being inherently artificial, particularly in contrast to the emerging free verse aesthetic. Few if any poets in our own century have written non-iambic meters that are subtly modulated and meant to be read aloud with natural speech stress, according to our twentieth-century preference. That fact, however, does not necessarily mean it cannot be done.

When I began to experiment with non-iambic meters in my own poetry, I found it extraordinarily difficult to conceive of a poem of indeterminate shape in a non-iambic meter (though I had written some sapphics), much less to sustain the rhythm; the poems would transform themselves into iambic pentameter or die on the page. I spent several years in the process of training my poetic ear (which had originally been trained in free verse and then in iambs) in meters other than iambic. Recently, I was asked to provide a series of poems for use in celebrations of the seasons. The project required me to provide eight poems, conveying very different moods, for the same audience at six-week intervals. I wrote each poem in a different non-iambic meter: trochees, alternating dactylic and anapestic stanzas, dipodic meter, cretics, and so on. In writing these poems, I found myself challenged and inspired by my rhythmical raw material, and the supposedly arcane meters provided pleasure to the audience as well.

The main source of difficulty with the non-iambic meters is the assumption that they are not "natural" to English. This view appears to have originated in the nineteenth-century reactions to dactylic verse in English.[1] It has held

---

1. I discuss these reactions at some length in *The Ghost of Meter.*

strong from Yvor Winters' conviction that the "iambic movement. . . appears to be natural to the language" (91) through most contemporary accounts. I have of course been taught, repeatedly, in the words of a poet who instructed me in graduate school, that "English falls naturally into iambics." To my ear, this sentence has a distinct triple rhythm. I would scan it as dactyls, ending in a trochee as many dactylic lines do, with one secondary stress or "cretic" substitution in the first foot: "English falls naturally into iambics." I find this the simplest scansion and the one that embodies the actual music of the line. I am well aware, however, that according to the most common system—whereby a line is accepted as innocent [i.e., iambic] until proven guilty [non-iambic]—the line should scan as an iambic pentameter with initial trochaic substitution and a falling ending, a reading I find jerky and decidedly "forced."

Is iambic meter the only natural meter? Though some contemporary poets believe that we no longer speak in iambic pentameter, others enjoy citing everyday examples of the meter to prove how ubiquitous and innate it really is.[2] One of my favorite such examples, Marilyn Hacker's "a glass of California chardonnay," was quoted at a recent conference. On the flight home, I began idly to wonder if the non-iambic meters could also be found easily in everyday speech. Only four or five minutes later, a flight attendant announced, "Please return to your seats and make sure that your seat belts are fastened securely." Perhaps, along with dactyls and trochees, the anapest constitutes just as "natural" a rhythm in English as the iamb.[3]

Of the many questions that have yet to be answered about the nature of non-iambic meters, perhaps the most essential is the question of their hospitality to metrical substitution. The prosodist Martin Halpern formalized in 1962 the idea, now a truism, that iambic meter is different from all the other meters because it alone can absorb substitutions with varying degrees of stress. As Timothy Steele puts it, "trochaics and triple meters . . . haven't the suppleness and the capacity for fluid modulation that iambic measures have, nor do they tolerate the sorts of variations (e.g., inverted feet at line beginnings or after mid-line pauses) that the texture of iambic verse readily

2. Galway Kinnell, for one, told me that people no longer speak iambic pentameter during a workshop held at the Poetry Society of America in 1980.

3. I have discussed this question over the years with numerous linguists, who tell me that there is no conclusive agreement among linguists either about the supposed iambic nature of English.

absorbs." Steele gives as an example a line from Longfellow: "The blue heron, the Shuh-shuh-gah," and comments, "it is unlikely that we would emphasize the two definite articles . . . but that is what Longfellow wishes us to do, since he is writing in trochaic tetrameter" (242). This line of reasoning constitutes a tautological trap in which to catch non-iambic meters; because the meter is trochaic, we assume the pronunciation is meant to be unnatural; then we damn the trochaic meter for forcing unnatural pronunciations. According to this common conception, "substitutions" in a non-iambic meter do not substitute at all, but actually demand that we "force" the pronunciation of certain words to fit the meter. Non-iambic meters are held to be so overbearing that they can't allow word-stresses an independent and counterpointing rhythm.

To me, the idea that non-iambic meters can't be modulated through substitution is a prejudice analogous to the Renaissance scholar Gascoigne's belief—described by John Thompson in *The Founding of English Meter*—that the iambic meter in the line, "your meaning I understand by your eye" is faulty because it forces us to stress "der" (72). Disproving such prejudices, the (relatively few) examples of skillfully modulated non-iambic meter available to us show that these meters are as capable of substitution as the iambic meter. To cite a well-known example, Clement Moore's line "[a]s dry leaves that before the wild hurricane fly" in *The Night Before Christmas*, employs two expressive substitutions of the pattern unstress-stress-stress in the anapestic base. These changes can be accepted as valid metrical substitutions, not explained away as clumsy anapests. Similarly, the line "the moon on the breast of the new-fallen snow" substitutes an iambic foot and a foot of the pattern stress-unstress-stress (it might be called a cretic) in the anapestic base. Isn't the counterpoint between speech and meter in such lines just as enjoyable as the counterpoint in iambic lines that employ substitution?

Distinctions between different metrical bases add immeasurably not only to accuracy in scanning individual poems, but also to the aesthetic pleasure the ear finds in metrical substitutions. The movement of metrical counterpoint, from which the beauty of accentual-syllabic prosody—in all meters—largely emerges, depends on the existence of distinct metrical norms that can play off of each other and stretch each others' limits, but never overtake each other completely. Metrically skillful poets play with the reader's perception of meter, testing and pushing it but never letting it lapse entirely, as when Shakespeare follows two lines including trochaic and spondaic substitutions with a strictly iambic one, in the very nick of time: "Let me not to the marriage of true minds/admit impediment. Love is not love/which alters when it alteration finds." The power of such effective substitution arises not from rhythmical variation alone but from the dangerously close presence of a conflicting meter which would, if indulged too excessively, undermine the poem's actual meter. The tension between conflicting meters, a source of beauty and excitement, would disappear without metrical diversity.

Even the boundaries that give metrical lines their identity would disappear without distinctly different metrical categories. Metrical feet are not all equally interchangeable. Dactyls and trochees, for instance, can't be substituted into a line of iambs (except after a caesura or line-break) without ruining the meter. That is why the trained ear finds the line "Ode to the West Wind by Percy Bysshe Shelley," to use a hypothetical example from Halle and Keyser's important essay on prosody, unrecognizable as iambic pentameter. But dactyls and trochees can easily be substituted, of course, in lines of falling meter. The kinds of substitutions the ear will accept in a line depend entirely on the line's metrical context. For this reason alone, it is necessary to preserve distinctions between meters.

Aspiring poets and creative writing students need to learn the full range of English prosodic possibilities. They will gain fluency and resourcefulness as writers, flexibility and sophistication as readers, from learning to hear the many different metrical patterns in English and the rhythmical variations on those patterns. My own prosody students hear anapestic, dactylic, and trochaic rhythms as different from the iambic. While some student poets write metrical poetry most easily and happily in iambs, an equal number (in my experience) write it most easily and happily in dactyls and trochees. Prosodic systems which maintain that only iambs can form a metrical base for substitution deny those students who might enjoy non-iambic meters the chance to develop skill in modulating them.

My current image of English prosody is a compass, with the duple and triple, rising and falling, rhythms constituting four primary compass points: trochaic, anapestic, iambic, dactylic. Interspersed among these fall the other meters and combinations of meters, accentual-syllabic and accentual, many possible ideals in relation to which poets and readers can situate the shifting and relative rhythms of actual poems. Rather than abandoning the non-iambic directions of the metrical compass, we can allow time for further experimentation to develop and refine these less-used meters with poetry and prosodic theory. Time may prove the falling and triple rhythms in written English to be sophisticated metrical idioms in their own right, worthy counterparts to the rising duple rhythm with which we are already so familiar.

WORKS CITED

Finch, Annie. *The Ghost of Meter: Culture and Prosody in American Free Verse*. Ann Arbor: University of Michigan Press, 1993.

Fussell, Paul. *Poetic Meter and Poetic Form*. NY: Random House, 1965.

Halle, Morris, and Samuel J. Keyser. "The Iambic Pentameter." *The Structure of Verse: Modern Essays on Prosody*. Ed Harvey Gross. New York: Ecco Press, 1979 (173 193).

Halpern, Martin. "On the Two Chief Metrical Modes in English." *PMLA* 77, no. 3 (1962): 177-86.

McAuley, James. *Versification: A Short Introduction*. Detroit: Michigan State University Press, 1966.

Southey, Robert. "Preface." *A Vision of Judgement*. 1821. *The Poetical Works of Robert Southey*. Vol. 10. London: Longman, Orme, Brown, Greer, and Longmans, 1838. 422-36. 10 vols.

Steele, Timothy. "Staunch Meter, Great Song." David Baker, Ed. *Meter in English: A Symposium*. Fayetteville: University of Arkansas Press, 1995. 221-247.

Thompson, John. *The Founding of English Meter*. New York: Columbia University Press, 1961.

Winters, Yvor. "The Audible Reading of Poetry." *The Function of Criticism*. Denver: Allen Swallow, 1957.

The Ghazal in America: May I?

Agha Shahid Ali

I will take back the gift outright: the Americans have got it quite wrong.

First, to be petty, the pronunciation: It is pronounced ghuzzle, the gh sounding like a cousin of the French r, the sound excavated near unnoticeably from deep in the throat. So imagine me at a writers' conference where a woman kept saying to me, "Oh, I just love ghazaaals, I'm gonna write a lot of ghazaaals," and I wanted to say, in utter pain, "OH PLEASE DON'T!"

Now, the desire to register a protest, an irritation at Paul Oppenheimer's assertion that the sonnet is "the oldest poetic form still in wide popular use"; he cites its origins in thirteenth century Italy. But the ghazal goes back to seventh century Arabia, and its descendants are found not only in Arabic but in various other languages including Farsi, Urdu, Turkish, Pashto, Hindi, and Spanish. The model most in use is the Persian, of which Hafiz (1325-1389) — that makes him a contemporary of Chaucer's — is the acknowledged master, his tomb in Shiraz a place of pilgrimage; Ghalib (1797-1869) is the acknowledged master of that model in Urdu — the only language I know whose mere mention evokes poetry. Lorca also wrote ghazals — gacelas — taking his cues from the Arabic form and thus citing in his catholic way the history of Muslim Andalusia.

Finally, to strike a pose of third-world snobbery: a free-verse ghazal is a contradiction in terms. As perhaps a free-verse sonnet, arguably, is not? At least those who arrive at free-verse sonnets have departed from some-where: from Petrarchan platforms or Elizabethan terminals. I mention the sonnet because the ghazal — somewhat arbitrarily — has been compared with it. But imagine a sestina without those six words. What would be the point? James Harrison and Adrienne Rich and so many others (I have a list) have either misunderstood or ignored the form, and those who have followed them have accepted their examples to represent the real thing. There have been no points of departure. But, as the Princeton Encyclopedia of Poetry & Poetics informs us, the ghazal was introduced to Western poetry "by the romanticists, mainly Fr. Schlegel, Ruckert, and von Platen (Ghaselen, 1821) in Germany, and was made more widely known by Goethe, who in his West-ostlicher Divan (1819) deliberately imitated Persian models."

So what is the Persian model — I mean the real thing? I will plagiarize from *The Practice of Poetry* (edited by Robin Behn and Chase Twichell), in which my not altogether correct entry, "Ghazal: The Charms of a Considered Disunity," quite correctly argues: "Because such charms often evade the Western penchant for unity—rather, the unities—I offer a truly liberating experience: the ghazal. . . . When students ask about a poem such as The Waste Land—How does it hold together?—I suggest a more compelling approach, a tease: How does it not hold together? I underscore how to emphasize craft. The ghazal has a stringently formal disunity, its thematically independent couplets held (as well as not held) together in a stunning fashion." The ghazal is made up of couplets, each autonomous, thematically and emotionally complete in itself: one couplet may be comic, another tragic, another romantic, another religious, another political. (There is, underlying a ghazal, a profound and complex cultural unity, built on association and memory and expectation, but that need not detain me here.) A couplet may be quoted by itself without in any way violating a context—there is no context, as such.

Then what saves the ghazal from what might be considered arbitrariness? A technical context, a formal unity based on rhyme and refrain and prosody. All the lines in a ghazal can appear to have—because of the quantitative meters of Persian and Urdu—the same number of syllables; to establish this metrical consistency, the poets follow an inner ear rather than any clearly established rules, as in English. To quote the Marxist historian Victor Kiernan—a translator of Iqbal and Faiz, two of Urdu's most important poets: "Urdu metres, mainly derived from Persian, are varied and effective. They are based on a quantitative system which divides the foot into sound-units composed of long vowels and vowelized or unvowelized consonants. Urdu has, properly, no accent; on the other hand, Urdu verse, evolved for public declamation, can be recited with a very strong accentual rhythm, the stresses falling on almost any syllable in accordance with the quantitative pattern. This pattern cannot be reproduced with much fidelity in English, where quantity plays a considerable but an undefined and unsystematic part, and where two 'long' (or 'strong') syllables cannot be made to stand side by side in a fixed order, as they do habitually in Urdu verse." However, some rules of the ghazal are clear and classically stringent. The opening couplet (called matla) sets up a scheme (of rhyme—called qafi; and refrain—radif) by having it occur in both lines, and then this scheme occurs only in the second line of each succeeding couplet. That is, once a poet establishes the scheme—with total freedom, I might add—s/he becomes its slave. What results in the rest of the poem is the alluring tension of a slave trying to master the master. A ghazal has five couplets at least; there is no maximum limit. A ghazal, as such, could go on forever.

The first real ghazal in English—the first authentic approximation of the form—is John Hollander's:

> For couplets the ghazal is prime; at the end
> Of each one's a refrain like a chime: "at the end."

Having seen or heard this opening couplet, one would know that the radif is "at the end" and the qafia a word or syllable that would rhyme with "prime" and "chime." Thus the second line of every following couplet will end with "at the end" preceded by a rhyme (which seems like a homonym) of "prime" and "chime." Hollander continues:

> But in subsequent couplets throughout the whole poem,
> It's this second line only will rhyme at the end.

He goes on with thematically autonomous couplets:

> On a string of such strange, unpronounceable fruits,
> How fine the familiar old lime at the end!
>
> All our writing is silent, the dance of the hand,
> So that what it comes down to's all mime, at the end.
>
> Dust and ashes? How dainty and dry! we decay
> To our messy primordial slime at the end.
>
> Two frail arms of your delicate form I pursue,
> Inaccessible, vibrant, sublime at the end.
>
> You gathered all manner of flowers all day,
> But your hands were most fragrant of thyme, at the end.
>
> There are so many sounds! A poem having one rhyme?
> A good life with a sad, minor crime at the end.
>
> Each new couplet's a different ascent: no great peak
> But a low hill quite easy to climb at the end.
>
> Two-armed bandits: start out with a great wad of green
> Thoughts, but you're left with a dime at the end.
>
> Each assertion's a knot which must shorten, alas,
> This long-worded rope of which I'm at the end.

To mark the end of the ghazal, often a poet has a signature couplet (makhta) in which s/he can invoke her/his name pseudonymously or otherwise. Hollander, charmingly, pseudonymizes:

> Now Qafia Radif has grown weary, like life,
> At the game he's been wasting his time at. THE END.

Notice that with the exception of the first and last couplets, the poem would not in any way suffer by a rearrangement of the couplets. Nor would the ghazal suffer if one would simply delete some of its couplets. Do such freedoms frighten some Americans?

Hollander has done something quite remarkable here, for by having "at the end" as his radif he has caught the particular spirit of the form. For, "within the ghazal, the poet almost always adopts the stance of a romantic hero of one kind or another: a desperate lover intoxicated with passion, a rapt visionary absorbed in mystic illumination, an iconoclastic drunkard celebrating the omnipotence of wine." In this century, especially among left-wing poets, the poet is often the committed revolutionary intoxicated with the struggle for freedom. "He presents himself as a solitary sufferer, sustained by brief flashes of ecstasy, defined by his desperate longing for some transcendant object of desire," which may be "human (female or male), divine, abstract, or ambiguous; its defining trait is its inaccessibility." Hollander's "at the end" is masterly, for it contains the possibility of being imbued with such longing and loss![1]

What is missing in unrhymed ghazals is the breathless excitement the original form can generate. The audience (the ghazal is recited a lot) waits to see what the poet will do with the scheme established in the opening couplet. At a mushaira—the traditional poetry gathering to which sometimes thousands of people come to hear the most cherished poets of the country—when the poet recites the first line of a couplet, the audience recites it back to him, and then the poet repeats it, and the audience again follows suit. This back and forth creates an immensely seductive tension because everyone is waiting to see how the suspense will be resolved in terms of the scheme established in the opening couplet. For example, if Hollander were to recite,

> You gathered all manner of flowers all day,
> the audience would repeat it and so on, and then when he'd come to
> But your hands were most fragrant of thyme . . .

the audience would be so primed and roused by this time that it would break in with "at the end" even before Hollander would have a chance to utter the phrase. And then, in raptures, it would keep on Vaah-Vaah-ing and Subhan-Allah-ing. If the resolution is an anti-climax, the audience may well respond with boos. I should mention that a ghazal is often sung. Some of the great singers of India have taken ghazals and placed them gently within the framework of a raga and then set the melodic phrase (which contains the individual lines of the ghazal) to a tala (cycle of beats). The greatest of them all was Begum Akhtar. This seemingly "light" form can lead to a lot of facile poetry (haiku-ish-ly, one could say), but in the hands of a master? Ghalib's ghazals reveal a great tragic poet, Faiz's a great political one.

To make abundantly clear why an unrhymed ghazal would be a contradiction in terms to an Urdu or Persian speaker, I will offer an unrhymed ghazal of mine (I have stolen some phrases from Laurence Hope's utterly sentimental "Kashmiri Love Lyric" which begins "[p]ale hands I loved beside the Shalimar"):

> Where are you now? Who lies beneath your spell tonight
> before you agonize him in farewell tonight?
>
> Pale hands that once loved me beside the Shalimar:
> Whom else from rapture's road will you expel tonight?
>
> Those "Fabrics of Cashmere—" "to make Me beautiful—"
> "Trinket"—to gem—"Me to adorn—How—tell"—tonight?
>
> I beg for haven: Prisons, let open your gates—
> A refugee from pity seeks a cell tonight.
>
> Lord, cried out the idols, Don't let us be broken;
> Only we can convert the infidel tonight.
>
> In the heart's veined temple all statues have been smashed.
> No priest in saffron's left to toll its knell tonight.
>
> And I, Shahid, only am escaped to tell thee—
> God sobs in my arms. Call me Ishmael tonight.

I think it is the seeming arbitrariness of the unrhymed ghazal that has kept it from becoming a necessary part of the American "mainstream" (I always put quotations around such words); it has led only to "exotic" dabblings. I think many Americans were tempted—as we all can be—by the freedom they thought they had gained without paying attention to the discipline freedom demands. And when they heard that an ancient culture sanctions a poem of thematically independent couplets, their surrealistic juices overflowed. It is the sort of thing that happens with haiku (Richard Howard is supposed to have said that as a poetry editor having to read 500 haikus a week was like being nibbled to death by goldfish, and James Merrill in his "Prose of Departure" has actually used rhyme for his haikus so that Americans would know that something is going on).

Further, there is a bonus for those willing to pursue the real ghazal. Through ghazals, Americans (and anyone else using English) can again employ full rhymes, even the most cliché-ridden, without embarrassment because the radif enables the rhyme to lose, through a transparent masking, its strained and clichéd element. What an incredible gift I am offering the Americans: all those rhymes they thought they could never use again. I am also offering Americans a chance to find a formal way, a "legal" out, to cultivate a profound respect for desperation—something the Americans have not altogether lost. As for the English, much of their poetry seems to have been at a cocktail party for almost 50 years now.

I do like Adrienne Rich's ghazals and could make a case for their discarding of the form in the context of the politics of the late sixties and early seventies in this country and see in her ghazals a desire to question all kinds of authorities by getting away from linearity and that crippling insistence on "unity." I also enjoyed her translations of Ghalib's ghazals—which is what I believe got her interested—as well as W. S. Merwin's. Now while translating an Urdu or Persian ghazal into English, I can see why one would have to use free verse (it would be impossible to sustain a convincing qafia—given the radif—when translating couplet after couplet). Anyway, I found their translations rather attractive because they often struck me not just as efforts but real accomplishments. But when Rich attempted her own original ghazals she simply did not bother with the form. This is how she explains the form in a note to her "Ghazals: Homage to Ghalib": "This poem began to be written after I read Aijaz Ahmad's literal English versions of the Urdu poetry of Mirza Ghalib (1797-1869). While the structure and metrics of the classic ghazal form as used by Ghalib are much stricter than mine [but hers are not strict at all!], I adhered to his use of a minimum five couplets to a ghazal, each couplet being autonomous and independent of the others. The continuity and unity [notice that she cannot get away from "unity"] flow from the associations and images playing back and forth among the couplets in any single ghazal. I have left the ghazals dated as I wrote them, during a month in the summer of 1968."

Notice how Rich creates a space for herself by—I would say deliberately—ignoring the fact of rhyme and refrain completely; it reminds me of what Harold Bloom says in *The Anxiety of Influence* (is there too much anxiety among American poets?) that poets deliberately misread other poets (a killing of the fathers) in order to create imaginative spaces for themselves. However, to be fair to Rich, I don't think she did this because she was suffering from any cultural anxiety of influence—her celebration of Otherness has been vivid again and again. I think that the business of rhyme and refrain just did not suit the aesthetic politics—and the political complexion—of her context in those days. The ghazal, as she practiced it, gave her the authority of a foreign and rich culture, it allowed her formally to question the authority of her own culture's often rigid proscriptions, and perhaps she saw in the thematic freedom of the couplets a chance for all kinds of liberation. What would have been paradoxical to many Westerners—the ghazal's blend "of unity and autonomy"—would have attracted her. (I hope it is clear that my use of "West" and "Westerners" assumes immensely deconstructive qualifications; Edward Said argues there is no such thing as the "West.")

I love forms, but I do not wish to come across as some kind of formalist. I am not, certainly not, the neo-kind who wishes to save Western civilization—with meters and rhymes! However, the issue here is that by following the form of the ghazal, the writer could find herself tantalizingly liberated, surprising herself with unusual discoveries by being stringent with herself as she goes from one theme to another in couplet after couplet. Form has been associated (remember the recent free verse vs. formalism debate)— and quite wrongly, really—with what holds truth back, especially political truth. But as Faiz said, there is nothing good or bad in any poetic form but the poet makes it so. And he used this very strict form to express an impassioned left-wing politics—using the stockfigure of the Belovéd to figure as the Revolution. And when Adrienne Rich was departing into open forms from the rather strict ones in her first books, it may have been inevitable that apart from this business of thematically autonomous couplets the actual technicalities of the form would simply not seem of the moment. As a matter of fact, her departure into the ghazal may even reveal her deeper political and cultural generosities.

But how far can one go with those free verse couplets with nothing but a seeming arbitrariness to guide one? Readers cannot but ask how the couplets are connected; they will automatically be looking for thematic unities. But the actual form, by its very nature, erases that expectation, pre-empts it. Recite Hollander's ghazal to anyone and notice how no one will ask for unities; the form seduces one into buying the authority of each couplet as thematically autonomous. When the Americans go crazy with the idea of composing thematically autonomous couplets in a free verse poem, they manage to forget what holds the couplets together—a classical exactness, a precision so stringent that it, when brilliant, surpasses the precision of the sonnet and the grandeur of the sestina (I love to say things like that) and dazzles the most untutored of audiences. That is why I think the free verse ghazal in America seems always a momentary exotic departure for a poet, nothing that is central to him or her, to their necessary way of dealing with the world of their poetry.

So while I do admire Adrienne Rich's "Ghazals: Homage to Ghalib" as well as some of the effects of Jim Harrison's ghazals and, more recently, of David Young's, it really is time the actual form found its way into American poetry. It really is. For one thing, as the narrator of Swann's Way phrases it, one can exact from a restriction a further refinement of thought, "as great poets do when the tyranny of rhyme forces them into the discovery of their finest lines." If one writes in free verse—and one should—to subvert Western civilization, surely one should write in forms to save oneself from Western civilization, which is a chimera. Why should one want to save Western civilization? When Mahatma Gandhi was asked what he thought of Western civilization, he answered: It would be a good idea.

NOTES

1. After a few years of relishing Hollander's ghazal and popularizing it among my poet-friends and students, I wrote to him (October 1, 1994) with a few complaints/suggestions:

Dear Mr. Hollander,

May I quarrel with you a bit, even though you don't know me?

First of all, I love your ghazal in *Rhyme's Reason*. It is the first real ghazal written in English, and it has given me the pluck to write a few myself. With "at the end" [as its radif] it captures the peculiar fragrance of the form, which has at its heart a constant longing. I have referred to your ghazal in *The Practice of Poetry* (edited by Robin Behn and Chase Twichell) and I also refer to it in an essay I wrote on translation. Then what is the quarrel about? All the lines of a ghazal must have the same syllabic length, and in yours though most have twelve syllables, some lines have eleven and one has thirteen and one has ten. Also, it is the repeated refrain — in this case "at the end"—which is the Radif; and it is the rhyming word or syllable which is the Qafia. Further, the form you have used is the ghazal that was domesticated in Iran and India; the Arabic ghazal is different in some ways (I don't know anything about the Turkish).

Before your ghazal, you say: "The poet signs his name pseudonymously in the final ghazal." Shouldn't that read "in the final couplet"? Besides, the poet need not sign his name pseudonymously, for often poets used and use their real names. And having the signature couplet—called Makhta—is not necessary though when it does occur the audience knows it's the last couplet.

Should you decide to have a further edition, I hope my comments will prove useful. (In the index, p. 6 is given next to "Ghazal" though it should be p. 66.) It would be nice to have one more couplet, one that says that each couplet can be and usually is thematically autonomous because my students (with whom I use your book very often)—despite your example—are so driven by all those unities that they don't notice the independence of each couplet.

Again I want to tell you that I love your ghazal and have memorized most of its couplets and have recited them by heart to various friends.

My letter continues for two more paragraphs. Some months after writing it, I realized I had made one wrong assertion—regarding the lines having the same number of syllables. The fact is—because of Urdu's quantitative syllables and meters—a ghazal usually seems to have the same number of syllables per line when recited or sung. Three months later I got a very fine letter from Hollander, in which he apologized for the delay and then went on most gracefully, making a particularly useful point about his line lengths:

Said lateness in no way reflects my pleasure at receiving your letter, and my acknowledgment of some errors in my entry on the ghazal in *Rhyme's Reason*. I fully intend to correct them at the next reprinting. The qafia/radif confusion I had already noted. The syllabic matter is different: I had not intended in my example, partially because of needing the stress-pattern to make the rhyming audible in English, to observe the strictest syllabic integrity (my lines had a four-stressed, largely anapestic rhythm, but a few iambic substitutions allowed for the divergent syllable-length on some occasions). I only observed syllabic length in the case of the haiku and, of course, English strict syllabics.

Your other suggestions deserve and will get due consideration. I know that I undertook risks in dealing with verse forms in languages I didn't know; in the case of the ghazal, with variant forms in different languages, it was even more risky; I'm most grateful for the corrections.

2. And there is now a nice convenience: "ghazal," pleasantly enough, is found in *Webster's Third International Dictionary*, so there is no need to italicize.

WORKS CITED

Agha Shahid Ali, *The Half-Inch Himalayas* (Wesleyan University Press, 1987).

Robin Behn and Chase Twichell, eds. *The Practice of Poetry* (Harper Perennial, 1992).

Shamsur Rahman Faruqi and Frances Pritchett, "Lyric Poetry in Urdu: The Ghazal," *Delos* (Winter 1991).

Amy Hempel and Jim Shepard, *Unleashed: Poems by Writers' Dogs* (Crown, 1995).

John Hollander, *Rhyme's Reason* (Yale University Press, 5th Edition, 1990).

Victor Kiernan, *Poems from Iqbal* (John Murray, 1955).

Princeton Encyclopedia of Poetry & Poetics.

Adrienne Rich, *Poems: Selected and New, 1950-1974* (W. W. Norton, 1975).

Calliope Music: Notes on the Sestina

James Cummins

The sestina, as the comedian might put it, don't get no respect. Or perhaps a paraphrase of Frank O'Hara's comment on opera is more to the point: the sestina is obvious as an ear. The sestina is ungainly somehow to us, to our sight as well as to our obvious ears. Bad poems importune, but any sestina seems to ask for too much: they're too tricked out, either over- or underdressed, Baby Huey lumbering up, giggling too loudly, or suddenly too earnest. Our comment about the sestina often has an edgy quality to it, too, as if the speaker not only is impatient to move on to more serious things, but also understands something important, even essential, about the form that the reader doesn't quite get; usually, the speaker dooon't feel required to put this knowledge into words. I wonder if maybe the sestina isn't secretly an embarrassment to formalists; it seems to mock their endeavor by its obviousness and lack of subtlety.

It intrigues me that of all the received forms that get talked about in our journals, only the sestina never gets anything interesting said about it. Or rarely. Often, it's used as a whipping post to flay writers somehow not as advanced as the writer making the comments. In a recent issue of *Poetry Pilot*, the Academy of American Poets' newsletter, Marilyn Hacker made some dismissive comments about those who write "unmetrical" sestinas. In the current issue of *Black Warrior Review*, Richard Wilbur made a number of comments about formal issues, including a few about the sestina. Again, though Mr. Wilbur's remarks were more substantive, he uses the sestina to target bad writers—the phrase "creative writing" rears its ugly head—and shows little sympathy for and much condescension to the form. Here is an excerpt from Mr. Wilbur's remarks:

> One thing that some people don't understand at present is that each form has a sort of implicit logic. I wouldn't dream of sitting down to "write a sonnet." Disgusting idea that someone should sit down with a determination to write in some form or other before he conceives of what the hell he's going to say. It's what you're going to say that tells you what formal means might further the utterance....
>
> It's one of the horrors of creative writing in America that people who have never written anything in form are often asked to write sestinas. They are often indulged in writing non-metrical sestinas, which is about as bad as you can get. But to sit down with the dire intent to write a sestina seems to me the

worst thing you can do unless there is something happening in your imagination that necessitated the form. And I do think, having thought about it a little, that there are some subjects that are suitable to the sestina—suitable to the taking of six key words and emphasizing them seven times each; I guess that's what happens. If you're writing out of obsession, I think the sestina might very well serve you very well. An inability to stay away from certain words and situations and [the need to] emphasize those things could be expressed by the sestina. The sort of experience which you just can't believe could be described very well in a sestina, you could say it first in one stanza and then say *I knew, really, it happened that way* and then go through the reshuffled key words once again. Alas, not all sestinas have that kind of logic.

Or one might say, *Thank goodness*. Now the rest of the interview from which this quote is taken contains some insights; however, it seems to me that he patronizes the sestina in this passage. This attitude has its roots in unspoken assumptions about received forms, I think, and helps account for the edginess of his remarks. Besides the desire for *permanence*—which is itself, of course, another way of stating the fear of impermanence—formalists want sport, play, not unlike Hemingway's ideas on the subject: an abstract field with clearly-delineated rules, wherein the cleanly-played game, the *artifice*, stands clear of the messiness of life, and comments on it. Corollary to this is the idea of the received form, brought to perfection by masters of an earlier time—Petrarch, Dante, Shakespeare—against whom one can be measured, with whom one can take one's place. One can *master* a form and, fetishized with our need to transcend ourselves, it can grant permanence.

Enter the sestina. Better yet, an unmetrical sestina. A formalist conceives of the sestina as a lyric, and hears the sound of it become distorted, go awry, if the basic metrical pattern, usually iambic pentameter, is tampered with—much like an air-raid siren blaring, going away, coming back in ellipses of sound that are uncomfortable to the ear. The metrical pattern is what holds the awkward, elliptical sound of the sestina together, in this view—counterpoints it, smooths it, gives it the polish and sheen of a lyric. Destroy the metrical pattern, and you've got a wounded, bleating animal on your hands—a *large* wounded, bleating animal. Add to this a lack of development—*change*—in the end-words, and you're listening to a large wounded bleating animal that's brain-dead. Few sounds are so nightmarish to an ear sensitive to poems.

But paradoxically that awful sound is a key to the power of the sestina: it can make that sound. Most poems can't, because they're too busy being what we want them to be: good. They're like children: they court us, want our approval, want to be like us. The sound of a bad sestina might be the sound of life leaving the beast, but at least it's life. Nature is cruel, after all. Maybe a hundred sestinas must die, so that one may live. In any case, the sestina is not a lyric form, though it has lyric aspects. It is a meditative, narrative, dramatic form, and we need to adjust our ears to hear it today.

I've tried to imagine what a sestina sounded like 8 or 900 years ago. With its high Middle Ages love of display, the lines looping out into the night, concerned only with what they would find, not in reinforcing preconceptions of rhyme; with its self-regard, the way it rhymes itself, as it repeats and develops itself; with its circularity, its connecting back to itself, and its way of thus presenting itself freed, self-referential: the numinous quality of such an adventure should not be slighted. If you consider some of the types of poems in the air preceding and during the time of the sestina, you see not only aspects of the form we've come to designate *sestina* (connection of each stanza with the foregoing one by repetition; rhymes of first stanza repeated in inverse order in the next, etc.), but also a sense of exploration, a sense of *becoming* on the part of the form. If you think of the first poems that used repetition in the way we can recognize as a primitive version of the sestina (indefinite number of stanzas, the last rhyme of each used in the first line of the next; the last rhyme of all corresponding to the first rhyme of the poem; etc.), you see the sense of circularity and completion — of Eliade's sacred and profane time — that resonated in the medieval mind, and resonates still. Basic to the sestina form are issues of time, the voyage out, the return, change, repetition-as-development, self-reference, self-consciousness. Evidently, these early poems were accompanied by a dance. How many poems, how many dances, how many years go by in the pleasure of this ritual, this developing form, as gradually (or maybe not so gradually) innovations are made *toward* what we think of as ours: the "final" fixed form of the sestina?

This sense of the *continuum* of form is often what is lacking when formalists speak so dogmatically about form. They want certain rules and regulations to apply. They want to be *right*. I've discovered in my life that at the exact, precise moment I feel myself to be 100 percent right about something, I'm invariably wrong. Always, when I focus on the one thing, I fail to see the many, the flux; I haven't allowed for the fact that, as has been noted, you can't step into the same river twice. The moment in which I am right must always be the moment in which I was right—whatever being right means, or meant—because by the time it gets to consciousness the moment has passed, and I no longer fit the requirements of the new moment. The poem, formal or free verse, is like that: it is the moment in which I was right, and also, by my definition, the moment in which I am wrong. It's why, I think, when we look at this ungainly form, the sestina, we often fail to see the possibilities: we are looking at the goofy, harshly-delineated inhabitant of this moment, not the mysterious voyager passing through our conscious-ness, whose form is not completely available to us. We want the sestina to be a certain thing, and we are disappointed when it eludes us.

The sonnet doesn't elude us; the sonnet reflects us, or at least reflects what we want to see about us. We can be brilliant in the sonnet, and the sonnet reflects our brilliance. Our argument can be allied with our verbal accomplishment; we can be unanswerable. We can have the last word. To return to the children again, sonnets are like our perfect children, or bril-liant pets (perfect children *are* brilliant pets, after all): they not only do what they're told, they do it *in league* with us. We ask one thing of every sonnet: uphold our idea of ourselves.

The sestina reflects us, too, much more accurately than we think. That's why we don't like it. Walker Percy has a trope in which he wonders why, after a lifetime of looking into mirrors, we are so surprised at our reflection in a clothier's three-way mirror. That perspective on us can't be us—can it? We walk out of a clothing store perplexed and shaken, our idea about our-selves a little more complicated than we'd imagined. What we need to rec-ognize, I think, is that the sestina is a form that humiliates you as a writer—a form that mocks you, mocks itself, is rueful, meditative, self-dramatiz-ing—in short, is *not* in league with you.

The formal principle of a sestina has nothing to do with metrics; it has everything to do with whether or not you can get said what you thought you wanted to say, as you find out what it is you *can* say. Mr. Wilbur calls it "disgusting" to sit down with a determination to write in a form before you know what you want to say. But he goes on in the next sentence to add that finding out what you want to say will tell you what formal means might help order your words. Which comes first, the chicken or the egg? The subtext here is a commonplace about organic form—expression finds its own form—transposed to formalist arguments, thus bridging a gap (or pre-empting one) in a politically-correct fashion. What it doesn't do is account for the mo-

ment when a given form rears its not-ugly but shaping head. Let's see: some-
one sits down with an unclear idea of what he or she is going to say; there-
fore, a sonnet is out. A lightbulb goes on, and the ideas come; therefore, a
sonnet is possibly the answer to the question of appropriate vessel. This is
all so, so ... *rational*. The phrase "what formal means might further the utter-
ance" buys into that false idea of "mastery," condescends to the very idea of
form that formalists formally espouse, yet secretly avoid: you *engage* form,
you don't *choose* it. It isn't an arrow in your quiver; it's an arrow in you, and
it quivers; it's a kind of love.

A sestina that flies into me is Elizabeth Bishop's poem, beautifully titled,
lest we forget, "Sestina." To savor this poem stanza by stanza is to appreci-
ate how a sestina can *mean*; and also to see, I think, a modern version of how
stanzas "mirror" each other in the sestina, something the medievals were
obsessed with. This "mirroring" is essential to the progression of a sestina;
and in this case, one way of seeing it work is to look closely at the teleutons,
especially "tears." First, the poem:

Sestina

September rain falls on the house.
In the failing light, the old grandmother
sits in the kitchen with the child
beside the Little Marvel Stove,
reading the jokes from the almanac,
laughing and talking to hide her tears.

She thinks that her equinoctial tears
and the rain that beats on the roof of the house
were both foretold by the almanac,
but only known to a grandmother.
The iron kettle sings on the stove.
She cuts some bread and says to the child,

It's time for tea now; but the child
is watching the teakettle's small hard tears
dance like mad on the hot black stove,
the way the rain must dance on the house.
Tidying up, the old grandmother
hangs up the clever almanac

on its string. Birdlike, the almanac
hovers half open above the child,
hovers above the old grandmother
and her teacup full of dark brown tears.
She shivers and says she thinks the house
feels chilly, and puts more wood in the stove.

It was to be, says the Marvel Stove.
I know what I know, says the almanac.
With crayons the child draws a rigid house
and a winding pathway. Then the child
puts in a man with buttons like tears
and shows it proudly to the grandmother.

But secretly, while the grandmother
busies herself about the stove,
the little moons fall down like tears
from between the pages of the almanac
into the flower bed the child
has carefully placed in the front of the house.

Time to plant tears, says the almanac.
The grandmother sings to the marvellous stove
and the child draws another inscrutable house.

The poem combines narrative, iconic, and meditative elements to present a static, yet highly-charged scene that moves slowly past us with all the power and pathos of achingly-lived life; and then is gone, unredeemed save by puny Art. The first stanza sets the scene: we are approaching the autumnal equinox ("September rain"), time of rhythms more powerful than the personal, and more noticed in a northern clime; the light is failing; and the grandmother is old. The mother—the *daughter*, after all—is gone; the grandmother—the *mother*, after all—hides her tears from the child. Her tears are natural, normal, and are for both, or for all three; and must be hidden to spare the child.

But those tears are a complex liquid. The heart and brain go on after tragedy—they *obsess*, as Mr. Wilbur would attest—and the grandmother has had to find reason in her grief. But for human reason to try to put a design on God's ways is to invite rigidness—or, ironically, madness—and the grandmother's claim to esoteric knowledge is based not only on a connection to the earth and its seasons, but also to a holy book, as well—the farmer's "Bible," the almanac. Such desperation—such *will*— is not enough; her action of offering the bread, and her directive that seeks to dictate time, are thus ineffective.

We tend to think of "time" in a sestina as "subject matter," but it goes beyond that; "time" is a structural component of the form. The sonnet holds the moment captive; any lyric, no matter how long its actual duration, asks that we suspend time for the *moment* of its cry. Of all the shorter forms, the sestina most self-consciously calls attention to its existence-in-time, as it makes its journey through its mirrored landscape. In Bishop's poem, the grandmother tries to control time by identifying herself with nature, and by reading the "signs" of a holy book. But nature has been distorted here—one generation has been removed from the picture—and fundamentalist typology cannot address the other, parallel "time" in the poem: the child's time. The child doesn't accept the "iron" kettle's contents—by extension, the brown tears of tea—but rather sees its "small hard tears" that have escaped—from the frying pan to fire, as it were—and are dancing, as she is, "like mad" with pain. She stares at them in a trance of psychological trauma, lesion, but also with some redemptive sense of the earth's power: she connects them to the dance of the rain on the roof. Here, the grandmother is "old" again, unsure of her explanations; and the almanac is "clever," a code word in such a household for the Devil's work.

In stanza four, the almanac is sinister, feral, "half open," not the solace the grandmother wanted from her "Book," but the source of deeper, truer knowledge that both threatens and comforts the child. From the child's perspective—and particularly for her adult self who serves as narrator of the poem—it is vitally important—ultimately, to her salvation—that the almanac know what it knows. Its knowledge is vaster than the typology the grandmother wishes to read there; and though the absence of the mother has left the child without a *translator* of this knowledge, the voices that begin to speak in stanza five, with their hard truths, must be heard. There has been a breach in the line of generation, through which painful truths surge; these truths turn the child, forever, into an artist. And though there is no mother to mitigate the flow and *charge* of these voices, there is no recourse to hearing them: not to listen would be to die.

The house the child produces in her art is "rigid," and she projects her fear and sadness into the "buttons like tears"; but the pride with which she shows her work to her grandmother signals the beginning of psychological integration, and a turning for home on the part of the sestina itself. Now we begin the return trip to the place we will know for the first time. The sixth stanza is magic: the nocturnal and diurnal processes come back into sync, as the almanac rains down its little moons like tears into the child's art. The last two lines of the envoy are an image of the parallel universes the grandmother and the child inhabit, with no mother to mediate between them; but the tears that have been planted do more than give hope. We have, after all, been reading one of their issue.

To understand finally those tears—and teleutons generally—we have to look at a certain process at work in sestinas. It is commonplace to say that we've lost the meaning of the number mysticism that the medieval mind associated with the sestina. The significance of the number 6 as a weak number, or of 7 as a number of mystical wholeness; of the sequence "615243"; or of the fact that each stanza is composed of three couplets, each of whose sum equals seven—these are not uninteresting facts to us, but they are shut off from us unless we can somehow *feel* their meaning in the poem. I don't claim to have rediscovered any of those old feelings, but if we remember that a seventh stanza, were we to go that far, would return us to the originating sequence of teleutons, ABCDEF (not the exact copy of the first stanza, but a mirror image)—and also that, at seven, we would have closed the circle perfectly—maybe we begin to get on the trail.

I have a feeling that the stanzas and teleutons of a sestina "mirror" themselves in a particular way, and to particular purpose; and that they do this primarily through the oddity of "rhyming themselves." Further, I think that this process is linked to the idea that "time" is a structural component of the form. It's a very strange thing, to rhyme a word with itself, and almost a taboo in ordinary rhyme. In a sestina, each teleuton mirrors itself in the previous stanza, thereby showing in itself gradation, change, progression. The mirror image "rhymes" itself, but is not "itself." The teleutons are signposts—each time you come around them you are made aware (one of their very important functions is to *make* you aware) of the passage of time: this word is the "same," but only in the sense a human being is the same at different ages. Time is the medium through which the teleutons pass, not only in the sense of *passage*, but also in the sense of duration of consciousness. Even self-consciousness.

To borrow Heraclitus again, you can't step into the same stanza twice. Or as Pound might put it, the teleutons of the fifth stanza are not the teleutons of the first, though they hang in the same way over the bridge-rail. This mirroring fascinated the medieval poets; I think they saw the sestina as a strange landscape of mirrors that refracted time and love with much more complexity than, say, the sonnet. In his poem, "West-Running Brook," Frost speaks of "that white wave [that] runs counter to itself" to describe a process of throwing back against oneself to progress—a process of "some strange resistance in itself" that pits the self against the self in order to grow.

The key here is progression, change. Each teleuton must change, grow, contain more or other than its previous incarnation, while it contains its own echo, another fascinating aspect of rhyming itself. Think what happens when a teleuton goes dead, doesn't progress: a sestina can stand — maybe — this happening once. But we hear the sound. Two teleutons die, and the air goes out of the ball; the game is over. In a larger sense, the stanzas work the same way; they progress and develop by commenting on what has gone before — on their previous formulation, as it were — then offering the new. Isn't this what's wrong with the many bad sestinas we've all read? The third or fourth stanza fails to deliver the new to us; or, like a sequence of too-similar adjectives, the "new" it offers hasn't changed, hasn't grown, enough.

So I chose to write in the sestina form; that was the first humiliation. There would be others to follow. Maybe that's why this old idea of "mastery" makes me laugh, makes me imagine myself holding a snowball while a high silk hat glides along the top of a fence. The sestina resists your "choosing" it as the "appropriate" vehicle for your "material"; it laughs at the whole process that compartmentalizes composition in this way. Because the sestina doesn't fit these ideas, people who need the notion of "mastery" find the sestina odd and confusing. I've mentioned Mr. Wilbur's notion that "obsession" has to drive a sestina. Paul Fussell has commented on the "dubious structural expressiveness in English" of the sestina, and Karl Shapiro also has decided sestinas reflect "obsessive vision." Whence this obsession about "obsession"? The sestina is an anomaly when seen from the perspective of "mastery": it won't play along. And thus it can't be seen for what it is, but only for what it isn't.

The sestina is a relic from an age of faith, and the meditative voice is never single. It's always dual because it posits God. It posits itself and a Listener; and the idea of someone listening to you — let alone someone omniscient — makes for a whole *dynamic*, more than an utterance. Much contemporary poetry has lost this sense of the dual (duet, duel?) — of the listening part of the mind that grows impatient with the earnestness of *I went, I saw, I thought.* (Not too unlike, after all, *I came, I saw, I conquered.*) A powerful intellect can seduce itself into believing that what it thinks is the final say; and by final say, I don't mean that it precludes what others might say later (in fact, it welcomes response, gaining legitimacy from it; *tradition*, and one's place in it, being the ultimate legitimacy), but only that, for the purposes of the poem, the poet is in control of all aspects of the material. This is vanity, anxiety. I said the sestina was an expression of an age of faith. I could add that it's a specific faith—it's Roman Catholic. The sestina has adornments, fetishes; it peddles influence and indulgences. It has about it the fat smacking sound of the Bishop's lips as he sets down his jewel-encrusted wine goblet and picks up a leg of mutton. This is disconcerting to the powerful Puritan intellect of our literature. The Puritan God doesn't find anything funny. No wonder he thinks the sestina can't express much. But with the duality of the meditative voice, the Listener can laugh at you—can find you absurd, ridiculous, give some measure to your outrageous earnestness, the comical seriousness with which you take yourself. When the meditative voice loses touch with the Other, the Listener, the "God" in whose presence and with whose assistance poems are made, the result is not *cry*, but *statement*. And statement, we know, partakes of the wrong kind of power. Bank statement. Bottom-line power.

The sestina is a vehicle for journeying, and as such its rhythms often lend themselves to decidedly unmetrical strategies. While it partakes of a version of rhyme by rhyming itself, it's open to all different sorts of "languages," since its overall desire is to deepen through repetition and change. As I conceive it, the sestina does not simply fire neural transmitters that come round in a regular way, but rather defeats your expectations of these very firings: it makes you miss your step, land slightly off; it truncates that seventh stanza. Purity—perfection—in this realm would be blasphemy. Several voices, different approaches to an issue, lyric riffs within stanzaic constraints; these extend and deepen the reach of the poem. I think a major strength of the contemporary sestina is its ability to assimilate prose rhythms.

Writing about Proust's masterpiece in *Aspects of the Novel*, E. M. Forster says: "The book is chaotic, ill constructed, it has and will have no external shape; and yet it hangs together because it is stitched internally, because it contains rhythms." He adds that he doubts "it [the quality of rhythm in the novel] can be achieved by the writers who plan their books beforehand, it has to depend on a local impulse when the right interval is reached." Writing on Forster writing on Proust, Frank Baldanza—who is writing on *Huckleberry Finn*—says:

> We ought to have a clearer idea of what Forster means by rhythm in the French novel. He selects as his example the "little phrase" from the sonata by Vinteuil, later incorporated into a sextet: Proust employs this musical phrase, which recurs innumerable times in the course of his narrative, in such a manner, says Forster, that in itself it has a "musical" function in the novel.... [W]e can see

that Forster has a clear definition of what he means by a "musical" function. The use of "repetition plus variation" is the key to this kind of rhythm. Simple repetition of a theme, such as Forster finds in [George] Meredith, is dead patterning; but repetition with variation and development, and especially with varying degrees of emphasis, is rhythm.

He goes on to quote Forster:

... the little phrase has a life of its own, unconnected with the lives of its auditors, as with the life of the man who composed it. It is almost an actor, but not quite, and that "not quite" means that its power has gone towards stitching Proust's book together from the inside, and towards the establishment of beauty and the ravishing of the reader's memory. There are times when the little phrase—from its gloomy inception, through the sonata into the sextet—means everything to the reader. There are times when it means nothing and is forgotten, and this seems to me the function of rhythm in fiction; not to be there all the time like a pattern, but by its lovely waxing and waning to fill us with surprise and freshness and hope.

Repetition, change, development—this is how the sestina goes out on its journey, and how it returns in a way different from any other form. The sestina seems to me to embody a very real mode of existing: conversation. In a conversation a concept or theme is introduced, then repeated several times throughout the course of the conversation—perhaps extend the concept of "conversation" to "evening"—a dinner party, perhaps, drinks before, coffee afterward. Each time this concept or theme comes up during the course of the evening, it's with a variation, a nuance, that deepens and extends the layering of the discourse. Then—often, not always—a crowning instance of it appears at the end; this can be overwhelmingly funny, and smart, even wise. We use this thematic agent as a means for "discovering" the "form" of the evening—organic form, of course, as the evening takes the shape it naturally takes, but with this thematic agent interacting with that natural form. The two interpenetrate, weave together the finished product: the night, but the night resounding with the human—with art, with human agency. This gentle, sometimes fierce, recognition of the ellipses that take us nearer to and farther from each other is what the sestina not only symbolizes, but embodies, for me.

Directions

Why We Need a New, Rhythm-Centered Theory of Poetry

Amittai Aviram

After teaching a basic undergraduate poetry class at my university for only a short time, I quickly surmised that my students' reasons for enrolling were quite at odds with my idea of what the class offered. These differences among their views, and between theirs and mine, reflect, I believe, distinct concepts of what poetry is. The concepts which my students held, however diverse, seem to me to be widely shared within our society, and they have very powerful consequences in the reading, understanding, teaching, and even writing of poetry—or, then again, in the widespread neglect of poetry. The most popular motivation for taking poetry, so far as I could guess, was that poems were short; there would be less reading. Even sincere admirers of poetry thought of it as having the advantage over prose of being more condensed or concise. Other concepts seemed more connected with Hallmark cards, although they may have nobler 19th-century origins: poetry is the direct, sincere expression of the personal feelings of its author, especially love. Poetry is a personal diary entry. Then again, poetry goes with sweet things like perfume and flowers (but still somehow utterly sincere). But whether conceived as concise formula or as personal expression, poetry is essentially, in these ways of thinking, a meaning-effect; poetry is a form of communication.

As I hope to show in this essay, poetry is not merely communication. A good half of the experience—the better half, so to speak—is not communication at all, but the experience of meaningless sound, and especially of rhythm. Rhythm is nonverbal, although words can be assembled to follow a rhythm. And, although rhythms can be associated with particular things, rhythm is not essentially symbolic—it does not have to mean anything, the way that words do have to mean something. In turn, this welding together of meaning and nonmeaning in poetry—words and rhythm—can have powerful implications, philosophically, socially, and even politically. In short, the rhythmic element of poetry is an instance of an ecstatic practice that enables the hearers or readers of poetry to experience a deep kind of freedom, which poetry uniquely provides. This is a freedom from the limits of individual subjectivity, a broadening of the sphere of possibilities, even as the words of poetry maintain our tie to the normal mode of social and individual being. In order to understand how poetry can do all this, we need a new theoretical approach to poetry, one that goes beyond poetry as mere communication.

The failure today to distinguish between what poetry and prose have to offer accounts for the very fact that, aside from choosing how to fulfill an undergraduate requirement, people today will rarely have anything to do with poetry. After all, prose communicates just fine. When we make an effort to communicate a message clearly, we invariably do so in prose. If poetry were nothing but meaningful communication, then my students would probably be right to prefer it over courses in the novel or drama because the readings would be shorter—except that this concept hardly takes into account some of the most famous and, in other times and places, best-loved poems, such as the *Iliad*, the *Odyssey*, the *Aeneid*, Ovid's *Amores* and *Metamorphoses*, and the *Ramayana* (not to mention *The Faerie Queene* and *Paradise Lost*). And there are long lyric poems, too, such as both the ancient Persian original and Edward Fitzgerald's once very popular English version of the *Rubáiyát of Omar Khayyam*.

The neglect of poetry throughout society is only partial, however. Our lives, the lives of my students, are saturated in poetry . . . in the form of popular song lyrics and raps, for example. When people express themselves in groups with the greatest political intensity and solidarity, they do so in poetry—in protest-chants and songs. But yet other social experiences are now lost: rereading, studying, pondering poetry, the habit of quoting verse (as some people still quote popular songs) as a resource of proverbial wisdom—and, with it, the sense of connection to other times and to a wealth of accumulated human experience over time. These are normal elements in the social life of many cultures today, including Latin American and East Asian societies—or were until recent inroads by television. One striking example is the tradition of composing, impromptu, a tanka poem (including a closing haiku) as one takes leave of a formal dinner to which one was invited in Japan. Puerto Ricans would make a pastime, not long ago, of vying for the best impromptu décimas—and of course, all competent contributions must scan and follow this elaborate form. One must assume that these cultures have a notion of poetry far different from, or at least beyond, our notion of poetry-as-communication. As my comments so far are intended to suggest, the neglect of poetry that has such consequences points to a theoretical problem: how we define poetry and its relation to meaning.

In short, what makes poetry distinct from prose, and what offers to poetry-lovers a pleasure not available elsewhere, is the fact that poetry does not consist entirely in meaning. Poetry is experienced simultaneously as a meaningful utterance and as a play of sounds—language, as it were, before meanings are assigned to the syllables, the sounds, the tones. But it has always been difficult for people, while they engage in rational discussions, to appreciate the value of such nonmeaning experience. Our evolution toward an information-based society makes it even more difficult. Hence the word "meaningless" usually has about the same effect as "worthless." In modern times, and generally since the eighteenth century, critics, writers, and teachers have responded to this problem in poetry by trying to interpret the sound of poetry as contributing somehow to its meaning. As Alexander Pope has it, "The sound must be an echo to the sense." Certainly, there are many passages in poetry (including the one immediately following Pope's remark in his *Essay on Criticism*) in which this approach works, and we can readily recognize some meaningful mimetic relationship between sound and meaning. But these passages stick out in our minds precisely because they're not normal. Normally, the sound of poetry is simply interesting, or attractive, or noticeable, without any possible reference to meaning. As a result, the experience of reading or hearing poetry is characterized precisely by the division of one's attention between two completely different, even unrelated, things: what the poem means and how it sounds. The unique pleasure that poetry excites is precisely in this conflict in our divided attention.

The sound of poetry: what is most noticeable and most ubiquitous in the sound of most poetry is precisely that aspect of sound least translatable into meaning. That is, rhythm. In most times, and in most places, where poetry has been practiced and where poetry has received attention, "poetry" has meant verse—that is, utterances whose sounds are so arranged as to express a musical, rhythmic pattern in time. The fact that rhythm is not foremost in the expectations of my students or other people today when they think of poetry has everything to do with both the modern drive to reduce experiences to communicable information and the inevitable decline of poetry as an object of thought and esteem. Definitions of poetry made to accommodate modern experiments in free verse have de-emphasized rhythm and shifted the balance almost entirely in favor of meaning. (Most of this modernist free verse poetry, by the way, is in one way or another rhythmic, despite how it is presented in the classroom or the manifesto.) Furthermore, the term "rhythm" in such modern contexts often takes on a vague, metaphoric sense, so that it no longer means the sort of musical experience which we could readily associate with such physical activities as, say, dancing or clapping hands. In other words, the very word "rhythm" is used in such derived or transferred senses that it no longer necessarily implies regularity and repetition of an event. Since this regular repetition is how, I think, most of us would define the literal meaning of the word "rhythm," the metaphoric uses of the word in teaching and criticism tend towards rendering the whole experience of rhythm in poetry inaccessible to discussion or even to notice.

The attitude toward poetry that places the emphasis on meaning to the virtual exclusion of rhythm also tends to view unmetrical writings as "free" in a political, not just a technical sense. From this point of view, "formal" verse is old-fashioned and politically conservative. (We may trace this critical rhetoric back to Walt Whitman, among others.) But this view is plainly contradicted by the facts. I have already mentioned the metrical chants of political demonstrations and the rhythmicity of rock and rap lyrics. Political positions of every sort have been expressed in words that follow a musical beat. As I have argued elsewhere, there is also a potential radicalism in the very existence of rhythm in poetry, precisely because it cannot be reduced to a meaning-effect alone. This challenge to the completeness of a world of pure meaning-effects may work even regardless of the ostensible, overt politics expressed in the words of a given poem, if any. But as a result of the theoretical prejudices that have dominated the teaching of poetry for more than a generation, our students will tend readily to associate unmetrical poems with freedom and rebellion, even when they cannot actually recognize a metrical poem as metrical when it is placed before them. In other words, the failure of theory has extended to the point both of falsifying politics and of rendering poetry itself inaccessible to experience.

If it is true that poetry divides our attention between its meaning and its rhythmic sound, this observation does, admittedly, beg a question for anyone who wishes to devise a better way of teaching and talking about poetry—one that works for poetry instead of against it. The question is: what do rhythm and meaning have to do with each other? Why should they co-exist in a poem, if they are so heterogeneous, so at odds with each other? The conventional ways of dealing with poetry by subordinating rhythm to meaning don't ultimately help in understanding this relationship and actually do harm. But they respond to a natural requirement we have to make sense out of something puzzling—an experience with two diverse natures, whose very duality of nature, so enigmatic, is precisely what engages poetry-lovers.

Although it may seem to be merely contrary, I believe that this problem can be solved by standing the conventional view on its head: making meaning subordinate to rhythm. In other words, the ideas and images expressed in a poem as its communicative content could be understood, ultimately, as metaphoric constructs representing and making partial sense of the nonverbal experience of rhythm which the very words are simultaneously realizing through their sounds. In this case, the nonverbal power of rhythm to engage the listener or reader in a virtually physical participation is represented or "figured" verbally by the interpretable aspect of the poem, its meaningful language. At the same time, since the poem is trying to represent metaphorically in words something that is powerful but not verbal—a sublime power—that power always exceeds the capabilities of language. Furthermore, the metaphorical language of poetry manages to get across this very failure of language in its struggle to represent the excessive power of rhythm.

The foregoing is a necessarily overcompressed account of a somewhat complicated theory. In my book, *Telling Rhythm: Body and Meaning in Poetry*, I call this theoretical approach to poetry "telling rhythm," and I present several kinds of argument, theoretical as well as practical, for why this notion of poetry, however odd it may seem initially, works and avoids the pitfalls of conventional theories. In the rest of this essay, I should like first to show (rather than to argue) the theory at work in the reading of a poem by a contemporary American poet. Neither the poem nor the poet is well known. Chris Llewellyn's "In Memoriam: Carolyn Johnson" is included in Judy Grahn's anthology of working-class women writers, *True to Life Adventure Stories*. My choice of this poem as the case in point serves several purposes. First, it should immediately dispel the prejudice that "formal" verse must express conservative politics. As a reflection upon aspects of modern secretarial work, in the context of working-class writing and experience, the poem addresses a kind of menial work shared by a very large number of people in our society today. What factory-work was to nineteenth-century poets, secretarial and other low-level white-collar work should be for our own. And even higher levels of work, such as the legal, educational, business, and even medical professions, share a great deal, especially at the entry level, of the tedium and pain of clerical work. Clerical work, after all, is characterized by the requirement to use one's mind to perform a task which one does not initiate, in which one usually doesn't believe, over which one has little or no control, and for which one gets little or no credit. And clerical work is one of those sites in society that is the focus of all the surveillance, policing, and control which Michel Foucault has so well analyzed. Given the centrality of the clerk in the typology of our work-lives, it is remarkable that so few writers have actually brought the subject up with any courage or candor.

At the same time, the poem has metrical, or rhythmic, features that make it relevant to this discussion, which are best pointed out after the text of the poem.

In Memoriam:

Carolyn Johnson
Carolyn Johnson:
you died two weeks ago.
I am the secretary
sent to take your place.
Your glasses and cupcakes
are still in your desk
and I write this
with your pen.
I am angry at your life.
I am angry at your death.
One workday I saw you
fifty shakey smokin too much
too overweight too lonely.
And I am too angry
at your life.

One afternoon you left
the office Alone you went
home Alone and
died Alone
in your Apartment.
It was two days before they
found you filed under A
(Alone).
I've finished transcribing and
typed final copy from your drafts.
Carolyn Johnson:

Who says women
can't be drafted?
Cause we're all drafts—
incomplete roughcopy
onionskin foolscap
manifold carboncopy
throwaway getanother
tissuetypewriter
womansecretary
officewife.

I take a clean sheet
rollit in the carriage
and center your name:
            Carolyn Johnson.
Then rollit up and smoke it
cause Carol I'm all keyed up
and I feel it in my bones
in my tissues in my
correctype liquidpaper brain.

Say after breathin whiteout
mimeofluid typecleaner
thirty (30) years were you
hi when you died?
Glad you were cremated
not filed ina drawer under
watermarked engraved letterhead:
Carolyn Johnson.
Stop.
Reachout fingers on homerows
deathrows of the world &
touch home touch my face touch
Carolyn's ashes somewhere in
Pennsylvania touch away
machinated lives mere extensions
of machines clicking tapping
thudding tiny nails in coffin lids
ticking clocks in mausoleumed
officebuildings and deliver us
from margins comma cleartabs
capitalize your periods don't reset
space bar lock shift index return
return
return
return:
Carolyn Johnson.

The poem follows a very clear binary beat structure. The verse is not
quite classical tetrameter, since the two fundamental beats are variously
subdivided or not, the number of offbeat syllables and their placement vary,

and there are some lines in which certain beats are not realized but implied. Also, there is one line, "typed final copy from your drafts," near the middle of the poem, that has three beats, and clearly can imply a silent fourth beat, the equivalent of two separate two-beat lines, simply written out as one. The fact that this poem is at once audible or readable as regularly rhythmic and yet that it does not seem to follow all the rules should also help us to move away from thinking of meter as a matter of following rules and towards a view of meter as an effective realization of a musical beat in words. Finally, this very powerful poem gives us an opportunity to consider the differences and relative merits between a theory that would have rhythm express meaning (the more conventional view) and one that would have content express rhythm, the theory which I hope to advance here.

The poem derives much of its power from indefinite but highly suggestive puns on the technical jargon of clerical work, puns out of which, in some instances, the imagery itself is derived: "keyedup," "carboncopy," "foolscap," "homerows"—and, of course, "return." Even the nonce-compounds such as "womansecretary" and "officewife" serve as puns, since they also imitate a common error in typing, where the space-bar isn't hit hard enough. Likewise, the word "Stop," occurring as a single-word line (and thus followed by implied silence in order to preserve the rhythm of the rest), recalls the use of that term to finish sentences in telegrams, in the days, not long ago, when telegrams were sent. It is striking how strongly these pun-images may speak to us despite the fact that office technology has changed so much as to make some of this relatively recent (1978) poem seem dated: although carbon copies and whiteout barely endure at the margins of the workplace, the fundamental features of the life of the cyborg remain the same.

Also noteworthy is how these puns seem to accumulate towards the end of the poem, contributing to a dissolution of syntax—so that the last line before the repeated "return," "space bar lock shift index return," is a catalogue with no apparent grammar. As the grammar disappears, so does the illusion of a subject who is speaking. It is as if the repetitive sounds and actions of office work numb the mind of the speaker and take over completely. The speaker's subjectivity or agency seems to return across the repetitions of "return," so that it serves, in effect, as a triple pun: carriage return (mechanical, impersonal), self-directed speech (a kind of therapy to bring the speaker back from turning into a machine), and an incantation directed toward the spirit of Carolyn Johnson (magic, in which the whole poem may be said to engage).

Indeed, the whole poem dramatizes a struggle between the impersonal system wherein the speaker is the secretary sent to take her dead predecessor's place — writing with the same pen — and the speaker's efforts to maintain her status as a thinking, acting, speaking subject. "I am angry at your life. / I am angry at your death." Here, the "I" comes out defiantly. But at other times, the speaker's irony suggests doubts as to her ability to maintain this status as more than a cog in a machine: "cause Carol I'm all keyedup / and I feel it in my bones / in my tissues in my / correctype liquidpaper brain." Carolyn Johnson is literally, physically dead; but the ironic puns in which the speaker takes delight also suggest how the speaker's very position as worker threatens the death of her subjectivity well before it threatens physical death. The womansecretary is in danger of having her physical tissue become paper, of her entire life becoming reduced to a file-letter such as "A" for "Alone," indeed, of the very syntax of her thoughts becoming simply impersonal mechanical actions with no subject in sight.

From this standpoint, the puns have a striking ambivalence. They, and their ironic tone, allow the speaker to be free of the deadening process about which she speaks. But they also represent that deadening process — a kind of metamorphosis in which a live body becomes a machine before our very eyes. This ambivalence reaches a poignant climax with the repetition of the word "return" near the poem's end. The word simultaneously draws the speaker and Carolyn Johnson out of death and mimics the process that deadens to begin with.

This repetition provides a good instance of how the binary rhythm of the poem holds an analogous ambivalence. On the one hand, the poem's rhythm, in twos or in fours, and its patterns of repetition, sweep us along as readers or listeners, the way rhythm in poetry always does. It is an intrinsic source of pleasure. It can be imagined as an instance of the speaker's finding something playful and thus pleasurable in a depressing situation, just as the puns serve the same purpose. On the other hand, the rhythm imitates the mechanicity of the workplace.

These ambivalences are necessary in order for the poem to have any power. For the poem must dramatize both the subject's struggle against the forces that threaten her and those forces themselves. Otherwise, we would not be able to experience the struggle as a struggle, and the poem would fall into mere telling—that is, it would be an essay.

But now, I seem to have contradicted my earlier comments. If both the rhythm of the poem and the speech of the poem express analogous ambivalences as part of the dramatization of the poem's struggle, then am I not conceding that rhythm does indeed express meaning? Isn't this an instance where the rhythm of the poem is actually part of the poem's representational language? Doesn't the conventional view of meter work just fine here—the very conventional view which I earlier criticized?

That would be putting the cart before the horse (to continue with outmoded technology!). The only way we know that the rhythm of the poem is supposed in any way to suggest the mechanicity of the clerical workplace is precisely because we've already paid attention to what the words say. If the words had said something different, then the binary rhythm would have to mean something else. So the rhythm still does not mean anything—at least not independently. Rather, the rhythm is available for us to pin meanings on it, based on what the poem says. The poem is making sense out of its own rhythm for us. The poem is telling its rhythm in words.

There is more.

It is not only in the workplace that regular rhythm threatens the individual subject. It is also in happier places, such as the dance-floor. Here, as people move, each in his or her own way, to the beat of the music, the individuality of the individuals fades as they become more or less one with each other and with the beat. This loss of the normal, individual self that presents itself as an individual in society is not a bad thing. In fact, it is something we cannot do without on occasion, even though we cannot do with it all the time. The loss of subjectivity experienced in ecstatic activities such as dance, meditation, sex, or physical games is a moment of freedom, a moment in which we feel no self-consciousness and no worries about whether we're doing the right thing. We don't have to worry about how much responsibility we bear for our actions, nor, on the other hand, about what may have caused our actions, because we are not quite ourselves to begin with. Both free will and causal determinism are only problems for a subject as such. I do not mean to say that we are completely brain-dead or senseless when we engage in such ecstatic practices. I mean simply that their ecstatic quality lies precisely in the interruption or fading or lessening of our individual subjectivities.

The rhythm of a machine is seductive. Machines attract us precisely because they offer this kind of freedom—even if, from another point of view, that very freedom from subjectivity is also the most degrading captivity that can be imposed on the self. We cannot but feel ambivalent to the rhythms of machinery—which are no different from the rhythms of nature or the rhythms of life—if we find ourselves in a position simultaneously to feel their attractions and to suffer our diminishment as selves. This is the very position of the speaker in a poem. For the speech of a poem is expected, generally, to make sense, to have both content and syntax—that is, to imitate qualities of a speaking human subject. But the words which the speaker utters are already determined to realize a metrical beat which does not depend on any particular meaning to exist. Likewise, the routines of secretaries will go on, even if one dies and another replaces her.

The ambivalence we have noted in the poem toward the mechanical rhythms of the office and its machines is thus an instance of an ambivalence that will always be at the heart of poetry. Does this mean that all poems mean the same thing? No. This poem takes that ambivalence as an opportunity to address a particular cluster of social issues and a particular struggle, one that is, moreover, at the very heart of modern work-life. But the observation that "In Memoriam: Carolyn Johnson" dramatizes an ambivalence that is in fact a particular realization of a kind of ambivalence built into poetry from the start does allow us to see, or to feel, something that we otherwise would not see or feel. This is how poetry affords us an experience not available in any other medium nor in any other form of language. Chris Llewellyn's masterful poem enables us at once to lose ourselves and to return to ourselves—part of the way in each direction. The subject—both the speaker and the reader—fades under the seductive power of rhythm; the subject—the speaker, the reader, and the remembered image of Carolyn Johnson—also struggles to return by constructing that rhythm, projecting onto it meaningful images and names. It is in this play of fading and return that the poem offers us a unique kind of freedom. And freedom, of course, is precisely the goal of the very political work of this poem.

WORKS CITED

Aviram, Amittai F. *Telling Rhythm: Body and Meaning in Poetry.* Ann Arbor: University of Michigan Press, 1994.

Llewellyn, Chris. "In Memoriam: Carolyn Johnson." *In True to Life Adventure Stories.* Ed. Judy Grahn. Vol. 1. Trumansburg, NY: The Crossing Press, 1983. 97-101.

Feminist Formalist :
A Critical Oxymoron?

Kathrine Varnes

The title of this essay does not mean to suggest that feminists cannot write in form or that formalists cannot consider themselves feminist. The anthology *A Formal Feeling Comes* provides ample material to suggest otherwise.[1] My focus is rather on what the critical arguments seem able to imagine about the aesthetic and political literature we call poetry. Therefore, I will juxtapose influential and groundbreaking critics in both feminist formulations of a women's poetry (Alicia Ostriker, Adrienne Rich) and new formalist defenses of a formalist poetry (Timothy Steele, Dana Gioia). This is not about ideological matchmaking, nor am I saying that opposites attract.[2] Rather I want to show how these critical positions can operate under a similar oppositional logic that closes them off from each other and from more complicated articulations of poetry's worth.

One source of this binary logic is the language of liberation that both movements employ. Generally speaking, Feminism presents itself as an overtly political movement which sometimes works to articulate a corresponding aesthetic position. New Formalism, on the other hand, presents its position as a primarily aesthetic one, while disclaiming any political agenda other than renewed interest in formal verse. Despite these differences, the critical arguments of both movements often hope for "real" social relevance, whether to more evenly distribute social power, or to gain a more popular audience for verse. Perhaps because of these broader-based desires, members of each group have a troubled, uncomfortable relationship with the academy even if employed in higher education. Both look for a sort of liberation, from either an institutionalized sexism or an institutionalized aesthetic bias, that will free more than a few students of higher education. Fighting the "institutions" of sexism and doctrinal free verse (often from

---

1. The full title is *A Formal Feeling Comes: Poems in Form by Contemporary Women* (Brownsville, Oregon: Story Line Press, 1994).

2. My resistance to this pairing is indebted to Judith Roof's article "How to Satisfy a Woman *Every Time*...," in *Feminism Beside Itself*, ed. Diane Elam and Robyn Wiegman (New York: Routledge, 1995), in which she extends Hayden White's theories of historical narrative with what Roof calls a "paradigm of conjoinder" that encourages opposites eventually to join and reproduce.

within their institutions), feminist and formalist critics also narrate the histories of their oppression in order to point toward their desires for either aesthetic or political freedoms. In line with Hayden White's description of history's narrative structure, these stories of liberation often rely upon uncovering the truth of oppression as a means of setting the liberation narrative into action.[3]

Consider Alicia Ostriker's important *Stealing the Language: The Emergence of Women's Poetry in America*. Providing a survey of women's poetry from the 1960s, Ostriker focuses on the "culturally repressed elements in female identity" (11). The first chapter effectively establishes the truth of the historical neglect of and condescension to American women poets since 1650. Narrating from this truth, Ostriker describes the liberation of contemporary poetry by motif: a divided self, primacy of the body, anger, intimacy, and the act of revisionary mythmaking. While questions of form occasionally come into her study, the primary focus is on content as it relates to identity and culturally inflected conceptions of the self. Indeed, Ostriker makes it clear that "[f]or most of the poems in this book, academic distinctions between the self and what we in the classroom call the 'persona' move to vanishing point." She continues, "When a woman poet today says 'I,' she is likely to mean herself, as intensely as her imagination and her verbal skills permit. . ."(12). The implication, here, is that if a woman poet today doesn't mean herself when she says "I," either she is not "likely," or she is lacking in verbal skills. Suddenly we have moved from Ostriker's preference for autobiographical women poets to a blanket aesthetic about women's writing that discounts all possibilities of narrative or dramatic verse even existing. Worse, this discarding of "what we in the classroom call the 'persona'" robs poets of their privacy and poetic license. Plus, it implies a kind of duplicity in the classroom. We tell these lies to our students, it seems to say, but we know better. But what is this thing we know? That language can reflect an authentic self? That poems accurately reflect real people? Psychoanalysis and poststructuralism aside (and that's a big aside), Ostriker's own metaphor for language as a patriarchal possession that must be "stolen" in order for women to use it, makes this shaky territory. In accepting an oppositional relationship to her own language, Ostriker begins a narrative of liberation

---

3. See "The Value of Narrativity in the Representation of Reality" in *On Narrative*, ed. W.J.T. Mitchell (Chicago: U of Chicago P, 1981): 1-23 and *The Content of the Form: Narrative Discourse and Historical Representation* (Baltimore: Johns Hopkins UP, 1987).

that asserts the primacy of the essential content — the 'self' — over language, and necessarily, over prosody.

Timothy Steele's *Missing Measures: Modern Poetry and the Revolt Against Meter* also details a revolution, but his project is to recast the intellectual positions of that revolt in a history that shows where the free verse propaganda perhaps mis-stepped. The book is powerful and revolutionary, overturning the assumptions of modernism's free verse champions by pointing out their associative flaws (Eliot's conflation of stilted Victorian idiom with meter, for example) as well as misleading influences from other cultural phenomena. Thus, *Missing Measures* has quickly become an authoritative defense of formal poetry, bringing to light the truth of a modernist oppression many have overlooked, furthered and even exaggerated. In this way, Steele enables the liberation of meter.

On the other hand, other measures are still missing from his history of modernism: Marianne Moore, Gertrude Stein, Djuna Barnes, Mina Loy, May Sinclair, and many others. H.D. is mentioned once; Amy Lowell twice. In fact, in the roughly 300-page book's $11^1/_2$, small-fonted, double-columned index, less than ten women poets' names appear with one or two page numbers listed. The entry for Emily Dickinson, as the only exception to this rule, refers the reader to four separate pages. Of course, my reader may respond that his dispute is with the perceived authorities of the revolt against meter. True enough. True also that one book can't do everything. Yet when such a persuasive and powerful voice in New Formalism neglects to explain this omission, when the movement itself already suffers from attacks of not only aesthetic but also political conservatism, I wonder if this counter-revolution is revolutionary enough for all of us.

In Steele's conclusion, he laments that ". . . in the absence of agreed upon standards of versification, poetry often is judged exclusively with respect to its intentions or subject matter." Certainly, the second half of his sentence is supportable. We could use Ostriker's focus on the self in women's poetry as an example of that very point. Yet can we know that this focus on subject matter is, in fact, a result of "the absence of agreed upon standards of versification"? It might be just as likely that the increasing focus on subject matter eventually worked to distract critical interest away from form. Even so, I'm not sure that a binary causal relationship is accurate here. Upset that meter and political content have become distinct poetic categories, Steele (and I) nevertheless continues to oppose them, along with

Ostriker. Yet this erroneous division has less to do with poetry than with our dependence — conscious or unconscious — on identity politics as the truths that set our liberation narratives into motion. Furthermore, this accidental or deliberate reliance on identity gets both the overtly political and the ostensibly aesthetic critical positions into trouble. (That's the truth of my narrative, but I don't promise to liberate any of us from it.)

To see more clearly how identity politics come into play in New Formalism, I want to quote from an otherwise lovely essay by Dana Gioia which appeared first in the *Hudson Review* and later, in slightly revised forms, in *Expansive Poetry* and his own *Can Poetry Matter?* Gioia begins by hailing the re-emergence of formal poetry in younger poets with a list of names: Charles Martin, Timothy Steele, Brad Leithauser, Vikram Seth. He then pokes fun at the worn out argument that metered and unmetered verse carry an inherent politics, identifies meter as an aural rather than a visual element in poetry, and demonstrates that William Carlos Williams wrote his famous free verse poem, "The Red Wheelbarrow", in iambic pentameter (162-3). It's a fun and lively read. Discussing the bias against metrical poetry, Gioia then writes:

> For up-to-date Americans it [rhyme and meter] becomes the province of the old, the eccentric, and the Anglophilic. It was a style that dared not speak its name, except in light verse. Even the trinominate, blue-haired lady laureates now write in free verse.*

After the last sentence, an asterisk directs the reader's attention to a footnote which reads:

> *The editors of *The Hudson Review* ask, as perhaps they should, if this statement is a sexist stereotype. I offer it rather as investigative journalism based on painful, first-hand knowledge of the work of such important contemporary poets as Sudie Stuart Hager, Winifred Hamrick Farrar, Maggie Culver Fry, Helen von Kolnitz Hyer, and the late Peggy Simpson Curry (the official poet laureates of Idaho, Mississippi, Oklahoma, South Carolina, and Wyoming respectively). When such rear-guard, middle-class poets write in free verse, how can that style not be said to belong to the establishment? (*Can Poetry Matter?* 37)[4]

The initial statement that "[e]ven the trinominate, blue-haired lady laureates now write in free verse" is what, in my adolescence, we used to call a real downer. The snide "trinominate," the superior "blue-haired," and the

---

4. This final version of the footnote varies only slightly from those appearing in *The Hudson Review* and *Expansive Poetry* through the deletion of one woman poet's name and the addition of the adjectives "rear-guard" and "middle-class."

scoffing "lady laureates" seem calculated to offend any moderately success-
ful writer of free verse, not to mention women and the elderly. What pains
me about this statement and its following defense is not that I assume these
authors might write poetry I'd enjoy, nor that they seem the most vulner-
able and least likely to defend themselves in this arena, but that the argu-
ment does not need this relatively gratuitous comment. In fact, it harms
rather than supports an essay and line of argument with which I agree.
Upon editorial questioning, Gioia pursues further this embedded sexism
(not to mention ageism) and throws in what reads as regionalism to boot.

What interests me most about this attack on older women poets who
have received recognition for their free verse is that, with the exception of
Adrienne Rich, the list of their names rectifies an otherwise complete ab-
sence of women poets in the essay. When looking for formalist poets to
praise, Gioia lists men; when looking for targets, women. "Painful, first-
hand knowledge" notwithstanding, the binary oppositions that this authen-
ticating detail reinforces mislead and damage writers, readers, and critics of
poetry, especially those who wish to promote New Formalism to more popu-
lar audiences. The fact that other of Gioia's writings work against the very
binarism set up here — his book's admiring chapter on Elizabeth Bishop as
a model poet, for instance — suggests, too, that the alienation of women
writers is far from Gioia's agenda. He often admires, encourages, even pro-
motes the work of women writers. Yet it seems his argument, here particu-
larly, partakes in a conversation that historically allows, even expects, this
sort of bias. While Gioia criticizes what he calls a utilitarian aesthetic based
on poets' political positions (241-2), it is also true that his arguments some-
times slip into aligning aesthetic positions with identities. That, too, is utili-
tarian and political. When we notice that the essay is reprinted in Frederick
Feirstein's *Expansive Poetry: Essays on the New Narrative and the New Formalism*
alongside 13 other essays, all written by men, the consistencies begin to add
up. These subtle infiltrations of an aesthetics predicated on identity make
it easier to imagine why Feminism has been historically suspicious of
formalism.

Consider Adrienne Rich, who has had an incalculable influence on how
critics of all persuasions imagine the relationship between Feminism and
aesthetic choices. In her oft-cited and reprinted, "When We Dead Awaken:
Writing as Revision," Rich tells the history of her own poetic development.
According to Rich, she moved from a formalism (as in "Aunt Jennifer's

Tigers") that, as she puts it, "like asbestos gloves, . . . allowed me to handle materials I couldn't pick up barehanded" (40-41), to the looser form of "Snapshots of a Daughter-in-Law" which still disappoints Rich since "I hadn't found the courage yet to do without authorities, or even to use the pronoun 'I' — the woman in the poem is always 'she'"(45). While form, in this context, can be read as liberating an otherwise suppressed content, Rich also represents formal prosody as a crutch to discard, or a hindrance to transcend. She narrates toward a more liberated state of writing when she is able to use the pronoun "I" rather than "she." Thus, her narrative suggests that discarding formal verse is a first step to owning identity. By fitting her work into the feminist argument for an identity-based, non-formal aesthetic, Rich literally authorizes this narrative of her liberation with her own "truth." And this essay is often cited as the proof that women working in form are likely to be denying some part of their identity.[5]

What, then, do these readings of feminist and formalist arguments have to do with each other? For my purposes, the most crucial connection is that arguments disputing New Formalism's alleged conservatism tend to conjure up poets' identities as a way to defend their politics. Robert McPhillips, for instance, challenges the attacks on New Formalism by arguing that critics have failed to "confront the poetry directly"(76).[6] A legitimate complaint, yet this position somewhat underestimates the power of critical context even as it works to change that context. Obviously, I agree with his assertion that aesthetics and politics do not form a stable paradigmatic relationship, and I find his essay one of the most thorough arguments I've seen on this subject. Yet, sometimes, I'm unclear on how politics and identity intersect in the essay. Providing three brief illustrations to prove that New Formalism is not, in fact, conservative, McPhillips writes:

> The political vision of Vikram Seth's *Golden Gate* is pro-gay and anti-nuke. Marilyn Hacker is an outspoken lesbian who sees no contradiction between her use of meter and rhyme, of villanelles and sonnets, and the feminist content of much of her poetry. Molly Peacock has argued, both in *Ecstatic*

---

5. For instance, Suzanne Juhasz suggests this in her groundbreaking and oft-cited *Naked and Fiery Forms: Modern American Poetry by Women, A New Tradition* (New York: Farrar, Straus and Giroux, 1978) as does Helen M. Dennis in "Adrienne Rich: Consciousness Raising as Poetic Method" in the collection *Contemporary Poetry Meets Modern Theory*, eds. Antony Easthope and John O. Thompson (New York: Harvester, 1991).

6. See "Reading the New Formalists," *Sewanee Review* 1989 (Winter, 97:1) 73-96. See also his essay included in *Expansive Poetry*.

Occasions, Expedient Forms and in *Poetry East*, that writing in form has paradoxically freed her to explore such delicate subjects as masturbation and abortion. (76)

This makes perfect common sense. It flies in the face of unsubstantiated accusations with factual, indisputable data. What strikes me as worrisome, however, is the way that the language shifts from describing the political vision of a book, *The Golden Gate*, to describing the sexual identity of Marilyn Hacker, to describing the "feminist content" of her work. This may seem trivial, a mere lack of parallelism for stylistic variation, but it results in a seeming interchangeability between identity and politics, especially since liberations from traditional taboos directly associated with sexual identity — gayness, lesbianism, and heterosexual women's enforced modesty — connect the three illustrations. The connection implies that certain identity groups are never conservative, always striving for some sort of liberation, which is then reflected in their work. If we agree that metered verse does not necessarily reproduce a conservative ideology, we cannot use a similar logic to argue that certain identities necessarily create a liberal ideology. If we do, we fall into another associative trap.

The construction of a New Formalist movement in contemporary poetry belongs, for the most part, to critical and poetic manifestos. Although feminist formalist poets exist, the critical material written either on feminism or on formalism rarely includes them. This comes about through, on Feminism's part, a traditionally "radical" oppositional positioning against so-called masculinist form which cannot reflect women's true experiences, and on New Formalism's part, a traditional conservatism which often forgets the contributions of women. Robert McPhillips and Annie Finch have started to correct these errors for New Formalism; Lynn Keller and Marilyn Hacker have started the process for Feminism.[7] But it will take more than a handful of critics, more than alliteration and identical scansion to put formalism and Feminism comfortably in the same title. We cannot use identity as a shortcut to political or aesthetic positions. And we must change the way we think about history.

Since I've somewhat presumptuously pointed out what I see as telling slippages in these important critical arguments, it only seems fair that I

---

7. See especially Keller's article on Hacker in *Feminist Measures: Soundings in Poetry and Theory*. ed. Lynn Keller and Cristanne Miller (Ann Arbor: Michigan UP, 1994), excerpted in this volume.

return that critical gaze upon myself. What have I accomplished and at what risk?

By emphasizing the gendered codes in these critical positions, to some degree I reinforce them: personifying a male formalism and a female feminism, which you know I wouldn't do unless I were hoping they'd somehow get together. You might expect me, in telling their condensed critical stories, to launch into a rousing rendition of the Brady Bunch theme, pushing formalism and Feminism into a happy critical sitcom marriage and a group of poets made family. Or maybe this is where I suggest that they've been having a successful affair the whole time and the critical neighborhood just hasn't figured it out yet. But I don't want to rely on a heterosexual model to get us out of this mess, although the terms of my argument may suggest it. Instead I want to suggest that in order to tell this story I, too, inevitably pushed my argument to a place where I could create identities out of abstractions. I did it because it makes a better story, but I hope I've also made the point that it's the story that, as critics, as poets, as readers, we all need to stop repeating.

Expansive Poetry and Postmodernism
Kevin Walzer

In the university today, postmodernist thought colors most discussions of contemporary literature. "Postmodernism," of course, refers to both a historical period—generally regarded as beginning in the 1960s—and a stream of thought, including rejection of universal reason, the dissolution of boundaries between elite and mass culture, and radical political commitments. Given the prevalence of these assumptions, one major question that critics of contemporary literature naturally ask in evaluating that literature is: Is it postmodern? Texts that receive a "yes" are automatically privileged.

The critical reception of two schools of poetry that emerged in the 1980s is a case in point. The first school, Language poetry, emerges directly from the avant-garde tradition in twentieth-century American poetry; Language poets see language as the source of perception, and therefore experience, and write poems that reject lucidity in favor of exploring the varieties of meaning that language creates. The second school, Expansive poetry, emerges from older traditions of meter, rhyme and narrative; Expansive poets seek to reach a broader audience by infusing their poems with novelistic narrative and traditional forms.

Because of its oppositional stance—characteristic of many postmodern thinkers—and aesthetic expression of recent literary theories, Language poetry has been privileged by such postmodern theorists as Frederic Jameson and Marjorie Perloff. In his influential book *Postmodernism, or, The Cultural Logic of Late Capitalism*, Jameson praises Language poets for seeming "to have adopted schizophrenic fragmentation as their fundamental aesthetic" (28). In contrast, Jameson completely ignores Expansive poetry. And other critics go much further, launching outright denunciations of Expansive poetry as being out of touch with postmodernist thought, as politically reactionary for trying to revive older forms such as meter and complex (as opposed to merely anecdotal and episodic) narrative in hopes of reaching the large general audience that still reads novels but leaves poetry aside. Ira Sadoff's charge of Expansive poetry's "dangerous nostalgia" is characteristic: "When they link pseudo-populism...to regular meter, they disguise their nostalgia for moral and linguistic certainty, for a universal...and univocal way of conserving culture" (7).

The critical milieu that gives rise to such automatic dismissals of literature that explicitly partakes of "tradition" is one thoroughly informed by the experimental, even radical spirit that followed modernism into the postmodern era. Within the field of poetry criticism, the most fully developed expression of this attitude can be seen in Antony Easthope's *Poetry as Discourse*. Easthope focuses on the development of iambic pentameter in English poetry since the Renaissance, linking blank verse with the emergence of the bourgeois, capitalistic society that is the hallmark of modernity. In Easthope's view, blank verse helped to create the very cultural conditions that bring on mass oppression: the tendency of capitalist culture to "naturalize" culture, regarding culture in all aspects as transcendent, unchanging, closed, fixed. Iambic pentameter emerged as an authoritative poetic form during the Renaissance, Easthope notes, and its authority has remained more or less undiminished ever since: "Like linear perspective in graphic art and Western harmony in music, the pentameter may be an epochal form, one co-terminus with bourgeois culture from the Renaissance till now" (53). Easthope argues that iambic pentameter furthers bourgeois culture by creating the illusion of a single poetic speaker, attempting to capture that individual's idiomatic voice by effacing the rhythm of the lines, rather than foregrounding the musical and communal quality of poetry that the older four-stress, oral poetic tradition emphasized: "*it would disclaim the voice speaking the poem in favor of the voice represented in the poem, speaking what it says*. Accordingly pentameter is able to promote representation of someone 'really' speaking" (74; emphasis Easthope's).

Easthope's implication is clear: iambic pentameter is complicit in the unjust, oppressive social structures that capitalist culture creates through its emphasis on individualism and discouragement of collective struggle. His sympathies are evident when he asks, "But if this [capitalist] epoch is over—or if not over, at least since 1848 in its terminal crisis—what happens to the poetic discourse most appropriate to it?" (161). The answer, according to many critics—from Jameson to Perloff—is to reject that poetic discourse. And, in the practice of most poets and the taste of most critics, that is exactly what has happened. Easthope champions the modernist experimentation of Pound and Eliot, which "comprehensively challenges the English poetic tradition, even if it does not succeed in overthrowing it. The whole field of inherited discourse is subverted in one way or another" (134). According to Easthope, to use iambic pentameter today, when bourgeois culture is in unmistakable decline through the efforts of social radicals like Marx and aesthetic radicals like Pound, "is in the strict sense reactionary" (76) because the historical moment that empowered pentameter as a poetic discourse has passed:

> Bourgeois poetic discourse now has no real audience. It is kept alive only in a tainted and complicit form. The state promotes it in secondary and higher education as part of the syllabus for public examinations and 'English' degrees. In Britain the state also subsidizes such poetry through the Arts Council, which gives money for readings and magazines. Meanwhile, people are much more interested in such genuinely contemporary media as cinema, television and popular song in its many varieties. (161)

Easthope's view is sweeping but reductive: he allows no possibility that iambic pentameter, or other traditional poetic form, can be used with any force in the postmodern era. To even attempt to do so is to, in effect, betray the revolution, to be "in the strict sense reactionary." Discussing Expansive poetry, Thomas B. Byers is less absolutist than Easthope; he understands the danger of establishing the kind of essentialist links between ideology and meter/narrative (401) that Easthope asserts, but he scolds Expansive poetry for being "far from progressive," at odds with what he describes as the mainstream of postmodern politics: "the preponderance of its utterances range from moderately conservative to virulently reactionary" (398).

Annie Finch, a feminist Expansive poet and critic, argues the opposite case: to her, given the postmodern emphasis on artifice, on the cultural constructedness of discourse, "the unabashedly stylized use of meter" is perfectly postmodern. Discussing Easthope at length, she believes that "epochal inappropriateness becomes an unconvincing aesthetic argument against meter" (124). And Byers at least allows that possibility; he concedes that meter, rhyme and narrative are not essentially incompatible with postmodernism:

> Narrative and dramatic, discursive and didactic modes might further undermine the lyric self and implicate the poet in a dialogic play of voices foregrounding history and community. These modes would also help undo the fetishization of the image and the reification of the poem itself. (401-402)

But Byers goes on to charge that

> the movement's laments about how poetry has become too intellectual and inaccessible for the common reader encode a nostalgia for an "ordinary language" theory of poetry, in opposition to the difficulties of both modernism and poststructuralism....It seems that what the Expansivists would like

postmodernism to mean is not that there has been a major paradigm shift in the ways we analyze the self, language and their relationship...but that we have, formally speaking, gotten over modernism. (403-404)

With certain people in the Expansive poetry movement, such an observation is true. Byers cites Gerald Harnett, whose journal *Hellas* calls for a "radical repudiation of the various schools of contemporary poetics — structuralism, semiotics, deconstruction, and even the New Criticism — that, with varying degrees of awareness, have established themselves on the ideological foundations of post-Kantian skepticism and 'constructivism,' the view that reality is in one way or another the construction of the human mind" (6). Vernon Shetley cites another: Timothy Steele, whose book *Missing Measures: Modern Poetry and the Revolt Against Meter* is "an indictment of poetic modernism tout court" (153).

Expansive poetry, however, cannot be reduced to a nostalgic, anti-modernist (or anti-postmodernist) monolith, seeking to avoid the inevitable pressures of history. Though Jameson ignores Expansive poetry in his discussion of postmodern aesthetics, a justification for the postmodernism of Expansive poetry can be constructed from his ideas. Furthermore, certain aspects of Expansive poetry — particularly the essays and poetry of Frederick Turner — call for a redefinition of postmodernism.

Jameson notes that a major component of postmodernism is "a weakening of historicity, both in our relationship to public History and in the new forms of our private temporality" (6) — the loss of a sense of historical continuity and unity, replaced with the sense of a constant present. Aesthetically, this leads to "the random cannibalization of all styles of the past, the play of random stylistic allusion, and in general what Henri Lefebvre has called the increasing primacy of the 'neo'" (18). Stylistic expressions, or images, of the past are all that we have left to evoke a historical sense, in this view; nostalgia films, for instance, approach "the 'past' through stylistic connotation, conveying 'pastness' by the glossy qualities of the image, and '1930s-ness' or '1950s-ness' by the attributes of fashion" (19).

Expansive poetry does not self-consciously conform to a theoretical postmodernist paradigm. But Dana Gioia's description of the practical strategies Expansive poets use to recapture a broader audience show the movement to be consistent with the postmodernist movement:

Having found high culture in shambles, the New Formalists looked to popular culture for perspective. In film, rock music, science fiction, and the other popular arts, they found the traditional forms and genres, which the academy had discredited for ideological reasons, still being actively used. Innocent of theory, the general public had somehow failed to appreciate that rhyme and meter, genre and narrative were elitist modes of discourse designed to subjugate their individuality....What the New Formalists—and their counterparts in music, art, sculpture, and theater—imagined was a new imaginative mode that took the materials of popular art—the accessible genres, the genuinely emotional subject matter, the irreverent humor, the narrative vitality, and the linguistic authenticity—and combined it with the precision, compression, and ambition of high art. (253)

Expansive poets make use of a number of elements of popular culture in their work. Turner writes epic science fiction poetry, *The New World* and *Genesis*. Vikram Seth's *The Golden Gate* is a novel-in-verse about Silicon Valley yuppies. Robert McDowell recounts the Lindbergh kidnapping case in *Quiet Money*. In *Take Heart*, Molly Peacock often explores feminist themes in daily life. Gioia has published dramatic monologues in the voices of characters from John Cheever and Raymond Chandler's fiction.

Although Gioia would likely not describe Expansive poetry as "the random cannibalization of all the styles of the past," the increased range of poetic modes of discourse that Expansive poetry makes possible demonstrates its consistency with postmodernism. That increased range—which partakes of popular culture—also points to the greatest historical context against which Expansive poetry rebels: poetic modernism. Certain critics, like Jonathan Holden in *The Fate of American Poetry*, dismiss Expansive poetry not on ideological grounds but on the belief that the movement does nothing new poetically. Holden sees Expansive poetry as one that "retrieved the strand of ironic, fixed-form, 'late-modernist' poetry, which had reigned briefly in the late fifties, a strand epitomized, perhaps, by the vintage work of Richard Wilbur" (37). But Gioia takes pains to note the different cultural assumptions of the two groups of formalists. Poets of the older generation, whose consciousness was formed by World War II, "saw themselves as guardians of the imperiled traditions of European high culture...they wrote poems that displayed their full command of the traditions of English literature, informed and energized by international modernism" (250-252); this was the poetry that the New Criticism was designed to explicate. In contrast, Expansive poets—largely comprised of baby boomers, the same generation whose literary critics contributed so heavily to the replacement of New Criticism with the various ideological approaches that so dominate critical discourse—came of age during the Vietnam era and the dissolution of cultural certainty that Gioia alluded to earlier; the different, postmodern culture they faced as writers led them to imagine their poetic audience, and to shape their poems, differently.

The fact that Expansive poets can use traditional forms like meter and modes like narrative and satire in such a way that they do not immediately evoke the weight of the entire Western tradition in poetry contradicts a central assumption of Byers' argument: that while there is no essential link between meter and ideological conservatism, the historical link between them is so strong that it might as well be essential. While Gioia and Jameson use different language, they are describing the same phenomenon: the recuperation of traditional aesthetics from past historical contexts. This putting of traditional aesthetics to postmodern use can be seen in a variety of Expansive poems.

"In Chandler Country," one of Gioia's poems from his collection *Daily Horoscope*, provides one example of Expansive poetry's postmodernism:

> California night. The Devil's wind,
> the Santa Ana, blows in from the east,
> raging through the canyon like a drunk
> screaming in a bar.
>   The air tastes like
> a stubbed-out cigarette. But why complain?
> The weather's fine as long as you don't breathe.
> Just lean back on the sweat-stained furniture,
> lights turned out, windows shut against the storm,
> and count your blessings.
>   Another sleepless night,
> when every wrinkle in the bedsheet scratches
> like a dry razor on a sunburned cheek,
> when even ten-year whiskey tastes like sand,
> and quiet women in the kitchen run
> their fingers on the edges of a knife
> and eye their husbands' necks. I wish them luck.
>
> Tonight it seems that if I took the coins
> out of my pocket and tossed them in the air
> they'd stay a moment glistening like a net
> slowly falling through dark water.
>   I remember
> the headlights of the cars parked on the beach,
> the narrow beams dissolving on the dark
> surface of the lake, voices arguing
> about the forms, the crackling radio,
> the sheeted body lying on the sand,
> the trawling net still damp beside it. No,
> she wasn't beautiful—but at that age

when youth itself becomes a kind of beauty—
"Taking good care of your client, Marlowe?"

Relentlessly the wind blows in. Next door
catching a scent, the dogs begin to howl.
Lean, furious, raw-eyed from the storm,
packs of coyotes come down from the hills
where there is nothing left to hunt. (7-8)

This poem is specifically postmodern in the way it adapts a traditional form—the blank-verse dramatic monologue speaker—and appropriates a pop-cultural icon. The speaker of the poem is Phillip Marlowe, the hard-boiled Los Angeles detective from Raymond Chandler's fiction. Gioia evokes both the stoic weariness of the detective—sleeping in his office on sweat-stained furniture, breathing smoggy air—and the haggard beauty of a dusty, stormy Southern California night, recalling the atmosphere of Chandler's fiction. But this is poetry, despite its casual language, appropriate for its character, the poem is written in a subtle iambic pentameter very different from that of Wilbur or James Merrill. Gioia's use of Marlowe's persona reflects, as Jameson says of postmodernism in general, a fascination "precisely by this whole 'degraded' landscape of schlock and kitsch, of TV series and Reader's Digest culture, of advertising and motels, of the late show and grade-B Hollywood film, of so-called paraliterature, with its airport paper-back categories of the gothic and the romance, the popular biography, the murder mystery, and the science fiction or fantasy novel: materials they no longer simply 'quote,' as a Joyce or a Mahler might have done, but incorporate into their very substance" (2-3). Gioia adopts the persona of Marlowe for several purposes: to evoke a particular mood about California through a familiar character, given the poem's placement in a group of poems about Gioia's childhood in California; to attract readers of fiction to poetry by animating a well-known author's work in verse; and to experiment formally. Robert McPhillips notes this aspect of the poem when he observes, "Gioia experiments with the shape of a poem written in particularly intense blank verse. In so playing with the lines of the poem, Gioia can simulate the looser lines of the hard-boiled prose that is the source of the poem's language, even as, by elevating the prose to the level of blank verse, he can comment on the poetic element in Raymond Chandler's fiction" (323). Clearly, the poem is not at odds with the postmodernist movement.

Another poem, "Say You Love Me" from Peacock's collection *Take Heart*, exemplifies another aspect of Expansive poetry's postmodernism. Written in terza rima, the poem narrates an incident with an abusive, alcoholic father. The drunken father hovers over the poem's speaker, his 15-year-old daughter, demanding she declare her affection for him:

> What happened earlier I'm not sure of.
> Of course he was drunk, but often he was.
> His face looked like a ham on a hook above
>
> me—I was pinned to the chair because
> he'd hunkered over me with arms like jaws
> pried open by the chair arms. "Do you love
>
> me?" he began to sob. "Say you love me!"
> I held out. I was probably fifteen. (9)

The speaker tries to resist her father's demands, but they begin to wear her down. "'DO YOU' was beginning to peel, as if live layers of skin" (9). His pathetic, drunken sobs overpower her anger: "my game/was breaking down because I couldn't do/anything, not escape into my own/refusal, *I won't, I won't*, not fantasize/a kind, rich father" (10). She gives in:

> unknown to me, a voice rose and leveled
> off, "I love you," I said. *"Say, 'I love you,
> Dad!'"* "I love you, Dad," I whispered, leveled
>
> by defeat into a cardboard image, untrue,
> unbending. (10)

At this point, the speaker tries to get up and leave the room, but her father still looms over the chair. She must depend on the intervention of her sister, who yells to her father that the phone is ringing. Although it is not ringing, he is too drunk to notice immediately and moves toward it, giving the narrator a chance to run. But though she is out of his shadow, there is still no chance for escape:

> He had a fit—
> "It's not ringing!"—but I was at the edge of it
> as he collapsed into the chair and blamed
>
> both of us at a distance. No, the phone
> was not ringing. There was no world out there,
> so there we remained, completely alone. (10)

This poem is postmodern in the way it uses terza rima to express a strikingly feminist content. In this poem, a young woman confronts oppression directly—an extorted declaration of love. Peacock makes use of an irregularly rhymed terza rima stanza to narrate the tense scene. The terza rima form is especially suitable for narrative poetry, as the rhyme and short stanzas (frequently enjambed in Peacock's use of the form) propel the poem forward—recalling Dante, who invented terza rima for his epic journey poem. Each stanza unfolds a small part of the scene, always ending without punctuation, driving the emotional battle between the speaker and her father: "my game/was breaking down because I couldn't do//anything,/....I was at the edge of it/as he collapsed into the chair and blamed//both of us at a distance" (10).

In the first example, the stanza break emphasizes the speaker's helplessness by placing "anything" in isolation; in the second example, the stanza break reinforces the speaker's alienation from her father, as blame is made over the literal distance from one stanza to the next. The breaks in stanzas, unfolding each part of the scene in isolation, are balanced by Peacock's use of rhyme, although many of them vary the standard terza rima scheme (the last three stanzas rhyme aba bba cdc, for instance); rhyme in this context serves to join the scene depicted, knitting a young woman's battle against patriarchy's power into a single whole. By establishing a structural tension between stasis and progress, the terza rima is not only useful but the most appropriate form for the feminist conflict depicted in the poem.

The flowering of the feminist poetry movement in America, ably described by Alicia Ostriker in *Stealing the Language*, clearly participates in the emergence of postmodern historical consciousness in American culture. To be sure, most poetry emerging from that movement has tended toward open form. In her introduction to *A Formal Feeling Comes: Poems in Form by Contemporary Women*, Finch acknowledges this point: "For serious twentieth-century women poets, traditional poetic form has had a troubled legacy" (1). But as Peacock's poem shows, contemporary women poets, with the history of modernist experimentation and feminist advances behind them, are finding genuinely contemporary, postmodern uses for tradition. Finch argues:

> At their best, these poets combine the intellectual strength, emotional freedom, and self-knowledge women have gained during the twentieth century with the poetic discipline and technique that have long been the female poet's province. These poems point the way to a true linking of the strengths of the

old with the strengths of the new: not a nostalgic return to the old forms but an unprecedented relationship with their infinite challenges. (5-6)

Gioia echoes these ideas in another essay, "Notes on the New Formalism," in which he addresses the broad concept of postmodernism, which he calls "an attractive term the meaning of which no two writers can agree on precisely because it does not yet have one" (39). But he draws connections between the emergence of Expansive poetry and the postmodern re-invigoration of modernity's other "epochal forms" (to use Easthope's term) — the "return to tonality in serious music, to representation in painting, to decorative detail and nonfunctional design in architecture" (39). He believes that "these revivals of traditional technique (whether linked or not to traditional aesthetics) both reject the specialization and intellectualization of the arts in the academy over the past forty years and affirm the need for a broader popular audience" (40). Gioia sees art as a distinct form of discourse engaging people on matters of fundamental human concern in a way no other mode of discourse can; though this view is a traditional one that modernism did not abandon, it has taken a pounding in postmodernist theory which insists on equating art with ideology, and Gioia's implicit hope is that the older viewpoint can be restored to respectability. And why not? When Byers dismisses Expansive poetry for being out of touch with postmodernism, he is, in effect, saying that it does not adhere to progressive ideology. But postmodernism is a cultural-historical concept as well as a set of ideological assumptions; if it encompasses all of contemporary culture as Jameson suggests it does, then it encompasses all political persuasions, including the center (where most Expansive poets, who argue for the separation of aesthetics and partisan politics, could be situated) and even the right.

In one sense, it is easy to understand why many postmodernist critics view Expansive poetry as simply a reaction against postmodernism; one of their key assumptions, that the Western tradition must be deconstructed, cannot lead them to see another conclusion. Even Jameson regards the postmodern use of tradition as the ransacking of tombs. But though Expansive poetry is postmodern, it contains an implicit critique of mainstream postmodern thought. First, and most obviously, Expansive poets believe that postmodernism must include a recognition that traditions are living, not dead. Turner makes a forceful argument for this point; he believes that traditional aesthetics such as poetic meter and musical tonality are part of a fundamental human nature that emerged as human culture and biology evolved together. He argues that a true synthesis of fundamental human traditions and contemporary culture are necessary for human society to move forward: "In this work ancient wisdom and traditional lore will join hands with the most sophisticated study of genetics, paleoanthropology, cognitive science, cultural anthropology, ethology, sociobiology, the oral tradition, and performance theory. The word that describes our historical experience of the joining of old and new is Renaissance" (*Tempest, Flute and Oz* 32). Turner is one of a group of thinkers who regard themselves as postmodern, but distinguish themselves from the postmodernist mainstream; David Griffin terms this group "constructive" postmodernists, as opposed to the "deconstructive" mainstream, because they regard deconstructive thought as ultimately paralyzing (20).

Expansive poetry critiques deconstructive postmodernism in another way also, through the sincerity of its commitment to mass culture. Despite the industriousness of scholars and theorists who discuss mass culture, their scholarship is seldom addressed to those who actually live in such culture. As Gioia perceptively notes, "While many influential literary theorists passionately discuss popular culture in general terms, they rarely show much enthusiasm about its gaudy particulars. Since their interest is primarily ideological, politics not pleasure becomes their governing principle. Unlike the actual audience for popular art, they view it in generically abstract terms— often with an unconscious element of professorial condescension" (254). In fact, Expansive poetry emerged in direct reaction against the entire academic culture that has been poetry's sole patron for half a century. Expansive poetry aims to reach a general audience, using the materials of mass culture. Of course, it goes without saying that poetry, Expansive or not, will not have as large an audience as Rosanne Arnold or Michael Jackson; not even Joyce Carol Oates, a novelist as popular as she is good, has enough readers to comprise a genuinely mass audience. But it may be possible for poets to reach an audience of the substantial size that Oates does command. And it seems logical that accessible, but still good, poetry has a greater chance of doing so than Language poetry, which actively rejects accessibility. Even though Language poetry also emerged outside the university, and thrives with a small audience of poets and followers of the avant-garde, it commands no substantial audience in the general culture—for all of its progressive, even radical, aims. Unless populism no longer suggests democracy, Expansive poetry cannot be faulted on ideological grounds.

As Gioia notes, "the dialectic of history is still moving too fast" to render final judgments about postmodernism (39). Turner views mainstream, deconstructive postmodernism as "an uneasy phase of transition" to the future world he envisions (*Tempest, Flute and Oz* 3). Even if Turner is ultimately wrong, however, it is clear that mainstream postmodern discourse is incomplete; even Byers acknowledges that "the politics of postmodern theory are as complicated as the politics of poetic form" (404). The question is not one of Language or Expansive poetry, but involves enough catholicity to recognize that both have things to say—and that the idea of tradition is still relevant. After all, does not Language poetry emerge from the avant-garde—itself America's most enduring artistic tradition?

WORKS CITED

Byers, Thomas B. "The Closing of the American Line: Expansive Poetry and Ideology." *Contemporary Literature* 33.2 (Summer 1992): 396-415.

Easthope, Antony. *Poetry as Discourse*. London: Methuen, 1983.

Finch, Annie (editor). *A Formal Feeling Comes: Poems in Form by Contemporary Women*. Brownsville, Oregon: Story Line Press, 1994.

——. "In Defense of Meter." *Hellas* 1.1 (1990): 21-25.

Gioia, Dana. *Can Poetry Matter? Essays on Poetry and American Culture*. Saint Paul: Graywolf, 1992.

——. *Daily Horoscope*. Saint Paul: Graywolf, 1986.

Griffin, David Ray. *God and Religion in the Postmodern World: Essays in Postmodern Theology*. Albany: SUNY Press, 1989.

Harnett, Gerald. "The New Classicism." *Hellas* 1.1 (1990): 3-8.

Holden, Jonathan. *The Fate of American Poetry*. Athens: University of Georgia Press, 1991.

Jameson, Frederic. *Postmodernism, or, The Cultural Logic of Late Capitalism*. Durham: Duke University Press, 1991.

McDowell, Robert. *Quiet Money*. New York: Henry Holt, 1987.

McPhillips, Robert. "Reading the New Formalists." *Poetry After Modernism*, Ed. Robert McDowell. Brownsville, Oregon: Story Line Press, 1991. 329-341.

Ostriker, Alicia. *Stealing the Language: The Emergence of Women's Poetry in America*. Boston: Beacon Press, 1986.

Peacock, Molly. *Take Heart*. New York: Random House, 1989.

Sadoff, Ira. "Neo-Formalism: A Dangerous Nostalgia." *American Poetry Review* 18.1 (January-February 1990): 7-13.

Seth, Vikram. *The Golden Gate*. New York: Random House, 1986.

Shetley, Vernon. *After the Death of Poetry: Poet and Audience in Contemporary America*. Durham: Duke University Press, 1993.

Steele, Timothy. *Missing Measures: Modern Poetry and the Revolt Against Meter*. Fayetteville: University of Arkansas Press, 1990.

Turner, Frederick. *Genesis*. Dallas: Saybrook Publishers, 1988.

——. *The New World: An Epic Poem*. Princeton: Princeton University Press, 1985.

——. *Tempest, Flute and Oz: Essays on the Future*. New York: Persea Books, 1991.

Psychoanalysis and Poetry

Frederick Feirstein

Over the past several decades, one of the justifications for abandoning the "formalist" techniques of meter and rhyme as well as genres such as the linear narrative came from a misunderstanding of what psychoanalysis has to tell us about the nature of the unconscious. The unconscious was perceived as being totally "free," as in another sentimental fiction psychotics were perceived to be "free." (As common sense tells us, the psychotic, far from being free, is imprisoned by repetitive cryptosymbols, in this case hallucinations and delusions.) This misperception about the nature of the unconscious originated with the early modernists. When the misunderstanding became the received wisdom of their descendants, it was used to attack form for being an artificial imposition on unconscious processes, considered the source of creativity. But psychoanalysts know from clinical data that such expressions of the "free" unconscious we find in dreams and "free associations" (which gave rise to such phenomena as automatic writing) are actually the derivatives of fixed unconscious fantasies. Not only the clinical work of psychoanalysts but the recent work of neuroscientists and dream researchers lead us to understand that the unconscious, far from being lawless, is much like the universe of chaos and complexity theories. It has its own rules which lead to order, if we are trained to observe them. We call these rules the "primary processes" of displacement and condensation, and they are the same rules that form metaphors of poetry and the action metaphors of narrative and drama. What truly liberates us is learning and practicing these rules in art, including the art of psychoanalysis where the primary processes come under the sway of a strengthening preconscious or ego.

Ironically, psychoanalysis, which for much of the century had been central to our culture, has been maligned in recent years by academia for much the same reasons as have "formal" and narrative poetry. The art of psychoanalysis is essentially a narrative one in which the story of a person's life unfolds backwards, like a Greek tragedy, from effect to cause. The story is played out dramatically and symbolically in the transference whereby the analyst is experienced as different projected selves and "objects," i.e., significant others in the analysand's emotional development, both as they really were or as they were imagined to be. The consulting room is filled with many different mothers and fathers, sisters and brothers, and many versions of the self. The fantasies and traumas that helped form such selves and internalized others also come up in dreams told to the analyst and in free associations to dreams and other material. As treatment progresses, and the unfolding narrative and key metaphors reveal the motivations of the various selves, the analysand comes to realize that he or she is living a double life: one of conscious intent, the other an elaborate fantasy life which, because it is unconscious, repeats itself in countless scenarios similar to one another and having a distinct plot and subplots, all invented by the child.

As a narrative poet will use stock plots to structure a work, so the psyche will use stereotypical plots to structure unconscious fantasies, usually in response both to forbidden wishes and to traumas. Like the narrative poet, the child will creatively elaborate these stereotypes with details from his or her own particular history. In the course of treatment, analysand and analyst together eventually come to uncover or reconstruct such stock plots as the Oedipus Complex or the fantasy of anal birth or the Cinderella fantasy, to name a few that become what Jacob Arlow calls "the personal myth," guiding large parts of a person's existence.

We can infer, from the way the child's psyche constructs such personal myths for survival and growth, a psychological foundation for the narrative impulse. As we are compelled to re-enact such fantasies throughout our lives for gratification and adaptation, so some of us are compelled to reproduce them as narrative art. Over a lifetime we unconsciously create new versions of such myths in a response to each new developmental phase and trauma. The psyche's re-working of such personal myths or fantasies finds a parallel in the maturing writer's repeating and developing key plot elements, themes, and patterns of imagery throughout a body of work. As all writers know, the act of exploring such fantasies creatively both helps resolve inner conflicts and leads to further thematic depth. When we are blocked or become boringly repetitive, it is because some aspects of the conflicts remain inaccessible to symbolic representation and instead lead to the cryptosymbols of symptoms, self-mimicry, and sometimes despair. (It's at these times that re-playing the fantasies in the transference help the writing block — much as a good director will help a playwright re-write a script; in this case a life-script.)

Because personal myths are based on stereotypes, i.e., universally shared myths, there's a resonance between the writer's work and the readers or audience who are themselves re-working such myths unconsciously day and night. When the lights dim in the theater or the reader creates an envelope of darkness around a book of poems, a trance-like state can develop in which the reader empathetically enters the writer's myth and can find solace and help with his or her own inner conflicts. We've all had the experience of a writer's inner life personally helping us when we were adolescents, and for some of us this experience has led us to become writers. For some reason, obscure to me now, reading Rimbaud's *Le Bateau Ivre* at 17 had just such an effect on me. This trance state is one in which the preconscious (that part of the psyche connected both to the unconscious and to waking reality) becomes intensely active and synergistic. As writers we experience this when we're in the heat of creation. We also experience such a state in practicing the art of psychoanalysis, especially when the analysand talks metaphorically and with hypnotic rhythms. The analyst enters into the state empathetically, using his or her own preconscious, much as a method actor will do when getting into a role. Such an experience often happens when resistance to treatment (reflecting the unconscious defenses) is lowered and unconscious fantasies and their derivatives emerge in a flow of free associations and metaphors.

Analysts, like myself, will from the very first session listen very carefully for metaphors because they lead to the unconscious whose symbolic organization must be re-worked for lasting change to take place. An analysand will use one or two central metaphors over and over again in treatment. They often will appear in seemingly casual comments about the self or reality as well as in dreams. Arlow finds that such central metaphors lead back to unconscious fantasies representing instinctual wishes and defenses against them. I've written about how such central metaphors lead back to traumas. These metaphors represent the self, traumas to the self, and the self's responses to the traumas. The psyche is poetic in its economical representation of disparate experiences. It will use a single metaphor to express an inner logic to the experience of several traumas, much as a poet writing a lyric sequence will elaborate a key metaphor to give the sequence a narrative contiguity.

Such metaphors expressing traumas often appear in the very first session as clichés, not only because the person has tapped into a stereotype but also because the preconscious hasn't been flexible enough to revitalize the cliché and turn it into a true metaphor. When analysis is successful, we usually notice that the cliché becomes deeply felt and is used in the last phase of treatment in a totally different way from the way it was used in the first session. Also, where the self was initially represented in the cliché as passive, by the end of treatment the self becomes an active agent in the very same metaphor. So, for example (as I've detailed in "Trauma, Fantasy, and Psychosomatosis), an analysand in his first session described how he was stuck in his obsessiveness by saying that he was "a car in neutral." The first dream he reported placed him in an old sportscar he couldn't start up. Throughout the course of his analysis, there were many dreams involving cars which we would learn represented various versions of his self. The metaphor of the sports car appeared in the last dream he reported and neatly illustrates the change in his unconscious that took place as a result of our work together: "I am driving a white BMW. I won it in a contest. I'm driving down a street with the windows open. It's a beautiful day. I never thought a car would make me feel so good. It's a statement of being well-off, things going well, Fred. I'm just cruising along. A BMW. This is nicer than I thought."

This analysand's preconscious (which Suzanne Langer calls the "symbolizing transformer") had been strengthened by learning and practicing the art of psychoanalysis. He came to understand the car metaphor so well that even in the state of dreaming it became more resonant. His strengthened preconscious, freed by sleep from the tasks of reality, began playing with variations of the metaphor for new purposes — as a poet plays with metaphors, turning them around to create meaning.

His preconscious also became stronger by the very act of his narrating his dreams to both of us. He showed me over the years what Ephron and Carrington had found in a study of a number of R.E.M. dreams — that as a person progresses in analysis, not only do the symbols in the dreams become more communicative but the dream itself becomes more and more narrative. In their fascinating essay, Ephron and Carrington proved that when many people first come into treatment their dreams are not only fragmentary and/or incoherent but often lack characters and have no linear action. But as the dreamers become healthier, characters appear in their dreams and so does plot; it is as if they were learning to use their preconscious processes, much as a narrative poet does in writing a poem.

I've found that not only do people learn to use metaphors, symbols, and narration in practicing the art of psychoanalysis with me, but they also learn to use form, as a "formal poet" will use rhyme and meter both for creating a work of art and as a means to explore inner reality. Those of us who use meter and rhyme know that these devices, far from constraining us, help create the trance-like states which give us access to deeper and deeper levels of our psyche. We know, for instance, that rhyme leads to connections of meaning that are often consciously inaccessible. That's because rhyme seems to be a way of condensing several associative paths upwards from our unconscious fantasies.

One analysand of mine, as innovative in his treatment as he was in inventing his pathology, hit on a method for free association far more effective than telling me his dreams or saying whatever came to mind. He would dim the light in his bedroom and make up rhymes which he would write down on long sheets of paper. He would keep the rhymes rolling till they led to startling material hitherto preconscious or unconscious. As his rhyming helped lift unconscious material more and more from the constraints of repression, he not only became healthier, his rhymes became primitive poems.

While working with him, I came across a book, now out of print, by an author quite brilliant and obscure named Theodore Thass-Thienemann who had found and proved in two volumes that etymology is another royal road to the unconscious. In a section entitled "Sound Association and Rhyme," he says (and I think this is worth quoting at length):

> When there is an association of sounds, there will also be an association of meanings.... If one inspects ... one or another treatise on rhyme, one will find again and again an unwitting affirmation of the psychological interpretation through philological data.... Medieval poetry preferred the stereotyped rhyme formulas. These formulas were scrutinized by countless speech experiences till they reached the general acceptance of a stereotype; consequently they display with special distinctiveness the very characteristics of the rhyme. In German medieval poetry the most general rhyme stereotype is the connection lip:wip (the modern German *Leib*: *Weib*, "body": "woman"). The German Leib, however, means not only "body" and "body-self" in the obsolete language, but also "womb"; *Mutter-leib*, properly "mother-body," means simply "womb." This rhyme was repeated with obsessive obstinacy over and over again in all German medieval poetry. In Wolfram's "Parzival" it is found one hundred and twenty-three times, and similarly in other poems. What is the reason for the repetitive use of the rhyme formula? One knows from pathological instances that such repetitiveness is the outflow of repression and anxiety. The "womb"-"woman" association is the great source of regressive fear and anxiety. There are many similar examples.
>
> In the centuries of increasing individualism such stereotyped rhyme for-

mulas were worn out so completely that they became the stigma of the poorest poetry. Every poet of respect avoided them carefully like taboos, but from the psychological viewpoint these taboo-rhymes which were avoided in the poetry of the eighteenth-century are as revealing as the stereotypes of the Middle Ages. I select just one of these trite rhymes as a control test for the above interpretation. In medieval times the German *muot-guot-tuot-bluot* (the modern German *Mut*, "boldness"-*gut*, "good"-*tut*, "does"-Blut, "blood") was a frequent formula; it seems to say simply that braveness (of the heart) does good things. This formula resulted in the trite taboo-rhyme *Blut-Mut*, "blood-boldness, bravery." I chose German rhyme words because the equivalent English words, *blood, boldness*, do not rhyme. If, however, these two concepts stick together in English too, then this association came about through the unconscious connection of the meanings. In this case, however, the German rhyme formula cannot be a mere sound association either. Looking into Shakespeare's language one will find that *blood and boldness*, though not forming a rhyme association appear as attracting one another. Shakespeare says: "The world will say, he is not Talbot's *blood* / That basely fled when noble Talbot *stood*." The rhyme is different but the association of the respective meanings is present nevertheless. Another instance in Shakespeare's language: "Be *bloody, bold* and resolute"; or "He is *bold* and *blushes* not at death"; or "O the *blood* more stirs to rouse a *lion* than to start a hare." Such instances could be multiplied and collected in a whole vocabulary proving the finding that phonemic associations are indicative of the meanings.

In summing up, one may say that these instances prove that the meanings in question are associated in English without rhyme; consequently, if they are connected by the rhyme, as in German, this rhyming supposes the "rhyming of meanings," too. This thesis has been vehemently denied by laboratory psychology, but became confirmed through interpretation of dreams.

Sound associations elicit some pleasure from the store of narcissistic echolalia as experienced by the small child. It springs upfrom the earliest unconscious layer of language. It is genuine with the forgotten language of unconscious fantasies. The analytical interpretation tries to translate the language of unconscious fantasies into the common spoken language. The rhyme is one of the characteristics of this almost forgotten and unknown language of fantasies. (173-75)

Thass-Thienemann is only one of many psychoanalytic writers who use terms from poetry to explain how the psyche works, both to create pathology and health. There are four (Susan Deri, Laurence Kubie, Henry Krystal, and Joyce McDougall) who are particularly interesting in describing how deficiencies in the use of symbols lead to pathology, and how a fluid use of symbols within the psyche and between the psyche and the outer world helps create health. Deri's model of health is the artist in the act of creation. When we are "healthy," the preconscious shuttles symbols back and forth between unconscious and conscious processes. When we become "unhealthy," it is because the preconscious has become too rigidly attached either to reality or to unconscious processes. Instead of negotiating inner and outer life with resonant symbols, the preconscious relies on cliches and signs which cut off affect or merely discharge it in random action.

So, for example, when severe or repeated trauma occurs, there follows such a gross inability to symbolize affect that the shocked psyche comes to rely almost totally on signs. A Vietnam Veteran I treated would try to read other people for emotions so he could guess at making the right response to situations. His manner of speech was what Krystal calls "aprosodic" — almost totally devoid of cadence. When I'd ask for associations to his dreams (which were few and minimal), he'd mechanically tell me more details without rhythmic coloring, much as a small child will tell the plot of a movie.

Joyce McDougall, in her book *Plea For A Measure Of Abnormality*, sees the formation of symptoms as crucial in helping such a numbed psyche survive — especially when the alternative is life-endangering psychosomatic illness, where the numbed psyche becomes driven to use the body mutely to communicate pain. McDougall helps such people ward off dangerous psychosomatosis with verbally-based, protective symptoms of neurosis. Once a neurosis is formed, McDougall then gradually helps bring the defended psyche to the true and flexible symbolization processes we call health.

Like most analysts today, particularly those who focus on narration and symbolization, McDougall is very careful not to use diagnostic categories to describe people. Instead, in her fascinating books *Theaters Of The Mind* and *Theaters Of The Body*, she elaborates a theater metaphor both for understanding failures in symbolization processes and for describing the inner voyages she and her patients go on to recover them:

> In taking the theater as a metaphor for psychic reality, I am hoping to avoid the standard psychiatric and psychoanalytic classification of clinical entities. These terms apply to symptoms, not to people. To designate someone as a "neurotic," a "psychotic," a "pervert," or a "psychosomatic" is little more than name-calling and is inadequate to describe anything as complex and subtle as a human personality. It not only fosters the illusion that we have said something pertinent about somebody, but implies that the rest of us are free of the psychic dramas that lie behind the symptoms to which these terms refer.

Each secret-theater self is ... engaged in repeatedly playing roles from the past, using techniques discovered in childhood and reproducing, with uncanny precision, the same tragedies and comedies, with the same outcomes and identical quota of pain and pleasure. What were once attempts at self-cure in the face of mental pain and conflict are now symptoms that the adult *I* produced, following forgotten childhood solutions. The resulting psychic scenarios may be called neuroses or narcissistic disorders, addictions or perversions, psychoses or psychosomatoses, but they originate from our childlike *I*'s need to protect itself from psychic suffering (3-7).

The analyst symbolically enters the analysand's poetic dramas with the view of helping to re-write them, so they do not remain fixed unconscious guides for constricted living. In order to do this safely, analysts must have an intimate knowledge of their own "inner characters and secret scenarios" which comes from their own analysis and subsequent self-analysis. The analyst, in effect, has to be analyzing two people in the session, the analysand and him or herself, with a full awareness that the analysand will be taking them on journeys into regions sometimes unknown and dangerous to both of them. In each analysis, somewhat of a joint cure will take place, if the analyst remains open and persistently questioning.

Roy Schafer in *The Analytic Attitude* calls psychoanalysis "a dialogue" and describes it as a narrative one in which the confused and confining story about the self that one has learned to live by is actively re-experienced in the transference and arduously revised, as a poet's narrative would be. Schafer says,

> People going through psychoanalysis — analysands — tell the analyst about themselves and others in the past and present. In making interpretations, the analyst retells these stories. In the retelling, certain features are accentuated while others are placed in parentheses; certain features are developed further, perhaps at great length. This retelling is one along psychoanalytic lines ... the division into analyst and analysand does not provide for the increasing extent to which the analysand becomes coanalyst of his or her own problems and, in certain respects, those of the analyst too. The analysand, that is, becomes a more daring and reliable narrator. (210-20)

In conclusion, we might say that the ultimate goal of analysis is to help people achieve self-cure by helping them become better narrative poets — with a seasoned ability to convert the cryptosymbols of symptoms into metaphors, and to re-write the motivations and aims of their inner characters so that the plot of their lives can change as best as the circumstances of reality will allow.

WORKS CITED

Arlow, Jacob. *Psychoanalysis: Clinical Theory and Practice*. Madison, Connecticut: International Universities Press, 1994.

Deri, Susan. *Symbolization and Creativity*. Madison, Connecticut., I.U.P, 1984.

Feirstein, Frederick. "Trauma, Fantasy, and Psychosomatosis." In: Janet Schumacher Finnell, (Ed.), *Psychoanalytic Treatment of Psychosomatic Disorders*. New Jersey: Jason Aaronson, Inc. 1996.

Ephron, Harmon, and Patricia Carrington. "Ego Functioning in Rapid Eye Movement Sleep: Implications for Dream Theory." In: Jules Masserman (Ed.), *Science and Psychoanalysis*, XI. New York: Grune & Stratton, 1967.

Krystal, Henry. *Integration and Self-Healing*. New Jersey: The Analytic Press, 1961.

Kubie, Lawrence. *Neurotic Distortions of the Creative Process*. New York: Noonday Press, 1961.

Langer, Suzanne. *Philosophy In A New Key*. New York: Mentor, 1951.

McDougall, Joyce. *Plea For A Measure Of Abnormality*. Madison, Connecticut. I.U.P., 1980.

——. *Theaters of the Mind*. New York: Basic Books, 1983.

——. *Theaters of the Body*. New York: W.W. Norton, 1984.

Schafer, Roy. *The Analytic Attitude*. New York: Basic Books, 1989.

Thass-Thienemann, Theodore. *The Interpretation of Language, v.1: Understanding The Symbolic Meaning of Language*. New Jersey: Jason Aaronson, 1968.

Playing Tennis in Asbestos Gloves: Women, Formalism and Subjectivity in the 1980s

Allison Cummings

Recent quarrels over the relative politics of one or another poetic form may be understood as expressions of a larger cultural struggle to define a self through language. In the case of recent women's poetry in traditional forms, the foremost question regarding subjectivity may concern the relation of gender to formalism. Women poets' descriptions of the interactions between gender, subjectivity, and set form, which often resemble feminist theorists' formulations of subjectivity, differ from New Formalist criticisms' most widely recognized stances on the self. This essay will suggest that gender, or conceptions of gendered identity, can play specific roles in relation to poetic form, roles that have not yet been defined fully either by critics or spokespeople for the New Formalism.

Since at least the 1960s, many women poets have associated set poetic forms and the western European tradition of formal verse with exclusive, patriarchal legacies. Adrienne Rich's well-known renunciation of the "asbestos gloves" of set form—which she believed blocked her access to "hot," controversial topics—influenced many subsequent women poets either to reject set forms in favor of free verse or to use set form but feel like "bad feminists" for doing so.[1] Even those feminist poets who do not regard the tradition of formal verse or individual set forms as necessarily patriarchal often express reluctance to embrace either that tradition or set forms wholeheartedly. The risk here is that assigning essential features to a poetic form (as Rich's stance may imply) is similar, in argument and consequence, to assigning essential features to (gendered) identity. Many feminist poets are wary of the theoretical and material consequences of such fixed definitions.

In contrast, recent male poets interested in set form seem untroubled by such concerns. Arguing since about 1975 for a renewed embrace of traditional forms, spokespeople for the New Formalism emphasize the democracy of formal rules and traditions. Often invoking Frost's observation that

---

1. See Adrienne Rich, "When We Dead Awaken: Writing as Revision." *On Lies, Secrets, and Silence: Selected Prose 1966-1978.* New York: W.W. Norton, 1979.

writing poetry without regular form and meter is like playing tennis without a net, these proponents of formalism imply that anyone can play the game with some study, practice and skill. Questions regarding gender or subjectivity rarely enter these spokespeoples' formulations of the "new formalism" explicitly, perhaps in part because the spokespeople—mostly spokesmen—have little impetus to consider women's relations to traditional poetic form. Despite outward equanimity, however, several spokespeople for the New Formalism imbue set form with masculine attributes in the process of advocating it. While their motives clearly differ from the feminist poets above, their gendered narrative is strikingly similar.

The 1994 anthology, *A Formal Feeling Comes: Poems in Form by Contemporary Women*, edited by Annie Finch, complicates the story by adding more views of formalism. This anthology gathers women's statements on poetics (rare finds), and modifies notions of subjectivity and form publicized by New Formalist essays and manifestoes. The contributors to this volume hold conflicting notions of gender and formalism's interactions. Some try to negotiate those conflicts in abstract terms while others describe their compositional processes through figurative language. Regardless of how they articulate the issues, most of the poets subscribe to one of several stances on gender and formalism. Some poets espouse a version of Rich's stance, viewing set forms and the Western tradition as masculine, oppressive and in need of subversion—but from *within* traditional form. Others regard the tradition and its formal structures as neither masculine nor feminine, but constructed and maintained by men and women equally. Still others view the formal tradition since the late nineteenth century as a predominantly feminine domain that has been dismissed by critics as aesthetically and politically regressive; these poets embrace and seek to revalue women's formal verse, including "sentimental" poetry.[2] A number of other poets situate their work in relation to other literary traditions, such as Native American chant, Latin American storytelling, or African American blues and jazz.[3]

These poets conceive of formalism in categories that parallel feminist theorists' disagreements over gender: is female identity essentially different from male, esentially the same, or a shifting constellation of socially-defined, intersecting characteristics of gender, race, class and other catego-

---

2. See Annie Finch, "Introduction", *A Formal Feeling Comes*.

3. See comments in *A Formal Feeling Comes* by Elizabeth Alexander, 9; Julia Alarez, 18; Sandra Cisneros, 45; Lenore Keeshig-Tobias, 107; and Leslie Simon, 208.

ries? Theorist Kathy Ferguson classifies two feminist strategies according to the terms "interpretation" and "genealogy." She defines interpretation as "articulations of women's experiences and women's voice" and genealogy as "deconstructions of the category of women". I believe the first two poetic stances, the most heavily represented in this anthology, illustrate Ferguson's two categories.

"Interpretation," or "articulations of women's experiences" and "voice," has become the province of lyric poetry by women. The lyric speaker seeks to project a self that coheres and precedes the poem. The subject may assert stable identity—in women's lyrics in particular—in order to claim the authority to speak from a traditionally masculine subject position, although that self need not embrace an essential or fixed identity.[4] In the process, the subject may cast the tradition, the auditor, or the chosen form as a foe to subvert or challenge. The process of claiming an authoritative subject position, then, appears motivated by a sense of personal and collective exclusion from the formal tradition and its customary subject positions.

In their essays, poets often suggest that poetic forms and gender have stable identities. Sharing Adrienne Rich's association of rhyme, meter and the literary tradition with specifically masculine, and often racially dominant, authority, Honor Moore writes, "I wasn't going to be incarcerated in 'their' forms, was how I saw it in 1970" (161). Moore goes on to suggest that she thinks of form differently now, though she maintains an opposition between the self and a language that is both enclosing and menacing: "[The sestina's] restraint became the walls of the room, the recurrence of end words a verbal equivalent for the relentlessness of the molester's intentions" (162). Cheryl Clarke appears to maintain a distance between her self and poetic form as well: "I do it—the form—to be rebellious and sometimes to be reserved. How can I reflect my black self in the form, how can I speak my contempt from inside the master's formula?" (FF 48). Julia Alvarez also implies a distinction between her self and language: "I wanted to go in that heavily mined and male labyrinth [the sonnet] with the string of my own voice. I wanted to explore and explode it, too" (17). Kelly Cherry also voices this distinction: "I began writing in forms after I had found, in my opinion

---

4. For much fuller explanations of lyric subjectivity and women's voices, see Rachel Blau DuPlessis, "'Corpses of Poesy': Some Modern Poets and Some Gender Ideologies of Lyric" *Feminist Measures: Soundings in Poetry and Theory*: 69-95, or Annie Finch, "The Sentimental Poetess in the World: Metaphor and Subjectivity in Lydia Sigourney's Nature Poetry" *Legacy* (Fall 1988): 3-18.

anyway, my own voice" (39). Alvarez alternately refers to poetic tradition as a foreign power: "I think of form as territory that has been colonized, but that you can free. . . . I feel subversive in formal verse. . . . The words belong to no one. . . . We have to take them back from those who think they own them" (16). In the manner of feminist poets since the 1960s who conceived of traditional form as a masculine, discrete entity, Clarke, Alvarez, Moore, Cherry and others differentiate the self, and its elusive signature "voice," from traditional poetic language. These poets associate the form itself, often explicitly, with various manifestations of domination—colonizers, restraint, a "male labyrinth." Reviewing *A Formal Feeling Comes* in *The Yale Review*, Langdon Hammer confirms that "for women poets in particular, to write free verse was to rebel against the male authority symbolized by rhyme and meter, which, like other poetic devices, were felt to discipline and disguise female identity" (126). As Hammer indicates, where Rich and other poets rejected formal verse based on its gendered and political implications, these poets use set forms but feel compelled to rebel against them in some way.

These associations of rhyme and meter with a "patriarchal tradition of male poetry" (Walzer 47) surface elsewhere in the essays in *A Formal Feeling Comes*, often in metaphors for order and structure. Through such metaphors, the anthology's contributors often erect binary oppositions between a masculine reverence for order and a feminine disorder or resistance to order. The writers then seek to invest that feminine resistance with value and legitimacy. Among other "feminine" categories, feminist poets attempt to revalue and insist on the significance of individual, contradictory experience by writing formal poetry about intimate subjects. These poets use poetic language to highlight the implications for women of a tension between traditional structure and the emotions of a private self. One possible implication of that tension is a reconceived sense of the importance and subversive potential of "private" emotion. Such "articulations of women's experience" have formed the basis of feminist writing's political resistance for several decades now and show few signs of abating.[5] Maxine Kumin, for instance, writes: "Constraints of rhyme and/ or meter liberate the poet to confront difficult or painful or elegiac material" (FF 143). Honor Moore puts it: "Embraced in [the sestina's] sure architecture, the violated child . . . is free to tell

---

5. For a recent critique of this model of feminist writing, see Joan Retallack's ":RE: THINKING: LITERARY: FEMINISM: (three essays onto shaky grounds)," Keller, *Feminist Measures*: 344-77.

her story" (163). Rita Dove comments: "I like how the sonnet comforts even while its prim borders . . . are stultifying; one is constantly bumping up against the Law" (58).

Employing similar metaphors for official power, Molly Peacock comments in an essay: "If I have a large and worldly structure, I shall be able to say small and private things without sentimentality" (Poetry East, 113). Peacock embellishes the notion of "small and private things" in *A Formal Feeling Comes*, using embroidery as a metaphor for a private, feminine activity composed of both tiny details and myriad flaws: "I began to think of writing poetry as doing needlework: embroidering . . . requires you to make tons of mistakes" (180). She compares the mistakes of embroidery to "a female embodiment of traditional verse. . . that acknowledges fluctuation and imperfection," while men seem to "admire rigor" more (182).

Peacock conflates the "small and private" with the realm of disorder and "imperfection" in the female body and psyche in the poem, "How I Had to Act." There she represents a tension between order and disorder both through regular and irregular rhymes and meter and through the speaker's wish for self-control and her compulsive lack of self-control. The speaker buys "a fake fur coat / from two old ladies in a discount shop" (184) as a tacky stand-in (which nevertheless exceeds her budget) for the real mink she desires. The mink signifies authentic selfhood: "I had promised myself a real fur coat / which I wanted as I did a real self" (185). Peacock's poem is rich with complex ironies concerning women's relations to appearance and clothing (as signifiers of identity), to other women, to their self-perception, and to their desires and actions. The poem articulates a common, realistic "woman's experience," and while the speaker suggests that her identity may be a mere reflection of desires constructed by family, commerce and the media, she still yearns for a stable self that has and knows its own desires and motives.

Peacock "value[s] the interplay between the chaos of emotion and the order of form" (182) and does not attempt to subordinate messy, personal details to exemplary tales for the tribe. New Formalist spokesmen certainly may value this interplay as well, but their rhetoric tends to shun or downplay chaos as it lobbies for greater order in contemporary poetry. As I mentioned at the outset of this essay, New Formalist spokesmen rarely discuss the role of gender in formalism explicitly; however, when they do discuss the self, they imply a narrative nearly as gendered as that of the poets above.

New Formalist spokespeople, too, associate set form with order, structure, and restraint, but they emulate rather than resist those masculine values. Put another way, where many women poets in *A Formal Feeling Comes* resist or ambivalently adopt set form's authoritative mantle, a number of male New Formalists proudly don it; both invest set forms and the tradition with power and authority, but they value those concepts quite differently.

In early definitions of the New Formalist movement, several spokespeople speak of set form, traditional meters, and narrative as techniques that enable poets to be objective, disciplined and less personal than do free verse techniques. They claim that set forms may help poets avoid the autobiographical, self-centered writing commonly attributed to mainstream lyric poetry.[6] In a special issue of *Verse*, Robert McPhillips reports the New Formalists' "resistance to the emotional extremism of the Confessional poets" (3). Elsewhere in that volume, he argues that narrative and formal poets must "eschew . . . solipsism . . . [by] turning outwards from the ego to tell stories about others in narrative poems, and from the subjectivity of 'organic' free forms to the objectivity of fixed forms" (22). In his essay, "Transcending the Self," Dick Allen echoes these ideas: "To escape the self-absorbed, often narcissistic poems characteristic since the 1960s, . . . Expansive [poetry] moves outward from the Self to reestablish identities with historical, social, religious and scientific realities" (*Crosscurrents*, 5).

Explicit references to masculine or feminine traits are nowhere found in these or other statements of the movement, but oppositions such as "subjective vs. objective" and "Self vs. historical, scientific realities" implicitly devalue personal experience in order to champion collective experience and authoritative, traditionally masculine discourses. Allen capitalizes "Self" to flag and criticize its omnipresence in mainstream free verse lyric poetry. Though Allen probably does not object to personal poetry in all cases, his efforts to differentiate a New Formalist agenda from the "narcissistic" mainstream lyric effectively denounce personal poetry. Personal poetry in *A Formal Feeling Comes* and elsewhere, however, is often precisely the vehicle chosen for feminist resistance to those masculine traditions which historically have erased the specificity of female experience. Allen's polemics overlook the aims and principles of much contemporary poetry by women and ironi-

---

6. See Frederick Feirstein and Frederick Turner, Introduction to *Expansive Poetry: Essays on the New Narrative and the New Formalism*; Brad Leithauser, "The Confinement of Free Verse," McCorkle, *Conversant Essays*, 1990.

cally, perhaps instructively, fail to transcend his own perspective.

Much as women's and men's gendered narratives for formalism resemble each other only superficially, women's and men's references to the restraining effects of set form echo each other only initially. For example, McPhillips writes, "traditional metrical and stanzaic patterns . . . impose restraint" on poets, enabling them to "render their personal emotions more universal in appeal" (*Verse*, 22). McPhillips' and other New Formalists' rhetoric strike many readers as antiquated because it resurrects and values concepts critical theorists have questioned for over a decade. The goal of universality, like that of objectivity, mentioned above, is no longer a literary value universally acknowledged. Though many contributors to *A Formal Feeling Comes* also speak of restraining emotion and controlling the self through form, their understandings of this aspiration and of what self is under control differ from those of New Formalist spokespeople. Where McPhillips' idea of restraint is to subordinate private experience to stories derived from a public, cultural domain, many poets in *A Formal Feeling Comes* view set form's restraint of emotion and self-expression ambivalently—as both "comforting" and "stultifying," "embracing" and limiting.

Thus far I have examined how women's statements about poetic form parallel the feminist strategy of "interpretation" and compared that strategy to male New Formalists' discussions of the self in formal poetry. Fewer women working in set forms adopt the other feminist stance—genealogy— but those who do generally seek to destabilize categories of identity and deny essential features of poetic form, gendered, political or otherwise. Marilyn Hacker is one such formalist. Hacker appears to see herself as inside of and heir to the formal tradition, perhaps because she defines tradition fluidly. In an interview, Hacker has said: "[T]he language we use was as much created by women as by men. . . . We've got to reclaim the language, demand acknowledgement of our part in it, and proceed from there" (Hammond, 22). By not assuming that the poetic tradition is male-dominated, Hacker avoids the kinds of gendered oppositions that many poets maintain. Hacker's essay in *A Formal Feeling Comes* avoids references to gender or female identity almost altogether. Indeed, Hacker opens her comments with "I have no political or aesthetic rationale for [the choice and use of a fixed or structured form], except that I like it" (87). Yet Judith Barrington has dubbed Hacker a "radical formalist" on the basis of feminist politics in her poetry, and Lynn Keller analyzes Hacker's "performative" formalism in terms of Judith Butler's notion that gender is continually constructed (and deconstructed) through its performance—a notion with radical political implications for women.[7] In other words, one may abstract a different narrative about gender and formalism from Hacker's poetry than from her essay.

Hacker's poems repeatedly represent gender and sexuality as shifting constellations of social and personal constructs. The speaker must name and rename herself in relation to, or often against, categories of identity furnished by American culture. In "Eight Days in April," Hacker playfully suggests that gendered identity is a chosen performance: "You're an exemplar / piss-elegance is not reserved for boys. / Tonight we'll go out in our gangster suits" (88). In contrast to Peacock's wish, however ironicized and undercut, for a real fur coat to establish a real, womanly identity, Hacker dons masculine clothing (and worn by men outside the law) to unmake the public's assumptions about womanhood and about clothing's ability to express authentic identities. In a poem not included in Finch's anthology, Hacker examines namelessness as an ambiguous alternative to performed identity. Her lesbian love unfolds in uncharted, unnamed territory: "Look what we're mak- / ing, besides love (that has a name to speak). / Its very openness keeps it from harm" (Love, 106). Rather than having an officially sanctioned contract such as marriage define their relationship, the poet and her partner must continually articulate and redefine the outlines of their relationship and their love:

> we must choose, and choose, and choose
> momently, daily. This moment my whole
> trajectory's toward you, and it's not los-
> ing momentum. Call it anything we want. (Love, 72)

In other poems Hacker also weighs the burdens of namelessness and self-definition against the political necessity of making oneself visible and titled. Numerous feminist theorists debate precisely these issues: do fixed identities encourage stigmatization or collective action? Do fluid identities escape scapegoating at the cost of social and political invisibility?[8] Hacker's

---

7. See Judith Barrington's review, "Feminist Formalist" in *The Women's Review of Books*, VII. 10-11 (July 1990): 28, and Lynn Keller's essay, "'Measured Feet in Gender-Bender Shoes': The Politics of Poetic Form in Marilyn Hacker's Love, Death, and the Changing of the Seasons" in *Feminist Measures*.

poetry may remind readers that not all women working in set poetic forms feel excluded from the formal tradition or conceive of gender and formalism as fixed, antithetical categories. In Hacker's view, the formal tradition's authority, though historically associated with men, resides in the office rather than in the gender of its most frequent occupants. Electing herself to draft and carry out formal laws and traditions, Hacker assumes this office confidently and rearranges the desk. In this light, Hacker treats set form in ways comparable to other feminist poets who wish to appropriate for themselves the power and authority that traditional forms may bestow. However, as Lynn Keller argues, Hacker's "formalist verse becomes radically innovative as she pursues the implications of nonorganicist assumptions about form and nonessentialist assumptions about gender" (264). As a collection, *A Formal Feeling Comes* demonstrates that many women poets, by situating their poetic practices in either these feminist contexts or others, may successfully challenge "organicist assumptions" that set or "closed" forms are politically conservative or regressive.

Of course Hacker is no more "inside" the tradition than Peacock is outside it, but where they think they are becomes definitive of women's relation to formalism, and of the critical interpretation of their poetic stances.[9] Similarly, even if Dick Allen's wish to "transcend the self" does not describe most actual formal poems, his rhetoric helps define the politics of the New Formalist movement. Moreover, when Robert McPhillips recommends form as a means to discipline emotion, his idea of his position in relation to the poetic tradition — and perhaps his actual position, if it can be known — differs from these women poets' notions of their positions.

Perhaps maintaining sexual tension in poetry (constructing form as masculine and opposed to a feminine self) is a means of displacing, enhancing or just articulating an aesthetic tension between self-expression and formal constraint that confronts any poet working in set forms. Where Wordsworth invoked a nun's convent room as a metaphor for the sonnet's constraints, contemporary women poets often liken the demands of set form to sexual,

---

8. For discussions of these questions in feminist theory, see essays in *Life/Lines: Theorizing Women's Autobiography*, ed. Brodzki and Schenck, 1988; Judith Butler, *Gender Trouble: Feminism and the Subversion of Identity*, 1990; Julia Kristeva, excerpts in New French Feminisms, ed. Marks and deCourtivron, 1981; Nancy K. Miller, *Subject to Change: Reading Feminist Writing*, 1988; or essays by different authors in *Feminism and Foucault: Reflections on Resistance*, 1988.

9. See also Lynn Keller: "how one approaches one's formalism. . . has more potential political significance than the formalism itself" (*Measures*, 264).

racial, and political oppression. Surely such metaphors reflect as much on our culture as on poetry. Women writing in traditional form may and do take up different notions of subjectivity, some of which have been outlined by feminist thought: is identity or gender inborn or performed, authentic or constructed, stable or shifting? In this diversity, they resemble women writing in experimental and free verse poetic forms, whose choices about poetic form almost inevitably raise questions about subjectivity, such as: what "I" speaks and on what grounds? By conceiving of the self as both the subject and agent of set form, and by implication of language, women who self-consciously write in form are productively wrestling with central contemporary debates over poetry and subjectivity.

WORKS CITED AND CONSULTED

Allen, Dick. "Transcending the Self." Special issue of *Crosscurrents: Expansionist Poetry: The New Formalism and The New Narrative* 8.2 (1989).

Annis, Claudia Gary. Review: *A Formal Feeling Comes. The Edge City Review: Books.* 1.3 (January 1995): 37-41.

Barrington, Judith. "Feminist Formalist." *The Women's Review of Books* 7. 10-11 (July 1990): 28.

Brodzki, Bella and Celeste Schenck, eds. *Life/Lines: Theorizing Women's Autobiography.* Ithaca: Cornell UP, 1988.

Butler, Judith. *Gender Trouble: Feminism and the Subversion of Identity.* New York: Routledge, 1990.

Byers, Thomas. "The Closing of the American Line: Expansive Poetry and Ideology." *Contemporary Literature* 33.2 (Summer 1992): 396-415.

Diamond, Irene and Lee Quinby, eds. *Feminism and Foucault: Reflections on Resistance.* Boston: Northeastern UP, 1988.

DuPlessis, Rachel Blau. "'Corpses of Poesy': Some Modern Poets and Some Gender Ideologies of Lyric." *Feminist Measures: Soundings in Poetry and Theory.* Ed. Lynn Keller and Christanne Miller. Ann Arbor: University of Michigan Press, 1994: 69-95.

Feirstein, Frederick and Frederick Turner, eds. Introduction. *Expansive Poetry: Essays on the New Narrative and the New Formalism.* Santa Cruz: Story Line Press, 1989.

Ferguson, Kathy. *The Man Question: Visions of Subjectivity in Feminist Theory.* Berkeley: Univ. of California Press, 1993.

Finch, Annie, Ed. and Introduction. *A Formal Feeling Comes: Poems in Form by Contemporary Women.* Brownsville, OR: Story Line Press, 1994.

—. "The Sentimental Poetess in the World: Metaphor and Subjectivity in Lydia Sigourney's

Nature Poetry." *Legacy* (Fall 1988): 3-18.

Gioia, Dana. "Symposium." *Crosscurrents*. 89.

Hacker, Marilyn. *Love, Death, and the Changing of the Seasons*. New York: Arbor House, 1986.

Hammer, Langdon. Review of *A Formal Feeling*. *The Yale Review* 83.1 (Jan 1995): 126-131.

Hammond, Karla. Interview with Marilyn Hacker. *Frontiers: A Journal of Women's Studies* 5 (Fall 1980): 22.

Keller, Lynn. "'Measured Feet in Gender-Bender Shoes': The Politics of Poetic Form in Marilyn Hacker's *Love, Death, and the Changing of the Seasons*." *Feminist Measures: Soundings in Poetry and Theory*. Ed. Lynn Keller and Christanne Miller. Ann Arbor: Univ. of Michigan Press, 1994: 260-86.

Leithauser, Brad. "The Confinement of Free Verse." *Conversant Essays: Contemporary Poets on Poetry*. Ed. James McCorkle. Detroit: Wayne State UP, 1990: 195-208.

Maas, Tomma Lou. "Multiformalism: An Interview with Annie Finch." *Poetry Flash*. No. 263 (Sept 1995): 1-10.

Marks, Elaine and Isabelle deCourtivron, eds. *New French Feminisms: An Anthology*. New York: Schocken Books, 1981.

McDowell, Robert, Ed. *Poetry After Modernism*. Oregon: Story Line Press, 1991.

McPhillips, Robert, Ed. *Verse: The New Formalism in American Poetry*. 7.3 (Winter 1990).

—. "Interview with Dana Gioia." *Verse* 9.2 (Summer 1992): 9-27.

Miller, Nancy K. *Subject to Change: Reading Feminist Writing*. New York: Columbia UP, 1988.

Peacock, Molly. "How I Had to Act." *A Formal Feeling Comes: Poems in Form by Contemporary Women*. Ed. Annie Finch. Brownsville, OR: Story Line Press, 1994.

—. "What the Mockingbird Said." *Poetry East* 20-21 (Fall 1986). Also in James McCorkle, Ed. *Conversant Essays*: 343-7.

Retallack, Joan. "RE: THINKING: LITERARY: FEMINISM: (three essays onto shaky grounds)." *Feminist Measures: Soundings in Poetry and Theory*: 344-77.

Rich, Adrienne. "When We Dead Awaken: Writing as Revision." *On Lies, Secrets, and Silence: Selected Prose 1966-1978*. New York: W.W. Norton, 1979.

Walzer, Kevin. "The Ghost of Tradition" (Review) *ELF* 4.4 (Winter 1994): 45-8.

The Inner Meaning of Poetic Form
Frederick Turner

As one of the founders and spokespersons of the "expansive" or "new formalist" movement, I nevertheless recognize that mere technique in poetic form and narrative, however skillful and admirable, is not enough; great poetry has been written in free verse, and trivial poetry has been written in tight, ingenious meters and cleverly organized narrative structures. The promise of the new trend will be realized only if poets and readers are able to take the formal elements of poetry at their deepest level, as talismans or psychic technologies designed to unlock the gates between the human and the natural, the conscious and the unconscious, the present and the past, the rational and the chaotic, life and death. Or rather, even to invoke these dualisms is to be betrayed by a language that is not truly poetic, not truly capable of the deep science in which the dualisms disappear.

When we respond to the meter or the mythic plot of a poem, we are doing so as a member of the species Homo sapiens, as a primate, a mammal, a vertebrate, a living organism, a marvellously intricate piece of carbon chemistry, a play of physical particles and forces, an involuted knot of spacetime. In other words, we are not confined, as we can be by unmeasured denotative statement, to the most recent level of biological evolution, that brought about the specialization of the linguistic areas of the left temporal cortex, but released into our entire evolutionary history.

The pleasure of meter, as I have shown by the research reported in my essay "The Neural Lyre," is based upon the three-second rhythm of the human information processing cycle or neural present, and mediated by the secretion of biologically ancient neurotransmitters. New research by Colwyn Trevarthen and Ellen Dissanayake shows that mothers and newborns conduct their prelinguistic conversations in a three-second antiphon of "motherese," and that mammals conduct their continuous little dance of movement, attention saccades, and expressive action in a three-second cycle. But meter is important at much deeper levels yet. As the psycholinguists Michael Lynch and Kim Oller have shown, within the three-second short-term memory window there is room for about ten shorter beats, corresponding to syllables, or to the shortest interval in which human action reflexes can still operate; within this 1/3 second period there are nested about ten yet shorter beats, corresponding to the minimum interval at which we can perceive the order of two different sounds; and within this tiny moment there is room for about ten tinier ones, the minimum interval at which we can identify anything at all. The brain uses the meter in which neural firings are exchanged as a carrier of precise information about what is perceived or remembered, and the enzyme and RNA factories that construct the body's proteins consult their central DNA library in an intricately hierarchical rhythmic pattern. Ilya Prigogine has shown that complex chemical reactions, especially those involving catalysts, have a rhythmic temporal structure, and quantum chemists and physicists have long known that matter can be described as the nodes where the different local periodicities of energy quanta find their harmonic resolution—matter as a kind of rhyme. . . .

So when a poet uses and an audience hears meter, we are taking a first step into an organic recognition of our unity with the physical universe; we are, if you like, celebrating our participation in the being of Gaia herself. We are also affirming our solidarity with the whole past of the world, and making it possible for our creations to be the issue of generative forces that go far beyond the capabilities of our clever little linguistic centers. Poetry becomes an accelerated version of evolution itself, of that miraculous feedback among variation, selection, and heredity which produced the orchid, the sperm whale, the tobacco mosaic virus, the giant panda and the coral reef.

Perhaps indeed this is the meaning of the myth of Orpheus, the first poet in the Greek mythology, who, like Solomon, or like Vyasa, the mythical poet of the Mahabharata, could speak the languages of animals and plants and stones. Orpheus' journey to the underworld and back (as Virgil says, any fool can go down there, but to return—this is the labor, this is the task) is more than just a search for his lost wife Eurydice. Or rather, the search for his lost wife means the recovery of the organic connection with the rest of the universe. The point is that Orpheus can make his journey only because he possesses and can use his lyre, the instrument by which Greek poets kept the measure of their meter and gave their lines a rhyme. It is the lyre that opens the gates of the underworld; and it is when Orpheus fails to trust its magic, and looks back to see if Eurydice is following, that he tragically loses her forever.

We can follow the mysterious logic of the myth still further; for the lyre of Orpheus (and of his father Apollo) was originally the invention of Hermes, who traded it for the caduceus, the snake-entwined rod by which he conducts mortals between the lands of the living and the dead. It so happens that the double helix of the two snakes is an exact model of the shape of the DNA molecule; and this is not just a coincidence, for the double helix is perhaps the best intuitive diagram of any feedback process, and DNA is the feedback process of feedback processes. If the lyre, then, is in some sense equivalent to the caduceus, we may infer that the meter of poetry is analogous to the meter of biological reproduction and evolution. This is the central insight of Rilke's Sonnets to Orpheus. Other versions of this talisman are the magic flute of Mozart and da Ponte, the golden bough of Virgil, the metatron of Moses (also a combination of rod and snake), the drum of the Asiatic shamans, the bagpipe of the ancient Magyar bards—even perhaps the "Mcguffin" of Alfred Hitchcock.

But this is perhaps to give too great an emphasis to meter. One could make much the same argument for narrative technique, that marvellous system by which time takes on its strange, unspacelike asymmetry. A story, like a melody, is any sequence of events that are retrodictable, that is, can be shown to have been inevitable once they have happened, but not predictable before they have happened; because the events themselves bring about a new kind of universe in which their antecedents now add up to an irreversible chain of causes. (The most crass example of this is the detective story, whose solution is obvious once the sleuth unveils it, but not before). In this sense we may perhaps take the rod of Hermes' caduceus to mean the fixed retrodictability of a story, and the snakes to mean its protean unpredictability. The unpredictability of a story is what makes us want to know what happens next—and this is why the Sultan spares the life of the storyteller Sheherezade, and Minos spares the life of Orpheus. In this light the duality of meter takes on a deeper significance still. The fixed pattern of stressed and unstressed syllables (or long and short syllables, or tone-changing and tone-unchanging ones as in Chinese verse) bears the same relation to the varying pattern of spoken cadence that floats above the fixed framework, that the predictable bears to the unpredictable elements of a story. Or one could even say that meter was micro-story, or that story was macrometer.

Thus if we are to take seriously the return to meter and narrative proclaimed by the new formalists and expansivists, a whole new set of intellectual, imaginative, and social responsibilities open up for the poet. Or perhaps it would be more accurate to say that the old responsibilities will come back in a new form. Essentially, the poets of the coming era must be shamans. A shaman is not just a private person voicing his or her personal angsts or expressing purely personal esthetic, philosophical, or political opinions. A shaman speaks to, and for, a whole culture, as the unifying mouthpiece of its own deepest collective musings, and as its representative when it consults its own dead sages and sibyls. Moreover it is part of the duty of the shaman to be to some extent public, even popular, to sell his or her visions in the marketplace, to hear and respond to the needs and yearnings of the patrons whose conscience they are.

The new shaman must also learn the dialects of the tribe—and that tribe is now global, the human race itself. The most important dialects are the ones that are shared among all peoples, and are taken as legitimate media of exchange and criteria of agreement—trade, law, technology, and above all, science. Science is the way we learn the languages of all of the rest of nature, beyond our human circle, and thus is even more important for a new poet to know than trade and law. Technology connects science with the others—the special technologies of the poet are meter, storytelling, and imagery (which I have not dealt with here because it is so well handled elsewhere).

Once we adopt the responsibilities of the shaman, many wonderful things that as poets we find increasingly difficult to achieve will suddenly become easy. One of them is finding a subject: we are engaged in the work of educating and healing our fellow-citizens, and we need only speak of what they need to know and hear. Another is being funny. The moment we recognize ourselves as the peculiar kind of primate mammalian animal that we are, trapped and incarnate in the material slapstick of physical existence, forced in the theater of human miscommunication to give and receive gifts from others in order to survive at all, laughter is hard to avoid. Shakespeare, perhaps the greatest shaman of all time, who fulfills all the difficult criteria I have tendentiously laid out here, knew all this very well. Another suddenly available resource will be vision. Instead of having to strain our humdrum daily perceptions for some little plankton-like smear of insight, we will have almost the opposite problem: how to make the miracle of existence, with its humming and ringing levels of concentric complexity, local enough to convey in an image or anecdote. Finally, the true shamans will find that rarest of all contemporary resources: a real audience, a public not drawn to the poet in hopes of recognition for its own poetic efforts, nor attracted by the fading glamor of another era's poetic achievements, nor hoping to share a fellowship of social and cultural failure; but coming together in the deeply pleasurable, ancient, ad hoc ritual of world-construction.

An Idea of Order

Christian Wiman

An anecdote, first of all. A few years ago I had an argument in a series of letters with a friend. The argument was instigated by a poem that I had sent her, which she thought was emotionally compelling but formally anachronistic. She meant her response to be strong praise with a slight caveat. I understood it as slight praise with a monumental objection. Our subsequent exchange centered on the meaning of form in a poem, and whether or not a poem whose form felt, as she put it, as if it could have been written 80 years ago could have any primary relevance for its own time. I argued that it could not. Even factoring in my obstinacy and fragile ego, I still believe I was right; not with regard to my own poem, perhaps, to which I was as blindly attached as most poets are to things they have just made, but rather in the general argument that ensued. I still feel that the form of a poem, no matter how "traditional," must make its claim as a living thing, its expressive capacity somehow adequate to contemporary experience. To say that a poem is formally anachronistic is, for me, to say that it's not much more than a curiosity.

I don't think my friend's beliefs are at all anomalous. Many poets and critics now almost automatically distrust any work which exhibits formal coherence, stylistic finish, and closure. Occasionally they simply dismiss such work as naive or reactionary. At other times, and probably more damagingly, they either subtly devalue or patronize the work in question, praising the craftsmanship of the poems in such terms as make it clear that this is not "important" poetry. The hardcore version of this argument goes something like this. Because our experience of the world is chaotic and fragmented, and because we've lost our faith not only in those abstractions by means of which men and women of the past ordered their lives, but in language itself, it would be naive to think that we could have such order in our art. A poet who persists in imposing order upon our uncertainty is either unconscious, ironic, or decadent. Even among many readers and writers who wouldn't altogether accept the premises of this argument, and who are often completely open to traditional forms, there is still a widespread tendency to distrust any form that seems too intact, to assume that it somehow distorts or evades the mental climate we inhabit. The range of such work is limited from the outset. It cannot speak to us with the immediacy or intensity of an art whose refusal of finish and closure more obviously accords with our experience of contemporary life.

There are a couple of different assumptions underlying such a conclusion. The first is that in order to be truly important the form of a work of art must somehow express something of the times in which it is created. With this I agree. It's why my response to my friend was so vehement. The second assumption, though, is that the form of a work of art expresses reality by imitating it. Our experience is fragmented and partial, therefore the forms with which we apprehend that experience must be similarly fragmented and partial. Yvor Winters termed this the "fallacy of imitative form," but Winters's alternative was genuinely reactionary. He thought of a good poem as one in which uncertainty had been forcibly eradicated. What I am interested in, and what I want to focus on here, is a kind of closure that compromises itself, a poetry whose order is contested, even undermined by its consciousness of the disorder which it at once repels and recognizes. I believe that there is no necessary contradiction between some of the ambitions and anxieties informing the work of a poet like John Ashbery — "The forms retain a strong measure of ideal beauty / As they forage in secret on our idea of distortion" — and the best work of some poets who work in what are called "closed forms" and whose poems exhibit no conspicuous stylistic opacity. I would even go one step farther: I believe that it's sometimes precisely in those works which exhibit the greatest degree of formal coherence, the greatest sense of closure, that a reader may experience, and thereby more likely endure, the most intense anxiety and uncertainty.

Because most of our ideas about formal instability and fragmentation derive from the Modernists, probably the best place to begin is with a reluctant one like Frost. Frost was in much of his work simply a dull period poet, sighing into formal and intellectual conventions as into warm bathwater. In his best work, though, he was as attuned to his own time as Pound or Eliot. There is a shift of cultural consciousness between two superficially similar poems such as Thomas Hardy's "The Darkling Thrush" and Frost's "The Most of It." It isn't that the former presents the natural world as a source of possible consolation for the speaker, attributing some "blessed Hope" to the bird's song at the end of the poem, whereas the latter is more obviously ambivalent about this. Both poems seem to me at their cores equally skeptical. The difference has more to do with the arrangement of the world with regard to the respective speakers. In "The Darkling Thrush," the entire natural world is made made into a metaphor for human life:

> The land's sharp features seemed to be
> The Century's corpse outleant,
> His crypt the cloudy canopy,
> The wind his death-lament.
> The ancient pulse of germ and birth
> Was shrunken hard and dry,
> And every spirit upon earth
> Seemed fervourless as I.

Much of Frost's work arises out of the same assumptions and employs the same technique, of course, but not "The Most of It." Hardy has fallen away from those poets who saw in the world the workings of God, but he can still see in the world the workings of his own mind, is still comfortable with a metaphor that links the two. Frost has fallen somewhat farther. He can't quite see the world in relation to himself, can't avoid his suspicion that the world and the terms with which he apprehends it have nothing to do with each other. In "The Most of It," the edge of uncertainty is the edge of the mind:

> He thought he kept the universe alone
> For all the voice in answer he could wake
> Was but the mocking echo of his own
> From some tree-hidden cliff across the lake.
> Some morning from the boulder-broken beach
> He would cry out on life, that what it wants
> Is not its own love back in copy speech,
> But counter-love, original response.
> And nothing ever came of what he cried
> Unless it was the embodiment that crashed
> In the cliff's talus on the other side,
> And then in the far distant water splashed,
> But after a time allowed for it to swim,
> Instead of proving human when it neared
> And someone else additional to him,
> As a great buck it powerfully appeared,
> Pushing the crumpled water up ahead,
> And landed pouring like a waterfall,
> And stumbled through the rocks with horny tread,
> And forced the underbrush — and that was all.

Something has been severed here, some sense of connectedness with the world and life, of the universe as a place that can be described or understood or — as with Hardy — at least suffered in human terms. The feeling isn't by any means forgotten, but it exists as a limb exists for a man who no longer has it, some phantom tingling telling him what is gone. There's something subtler than a simple disjunction between form and subject matter going on in this poem. That is one way to enliven traditional forms, sometimes a very powerful one, as Thom Gunn's *The Man With Night Sweats* attests. I also mean to distinguish the effect of Frost's poem from the poetry of such deliberately clenched and defensive poets such as Winters or J. V. Cunningham. Both of these poets were acutely conscious of the chaos outside of the mind, but this anxiety expresses itself in their forms only as an exclusion. Some poets survive as turtles survive, by pulling their extremities in.

Frost was more ambitious, and consequently more vulnerable. Look at Frost's poem one way and it seems to be saying that the world did respond to the self, if in an ambiguous form. Within that word unless is a whole world of hope and possibility. Change the angle slightly, though, and the poem is saying exactly the opposite. Nothing ever came of what he cried but this buck, which, in human terms, is nothing. The concluding phrase — "and that was all" — contains a similar sort of apparently mutually exclusive meanings. The poem is at once an assertion of connection with the world and a recognition of existential isolation. It straddles these two possibilities, and it does so formally. The rhymes reiterate the voice that is the mocking echo of the poet's own. Each seems to answer a cry that comes before it, but it does so with such unvarying regularity that it suggests itself as merely an echo. The effect would be quite different if even one of the rhymes were off. Stylistic roughness or overt formal distortion would have the paradoxical effect of *diminishing* the uncertainty and anxiety in this poem. It would seem like life had definitively answered. In a very real sense, the tension between the closure of "The Most of It" and the uneasy feeling which that closure creates is an example of, to use a word that is often used to justify merely incoherent art, dissonance.

"The Most of It" is one of Frost's momentary stays against confusion. It aims in art at a calm and coherence that its writer lacked in life, and it's interesting to consider the poem in light of an essay that Auden once wrote on Tennyson. In the essay Auden criticizes poets who attempt to use poetry to fulfill needs which can only be properly fulfilled outside of poetry — through direct action, religious belief, personal relationships, or some other area of "life." The point is well-taken. Poets who confuse art and life often make a mess of both. But there are dangers as well for poets who accept too readily Auden's clean distinction between art and life. They may become esoteric. They may become emotionally and technically glib. They may become Auden.

Most artists make art precisely because they feel some sort of absence or incoherence in their lives. It seems not simply inevitable but necessary that the art they produce in some way seek to contain or heal whatever is missing or wounded or wrongful in them. For those poets whose confusion in life inclines them to closure in art, the key to avoiding Auden's criticism and example lies, I think, in the kind of self-contested quality that I find in "The Most of It." This is obvious enough when the surface of the poem is disrupted, so that there is a pronounced disjunction between the sense of closure and the effort it took to get there, or between the finish of art and the roughness of life: early Lowell, Bunting, Hart Crane, Hopkins. It is less easily perceived when the surface of the poem is completely clear. "The Most of It," for a moment at least, seems to be the order in which it can't quite believe. Its closed world of metrical regularity, of rhymes that confuse answers and echoes, is a kind of refuge from the flux and profusion of a world for which it can't keep itself from reaching. Both its aspiration and its doubt are part of its form, as are its effects of seeming at once compensatory and comfortless.

Among those poets inclined to closure and finish, perhaps this distinction may be drawn. There are those who seek to replace whatever they have lost in their lives, and there are those who seek in their art a form within their loss may be felt. The former will either be a clenched, occasional poet like Winters and Cunningham, or the sort of poet of whom it is said, "He lives for his art." He may be great, as Rilke was great, but there will be about the work a palpable sense of separation and enclosure, something of what the art critic Edgar Wind called "an emotionally untainted sense of form." The latter kind of poets — and the poets I'm talking about in this essay are the latter kind — will usually have some sort of deep ambivalence about the value and efficacy of poetry itself, and this ambivalence will make itself felt formally. They are also enclosed in a kind of cell, but from beyond the wall on which they practice their half-learned language of taps and scratches there sometimes comes something like an answer, something that, in their better moments, they can almost believe is an "original response." The wall is poetry. Life is on the other side. The wall is what separates the poet from life, but it is also the means by which life is apprehended and understood.

The figure is Simone Weil's. The tenor of her metaphor is grander — "It is thus with us and God. Every separation is a link. — but the idea of isolation and communication as coextensive is the same. Weil found a language for a kind of belief that had outlived or otherwise lost its object, and in my attempts to explain to myself why I experience a certain kind of closure and formal coherence in poetry as both fulfillment and deprivation, presence and absence, she is one of two or three prose writers who have been very important to me. Another is Proust, whose *Remembrance of Things Past* is a monumental effort at formalizing loss, at making a place in language wherein the past can be lost instead of simply forgotten and unfelt. My deepest sense of this book, though much of it is comical and ironic, is of abiding sadness. Its source is less in the specific characters and events themselves than in Proust's constant consciousness of his own failure, his inability to fully recreate and retain whatever it was that made his losses "life": "But to release that fount of sorrow," he writes in *Within a Budding Grove,* "that sense of the irreparable, those agonies which prepare the way for love, there must be — and this is, perhaps, more than any other person can be, the actual object which our passion seeks so anxiously to embrace — the risk of an impossibility."

I'm trying to describe a similar effect in form, one arising from a belief or need that has outlived or lost its object, a formal coherence whose reach exceeds its grasp:

> The garden of the world, which no one sees,
> Never had walls, is fugitive with lives;
> Its shapes escape our simplest symmetries;
> There is no resting where it rots and thrives.

That's the last stanza of Richard Wilbur's "Caserta Garden," a poem which, in this last stanza at any rate, expresses more compellingly the inadequacy of language, indeed of all human ordering, than anything that I have read by the Language poets. The poem is itself one of the "simplest symmetries" which the world escapes. It wants to be the rest or "stay" which it admits does not exist beyond its own borders, but by such an admission it makes those borders at least partially permeable. Its strength inheres in the balance it maintains between a consciousness of its limitations and the assertion of formal order it makes in the face of them. Like "The Most of It,"

"Caserta Garden" has the poignancy of impossibility about it.

One might compare these two poems, and particularly "The Most of It," with a contemporary poem which has a similar theme but more relaxed form. I take A. R. Ammons's poem "Gravelly Run," in which Ammons seeks to know the self "as it is known / by galaxy and cedar cone," to be in a direct line that runs from Hardy and Frost. Ammons's poem, though, ends much less ambiguously than "The Most of It":

> no use to make any philosophies here:
> I see no
> god in the holly, hear no song from
> the snowbroken weeds: Hegel is not the winter
> yellow in the pines: the sunlight has never
> heard of trees: surrendered self among
> unwelcoming forms: stranger,
> hoist your burdens, get on down the road

"Gravelly Run" is a poem that is certain about the mind's inability to be certain of anything beyond its own borders. It gestures toward the order from which Frost's poem has fallen away, but the nerves are number now, both the expectations and anxieties diminished. This difference expresses itself formally. Although Ammons's poem is clearly "formal" in its way, cohesive in its sounds and shape, it does not have the kind of symmetrical urgency of "The Most of It" or "Caserta Garden." There is no sense of impossibility about it, of some abstract order articulating itself with a kind of beautiful futility in spite of what the poet knows, or doesn't know. I don't mean for this distinction to be necessarily a qualitative one; "Gravelly Run" is a very good poem. The point I want to make is that there are effects available to traditionally formal poems which aren't available to other forms, and that one of these effects has to do with an intensification of the uncertainty and even open-endedness that we normally associate with looser forms. "To crave and to have are as like as a thing and its shadow," Marilynne Robinson has written, "… and when do our senses know any thing so utterly as when we lack it?" Both "The Most of It" and "Caserta Garden" shadow an order which they suggest does not exist. Their forms make us feel physically this lack, at once easing and intensifying our perception of the disorder that is the reason for this lack. The disorder of "Gravelly Run," by contrast, is an idea.

The poems that I have discussed so far are not really "contemporary." "The Most of It" was first published in 1946, "Caserta Garden" in 1947.

Ammons's poem is more recent, and it raises the question of whether faith in the mind's ability to find meaning in the world hasn't eroded to such an extent that the comparison is unfair or irrelevant. I want to look now at a couple of contemporary sonnets which I believe accomplish similar effects to the Frost and Wilbur poems, while being very much of their own times. I want to reiterate that the effect that I am describing has to do with getting something of contemporary consciousness into the form, which may have nothing to do with the details of contemporary life — quatrains crammed with brand-names, colloquialisms, and such. I'm after something more subtle, powerful, and, I think, more lasting.

Here is Marilyn Nelson's "Balance":

> He watch her like a coonhound watch a tree.
> What might explain the metamorphosis
> he underwent when she paraded by
> with tea-cakes, in her fresh and shabby dress?
> (As one would carry water from a well —
> straight-backed, high-headed, like a diadem,
> with careful grace so that no drop will spill —
> she balanced, almost brimming, her one name.)
>
> She think she something, stuck-up island bitch.
> Chopping wood, hanging laundry on the line,
> and tantalizingly within his reach,
> she honed his body's yearning to a keen,
> sharp point. And on that point she balanced life.
> That hoe Diverne think she Marse Tyler's wife.

This poem draws a thematic line — between aesthetic beauty as a source of power and beauty as power's object — which it walks in form. The sensuous descriptions of Diverne elicit our admiration for her even as they "hone" our sense of the historical context in which they occur. This is no ordinary courtship. Marse Tyler can rape Diverne if he chooses. The form of the poem elicits a similar sort of troubled admiration. I have said that "The Most of It" and "Caserta Garden" draw their strength from their consciousness of their own limitations as forms. Although "Balance" isn't as directly self-referential as either of those poems, I think its techniques — the italicized speech of the other slaves rendered in perfect iambic pentameter, those lines juxtaposed with the language of the educated poet ("metamorphosis," "diadem") — make it impossible to ignore the context in which it was written: a contemporary African-American woman employing a form that is the product of a culture which has traditionally excluded and exploited African-Americans. (The form itself has no inherent political meaning, but that doesn't mean that a poet's treatment of the form can't give it a political meaning. And when a poet inhabits a form as uneasily as Nelson does in "Balance," calling deliberate attention to this uneasiness, I don't see how this dimension of the poem can be avoided.) It's simplistic to say that Nelson is "subverting" the form, as it is to say that she is submitting to it. The poem contains both possibilities. The stakes aren't as immediately high for Nelson as they are for Diverne (though anyone who has found that her confusion in life finds both expression and alleviation in form knows that the stakes are indeed high), but the line between power and powerlessness, control and chaos is being walked by both of them. I take the slant rhymes of the first twelve lines to be a kind of conscious wobbling. The final full rhyme — coming after the explicit, coarse sexual reference in the last line and the revelation of the fact that this is a white man watching a slave (without the "Marse Tyler," this would be unclear) — is a very qualified sort of control. The form is both finished and painfully insufficient, locked but volatile.

"Balance," then, is a good example of what I mean by a kind of closure that compromises itself. There is a discrepancy between the finality with which the poem concludes and the possibility of disorder which it contains. The disorder that threatens the formal order of "Balance" is more cultural and political than epistemological (though it is inevitably this as well), but the discrepancy between the two is roughly analogous to the distance between the echoes and original response of "The Most of It," or between the formal self-containment of "Caserta Garden" and the formless world that is its subject. I have come to think of this discrepancy as a kind of space within the form itself, some core of air that isn't order and isn't disorder, some absolute emptiness which the form can neither eradicate nor fill. Engineers know that some structures are sturdier if some give is built into them, that sometimes a frame that's hollow rather than solid will bear a greater strain. Perhaps a similar principle applies to the forms of some poems.

In the last sonnet of Seamus Heaney's elegiac sequence to his mother, "Clearances" (and, in a more unequivocally positive sense, in his essay on Larkin), something like this space becomes the poem's subject:

> I thought of walking round and round a space
> Utterly empty, utterly a source
> Where the decked chestnut tree had lost its place

In our front hedge above the wallflowers.
The white chips jumped and jumped and skited high.
I heard the hatchet's differentiated
Accurate cut, the crack, the sigh
And collapse of what luxuriated
Through the shocked tips and wreckage of it all.
Deep planted and long gone, my coeval
Chestnut from a jam jar in a hole,
Its heft and hush become a bright nowhere,
A soul ramifying and forever
Silent, beyond silence listened for.

Christopher Middleton has written that most poetry, even great poetry, tends to perpetuate clichés, and we might reduce the cliché behind this poem to something like this: "She's gone but will live forever in my heart." There's something more complicated going on in the poem, I think, something having to do with the form and its relation to that final line. To listen for a silence requires contrast. A silence that is "listened for," then, is everything outside of sound. It is what surrounds the words we use, the poems we write. A silence that is "beyond silence listened for," it follows, must be a silence that is imperceptible. It is either the complete absence of sound, or it is some stillness inside of sound itself, some final silence haunting all our words, all our poems, something not dissimilar from the silence that Wittgenstein was referring to (or trying to refer to) when he said, "Whereof one cannot speak, thereof one must be silent." Heaney's poem tries to speak of this annihilating silence, tries to make it *mean*. That in some ultimate sense he fails is part of that meaning.

To understand what the form of Heaney's poem has to do with this meaning, a comparison with another contemporary poem might help. In Robert Hass's well-known "Meditation at Lagunitas," the speaker addresses the problem of language's referentiality and "truth" directly, wondering if, since the word "blackberry" has no definitive denotative capacity, "a word is elegy to what it signifies." Recognizing the corrosive effect of this premise upon language and, if one believes that language is the only means by which we secure our experience, upon life, the speaker eventually offers up with equal parts helplessness and tenderness the details of a remembered relationship:

Longing, we say, because desire is full
of endless distances. I must have been the same to her.
But I remember so much, the way her hands dismantled bread,
the thing her father said that hurt her, what

she dreamed. There are moments when the body is as
numinous
as words, days that are the good flesh continuing.
Such tenderness, those afternoons and evenings,
saying blackberry, blackberry, blackberry.

Like Heaney's sonnet, and like the other poems that I have mentioned,
"Meditation at Lagunitas" is conscious of its own inherent limitations as a
piece of language yet persists in trying to make meaning in the face of them.
Unlike those other poems, though, which counter their consciousness of
disorder with an urge toward some ideal order in their forms, the tension
between order and disorder in Hass's poem is merely a matter of competing
assertions. It's like Ammons's poem in this respect, except that Ammons
recognizes the world's unknowability and says in effect: "Get over it." Hass,
like Heaney, can't quite get over it, but he has nothing to counter his doubt
but the fact of his own deep feeling, nothing to offer up against the inad-
equacy of language but a piece of pretty writing. There is consequently a
softness at the center of the poem. Heaney's poem contains the same sort of
competing literal assertions ("Utterly empty, utterly a source"), but there is
an austerity about it, some deeper meaning, and deeper emptiness, in its
form. Though it is more rough-hewn than the other poems that I have looked
at, it nevertheless aims at the abstract order of a sonnet, making itself into a
space analogous to the one that is the poem's subject. The poem admits that
there is nothing to hold, and holds it. "Grace fills empty spaces," writes
Simone Weil, "but it can only enter where there is a void to receive it."

Whatever one thinks about the religious implications of that sentence,
there is a kind of faith which a poet had better not lose. It is a faith in the
mind's ability to find meaning in a world that exists independently of itself,
and a concomitant faith in language to serve as a means of doing so. In the
absence of this, poetry can only be at best a diversion within life; at worst it
is a complete evasion of it. Yet even for those poets who manage to retain
such faith, who in their better moments believe in the value of poetry and in
its capacity to formalize some fragment of living reality, the prospect of
spending a life trying to articulate sweet sounds together ought to be fraught
with doubt and uncertainty, some unshakable sense that, in the face of real
suffering and chaos, poetry may be irrelevant. It is this tension that keeps
talent alive.

It is also this tension that keeps forms alive. The least satisfying forms
are those that are the most satisfied with themselves. Edward O. Wilson

has written that there are always two kinds of original thinkers, "those who upon viewing disorder try to create order, and those who upon encountering order try to create disorder." Those who merely imitate the order they see around them are ornamentalists. There are pleasures to be had from such work, but they are the pleasures of amenities. At the same time, formal distortion is interesting and meaningful only when it occurs in a poet for whom formal coherence seems a real possibility. (This is what distinguishes Ashbery from his imitators. It is also what distinguishes Ashbery from Ashbery.) It requires no great talent to imitate chaos, or to illustrate the inability of the mind and language to make meaning. Those who do so, as Wallace Stevens suggested, are simply exacerbating our confusion:

> This structure of ideas, these ghostly sequences
> Of the mind, result only in disaster. It follows,
> Casual poet, that to add your own disorder to disaster
>
> Makes more of it.

I have not intended this to be an argument in favor of a "return to traditional forms." Much of the self-satisfied metrical poetry that I read makes me nostalgic for Dadaism. I have focused on these forms for the sake of clarity and economy, and because they seem to provoke the strongest animus. I do feel that, whether one writes in traditional forms or free verse, it's probably time to get beyond this automatic resistance to finish and closure in poetry, that the idea of form as somehow more authentic if rough and unfinished has itself become something of a convention. If one's experience of life is truly confusing and chaotic, and if one's feeling for the inadequacy of language is something more than an academic idea, perhaps the proper response is either silence or coherence. Not the kind of coherence that eliminates uncertainty, not the kind of closure that congratulates itself, but something sharper, some only momentary peace which, because it comes with a consciousness of its loss, is also pain.

My friend thought that to write in traditional forms was to cleave to a vanished past, to insulate oneself and one's work against one's own time. I have tried to make a case for them as bearers of contemporary consciousness, though I do admit that one can't use these forms without referring to the past. So long as it isn't merely a sentimental attachment to the antique, I think of this reference as a strength. I also think that there is a sense in which to work toward some ideal order is to claim a connectedness with the future as well as the past, that a poem may foreshadow formally a time in which one's world and mind will — and I'm paraphrasing Marilynne Robinson here — be made whole. To reach for is not to grasp. Simone Weil writes that "we must believe in a God who is like the true God in everything, except that He does not exist, since we have not reached the point where God exists." I think perhaps the poems that I've been talking about in this essay were written by poets who believed in an absolute formal coherence in every way except that it did not exist. To experience such forms is to experience both consolation and provocation. It is to come into a place of language that is easeful and unchanging and will not let you forget the fact that it is not a place. It is to be given an image of life that you have lost or long dreamed of, to hear as sound something of the farthest sorrows that you are, and to know in that moment that what you've been given is not enough.

The Trouble With a Word Like Formalism

Anne Stevenson

It is no secret that literature since the mid-century has been overshadowed by isms. One hardly needs to list them. At the heels of modernism nipped "the new criticism," which in the 1960s ceded ground, *pace* anthropology, to the sign-theory of structuralism. Hardly had we got used to structuralism, when Barthes, Derrida & Co. began to tease us with deconstruction. And now, in the 1990s? In England, you can't so much as glance at a serious literary or intellectual journal without being overcome by a cloud of jargon. The pollution emanates chiefly from a clutter of posts: "post-modernism," "post-structuralism," "post-colonialism," "post-Freudianism," " post-Marxism," "post-Lacanian feminism." One has a sense of living through a post-literary decline; call it interminalism. This essay argues that isms, not to mention post-isms, are creations of academics, not writers. If we seek to dispel the smoke and rescue poetry from ideology, it would be folly to cover ourselves defensively with academic fug. To me, a phrase like "the new formalism" feels like fug.

To be fair we have to acknowledge that abstract thinking (as distinct from over-theorizing) has long been vital to literature. If it were simply the job of writers to write and of critics to enlighten the public about the nature of writing, few problems would arise. But of course no such simple dichotomy exists. Not many academic critics today dare expose themselves by writing poems, yet their debate about the nature of language has importantly affected contemporary practice. As for the other side, since the time of Aristotle poets have felt compelled to offer the world apologias. For us in England, Coleridge's criticism has been as influential as his verse. Matthew Arnold's perceptions regarding literature and culture are to some extent still relevant. No one presents a better example of a modern critic-poet than T.S. Eliot, whose essays may be regarded as rational explorations undertaken as relief from the excruciating psychological pressures of making poetry: "the intolerable wrestle with words and meanings."

Formalists may complain that Eliot and the modernists were the source of the trouble, that they are still to blame for the way "difficult" poetry puts people off. Again, anyone who has experienced that "intolerable wrestle" must find such a view facile. Poetry really is more difficult to write than it was when civilization was younger and artists were less self-conscious. The modernist defense still holds: by the turn of the last century it did become obvious to the more sensitive that advanced technology—in industry, in communication, in warfare—was about to tear apart the presuppositions of Western society. Changes in traditional forms of living were bound to challenge traditional forms of art. Today, when we look back to the writers who gave radical definition to their feelings after the First World War, it is easy enough to lump them into a category: "the modernists". In actuality, what looks to have been a stylistic revolution represented an extraordinary congruity of response. Everybody was challenged. The most original reacted most vigorously, by "making it new"—and poets naturally "made it new" with language.

Stylistic innovation, then, was a way of showing that new realities demanded new forms. But not only style distinguishes those poets we call "modernists" from "traditionalists" such as Frost and Graves. Both the latter—fine, energetic writers as they were—can be said to have cultivated a dying garden. Frost preserved his growly Yankee voice by holing up north of Boston and writing almost exclusively of (old) rural, not (new) urban experience. Graves disappeared into his own version of Greek mythology. The modernists (Pound, Eliot, Joyce, Stevens) on the other hand, broke with tradition (a better metaphor might be pruned it back to its roots) in order to renew it.

Three-quarters of a century later, it is as important for us to reassess that poetry of innovation as it was for Pound and Eliot to attack the pastorals of the Georgians. Yet it is incumbent upon us, too, not to oversimplify what modernism meant—not, that is, to treat the modernists (or the Georgians, or the Romantics either) in blocks as "a good thing" or "a bad thing" as if they were items in a literary *1066 And All That*. We would do better instead to examine our own attitudes towards particular poems: to ask ourselves, for example, why *some* of *The Cantos* satisfy us while others do not; or why reading the poems of Wallace Stevens with a fresh eye for their strengths and weaknesses is worth any amount of poring over heaps of Stevens-criticism. What I am advocating, in short, is an approach to poetry that resembles the creative process itself. Why not read it as we would write it—aloud for the feeling of speech-sounds and the subtleties of rhythm? Let's freely admit to liking or disliking actual poems without labelling them first. Let's approach poetry boldly, at first hand, without recourse to specialist introductions that suggest, in many cases, that a poet's *name* summarizes some inflexible position in a hierarchy of "importance."

If readers of poetry (a group which must include everyone who hopes to write it) could free their minds of the stereotyped universals so dear to theorizers, they would be in a better position to understand how the form of a successful poem embodies its meaning. In a good poem, as everybody knows, form is inseparable from sense and tone. No poem worthy of the name can be formless, whether it is written according to metrical rules or in free verse. The sounds, rhythms, pitch and intensity of the lines ARE the poem. Every poem IS its form. A bad or failed poem is one whose form has either been too much imposed upon it, or neglected through ignorance and lack of an ear—or perhaps because the poet just didn't bring it off. (Shakespeare himself wrote some pretty indifferent verse.)

The trouble with a word like "formalism" is that it seems to impose restrictions on the making of poetry without taking into consideration the conditions a poem sets for itself. As Douglas Dunn commented recently, "There are other ways of making well than those of versification, and, at times, I've suspected that too heavy an emphasis on the technical side of poetry reduces it to the level of car maintenance or flower arranging." Significantly, Dunn goes on, "But what versification offers the writer and reader is a constant re-engagement with the artistry of the past. Conducting that creative investigation in the present could—or so I'd like to believe—help to articulate contemporary life without too much of the dishonour of bad craftsmanship." (1)

Dunn's untrammelled attitude of mind towards "the artistry of the past" keeps the door open to the present. It is perhaps only possible to begin afresh by keeping poetry's roots alive while encouraging it to put forth new variations. By now, though, those roots are so deep and so hideously built over that many are forgotten. The English "intellectual" tradition that modernism is accused of foisting on us (let's avoid that overused and meaningless term "canon") extends back to Greek metrics and Latin hexameters on one hand and to Anglo-Saxon kennings on the other. It embraces the medieval poets (those who wrote in Latin, and those who wrote middle English); then Chaucer; then the Elizabethans and the metaphysicals. No one with an ear for speech rhythms would underestimate, either, the pervasive influence of the King James Bible. I myself would add an unfashionable plug for Milton. So by the time we arrive at the formal metrics of the eighteenth/nineteenth centuries, we are looking back over a long, nourishing heritage of variant patterns—and that before we even approach the Americans and the influence that, after Whitman, American English has wielded everywhere in the world.

Any valid ideology behind formalism, one must suppose, would encompass all such patterns as models. Yet the term is pretty well doomed to misinterpretation in our present world, in which historical imagination and sensibility play so small a part. Uninformed people of a politically correct persuasion are bound to associate a term like formalism with political conservatism—as, in another context, Douglas Dunn sharply points out (2).

More importantly, many well-meaning contemporaries use the term "formalism" as if it meant merely writing in rhyme and meter—merely learning to scan, or count syllables and stresses so as to qualify as a producer of sonnets, couplets, narrative epics and so on. Alas, most beginners who try out "form" in poetry achieve only exercises in verse—and probably not very good verse at that. They would almost certainly write better poetry if they followed their instincts in free verse, if free verse is what they were brought up hearing. It's not so much that poetic technique or craft cannot be taught (for indeed it can and should be) as that the process of absorbing and assimilating the feel of poetry is so psychologically complex. It takes a long time—half a lifetime maybe—to *overhear* those hardly definable facets of a language that give it a distinctive music. Writing poetry is inseparable from a poet's unconscious "at homeness" with the sounds, inflections, pitches and textures of a language. The pulse of its rhythms, the different weights and lengths of its vowels— these have to accumulate in a poet's consciousness without his knowing how. Hence, the mysterious instinctual element that tradition associates with the muse. Inspiration truly does make poetry possible. And that is why, as many poets have testified, "creative writing" cannot be taught, and why a real poem almost always feels like a donée when it arrives.

Yet despite the temptations of metaphor, there is really nothing organic about poetry. Keats never said that poetry was a tree; he said that "unless poetry *comes to the poet as easily as leaves to the tree* it had better not come at all." [My italics.] The emphasis is all on the poet's unconscious mind, which *like* a tree roots itself in common verbal experience and yet creates, in poetry, memorable patterns of language. Keats listened to the rhythms of "past art-istry" in Shakespeare and Spenser; the leaves he put forth derived from his passional instinct for knowing what music to overhear and what words to write down. Such a practice requires a different order of self-discipline from mechanically counting syllables or stresses in a line, or learning to tell the difference between iambic and anapestic feet.

Robert Wells, a contemporary English poet who is acutely conscious of form, suggests that, for him, writing poetry is the result of a personal need to get something clear. What lures him on, he says, "is the promise of form which allows that to happen." Clarification means finding a form of language that will tell him what he feels. Earlier in the same essay, he writes:

> It may be possible to look at the result [of a poem] and detect a set of principles at work, but in the actual writing I'm simply out to please myself. Within the form I've chosen I work entirely by ear, and choosing the form too is largely a matter for the ear, of hearing the potential for shape within a body of material which may itself be only vaguely apprehended, so that I have the form of a poem sometimes before I discover the content.

And he goes on,

> The terminology of meter provides a useful way of describing poems once they are written, but I seldom feel the need for it when writing. I will count syllables and listen for pauses, but I've never asked myself in so many words whether an iamb or trochee is required in such-and-such a place, or where the caesura should occur in a particluar line. The work of getting the poem right is done by the ear, or rather by the ear and voice together, as one hears oneself when one is speaking. Of course, the ear's instinct isn't an innocent one. Reading, observations and practice all play their part in it. (3)

Where, then, is your need for "formalism"? The case for form is won with every good poem that's written—and then sensitively read by readers who can judge for themselves whether it is worth re-reading. What should be taught are techniques of reading such as actors learn when they study Shakespeare, or that children used to be taught when they were encouraged to recite poems in grade school. If, as may happen, the culture of the past is wholly lost and our children grow up knowing nothing of literature but the popular entertainments they see on television, there will be no point at all in teaching them to write in archaic meters. The rules of English metrics were, in any case, derived from the long and short vowel-pattern of Greek and Latin verse; they have never perfectly adapted to the stress-patterns of English.

As long as poetry remains part of our culture (and there's an awful lot of poetry about these days), *some* poets will write by ear. In the past, poetry has been primarily sound (4). Today a lot is published (pretty much of it mediocre) that relies purely on imagery, or in periodicals like the TLS, on fairly obscure insider references and allusions. Meanwhile, other new poetries—from the Caribbean, for example, and from Africa and Australia—are introducing new rhythms into English, and thus extending its potential for energy. The "English" poetry of the future is bound to take on and mix influxes from even more cultures. What a mistake it would be— how impossible it already is —to attempt to channel the flood within the narrow banks of "traditional form," in the most limited, archaic sense of that formula.

The best poetry of the past will last anyway; and it will last longer if it is not forced to retreat and inbreed (to change the metaphor) but instead is encouraged to take its chances in a changing world and survive by adaptation. I am writing this essay early in the spring of 1994. The weather is hostile, freezing cold with snow showers battering the daffodils— those English daffodils that over the centuries have been celebrated by Shakespeare, Herrick, Wordsworth, Masefield. This morning I came to life with some lines in my head:

> Daffodils...that come before the swallow dares
> And take the winds of March with beauty....

Once I was fully awake, I recognized them: *The Winter's Tale*. But where exactly? I rose and found the play. The passage occurs in Act IV, scene iv, which takes place, you may recall, in a very English Bohemia where Florizel and Perdita are improbably brought together in a shepherd's cottage. Perdita coyly wishes that the flowers of the mid-summer harvest were more suitable for virgin shepherdesses. On the page, the famous passage looks like this:

> O Proserpina,
> For the flow'rs now, that, frighted, thou let's fall
> From Dis's wagon! Daffodils,
> That come before the swallow dares, and take
> The winds of March with beauty; violets, dim,
> But sweeter than the lids of Juno's eyes,
> Or Cythera's breath; pale primroses
> That die unmarried ere they can behold
> Bright Phoebus in his strength....

The classical references, the conceits, the flowery rhetoric sound arcane; no one could write like this today and get away with it. And yet a few lines stick so fast in the mind that one forgets they belong to their period and are written in iambic pentameter. But are they iambic pentameter? The line in which "daffodils" appears is foreshortened—only eight syllables, with four stresses. The next line fills out the pentameter, but with "and take" and the short pause that precedes it, it runs over into the following one: four stresses ending with the falling sound of "beauty." To the ear, then, the lines look as I remembered them:

> ´ ˘ ˘   ´ ˘ ´ ˘ ´ ˘ ˘
> Daffodils, that come before the swallow dares,
> ˘ ´ ˘ ´ ˘ ´ ˘ ´ ˘
> And take the winds of march with beauty....

Iambic pentameter hardly accounts for the delicate parallel and lowering of vowel-pitch between "Daffodils" (then a pause) and "swallow dares" ("swallows dare" would ruin it); nor for the repeated a's and d's of the diction. To the ear, the first line sounds like Hopkins's sprung rhythm or an Englished *cynghanedd*; and although the second line is iambic, the feminine trailing off of "beauty," with its longer vowel after the short a and i of "take" and "wind," gives it emphasis, like a sigh.

It has taken me half a day to work out why I remember those Shakespearean lines that I have known "by heart" for years. Yet it doesn't matter "why"; the lines do not belong to "literature" but to my life—mine and many other people's, down, as they say, through the ages.

NOTES

1. "Public and private realms—a comment on his new collection from Douglas Dunn" in *The Poetry Book Society Bulletin* no. 159 (London: Winter 1993), p. 12.

2. Douglas Dunn, "Writing Things Down" in *The Poet's Voice and Craft*, Ed. C.B. McCully (Manchester: Carcanet), 1994, p. 100.

3. Robert Wells, "Distinctive Anonymity" in *Ibid.*, p. 168.

4. For a thorough exposition of this view, see Francis Berry, *Poetry and the Physical Voice* (London: OUP) 1962, esp. chapter I, "Problems and Hearing and Saying."

Contributors

Agha Shahid Ali is on the MFA poetry faculty of the University of Massachusetts, Amherst, and the author of seven collections of poetry, including *The Half-Inch Himalayas*, *A Nostalgist's Map of America* (Norton), and *The Country Without a Post Office* (Norton). He has received several fellowships including an Ingram Merrill grant and a Guggenheim. His translation of Faiz Ahmed Faiz, *The R;*

Amittai F. Aviram is associate professor of English and Comparative Literature at the University of South Carolina, where he teaches literary theory and poetics. His book *Telling Rhythm; Body and Meaning in Poetry* (Ann Arbor: University of Michigan Press, 1994) presents a theory of poetry within a Nietzschean tradition, and his poetry chapbook *Tender Phrases, Brassy Moans* (Charlotte: Sandstone Publishing, 1994) was finalist in a first chapbook competition. He is now at work on a new book on poetics, *Poetry Lessons*; two of his poems are forthcoming in *Paris Review*. More on recent work, including New Formalist Criticism, at his web address, http://www.cla.sc.edu/ENGL/faculty/avirama.

Allison M. Cummings is currently teaching at Hampden-Sydney College in Virginia. Previously she was Associate Director of The Center for Research on Women at Barnard College. She has presented conference papers and published articles on contemporary American women's poetry and on pedagogy, including an essay about recent lyric poetry by women in the volume, *New Definitions of Lyric: Theory, Technology, and Culture*. She has also published poetry and was formerly a poetry editor at *The Madison Review*.

James Cummins is curator of the Elliston Poetry Collection at the University of Cincinnati, where he also teaches literature and writing. His first book, *The Whole Truth*, was published by North Point Press in 1986; his second, *Portrait in a Spoon*, came out in 1997 from the University of South Carolina Press. His poems have appeared in three volumes of *Best American Poetry* (1994, 1995, and 1998), and he has received grants from the National Endowment for the Arts, the Ingram Merrill Foundation, and the Ohio Arts Council.

Frederick Feirstein has published seven books of poetry, the most recent of which is *New and Selected Poems* (Story Line Press, 1998). He has produced ten plays and has won such awards as the Guggenheim in poetry and the Rocheffer OADR in playwriting. He is a psychoanalyst in private practice in New York City and is also on the faculty of the National Psychological Association for Psychoanalysis, where he teaches symbolization and creativity.

Annie Finch's collection of poems, *Eve*, was published by Story Line Press in 1997. She is also the author of *The Ghost of Meter; Culture and Prosody in American Free Verse* (Michigan, 1993) and editor of *A Formal Feeling Comes: Poems in Form by Contemporary Women* (Story Line Press, 1994) and, with Kathrine Varnes, of *An Exaltation of Forms: Contemporary Poets Celebrate the Diversity of Their Art* (Michigan, 1999). She teaches at Miami University, Ohio.

Dana Gioia has published two books of poetry, *Daily Horoscope* (1986) and *The Gods of Winter (1991)*, as well as a critical collection, *Can Poetry Matter?: Essays on American Poetry and Culture* (1992). He co-edits (with X.J. Kennedy) a series of college anthologies, including *An Introduction to Poetry*. He is currently finishing a book on contemporary British Poetry, *The Barrier of a Common Language*, for University of Michigan Press.

Daniel Hoffman was the 1973-74 Poet Laureate of the United States, the appointment then designated Consultant in Poetry of The Library of Congress. The latest of his ten books of poetry is the verse novel, *Middens of the Tribe*.

Mark Jarman's latest collection of poetry, *Questions for Ecclesiastes*, won the Lenore Marshall Poetry Prize for 1998 and was a finalist for the 1997 National Book Critics Circle Award. He is co-editor of *Rebel Angels: 25 Poets of the New Formalism* and co-author of *The Reaper Essays*. His book of essays, *The Secret of Poetry*, is forthcoming from Story Line Press, as is his next collection of poetry, *Unholy Sonnets*. He teaches at Vanderbilt University.

Paul Lake's books include *Another Kind of Travel*, published in Chicago's Phoenix poetry series, and a novel, *Among the Immortals* (Story Line Press) as well as a new collection of poems, *Walking Backwards*, also from Story Line Press. He teaches at Arkansas Technical University.

David Mason's first book of poems, *The Buried Houses*, was co-winner of the 1991 Nicholas Roerich Prize. His second, *The Country I Remember*, includes a long poem that won the 1993 Alice Fay Di Castagnola Prize from the Poetry Society of America. He is co-editor, with Mark Jarman, of *Rebel Angels*, and co-editor, with John Frederick Nims, of the fourth edition of *Western Wind: An Introduction to Poetry*. His latest book is a collection of essays, *The Poetry of Life and the Life of Poetry* (Story Line Press, 1999).

Robert McPhillips teaches at Iona College. His essays and reviews have appeared in *Sewanee Review, Prairie Schooner, The Nation, Washington Post Book World,* and *The New York Post*. He is currently writing a book on the new formalism.

Carol E. Miller is visiting assistant professor of English at Benedictine University. Author of the poetry manuscript, "Woman's Head," she has published poems in *The Muse Strikes Back* (Story Line Press) as well as in *Partisan Review* and other journals. Her article, "Bishop and National Geographic: Questions of Travel and Imperialism", appears in *Worcester, Massachusetts: Essays from the 1997 Elizabeth Bishop Conference* (Peter Lang).

Marilyn Nelson (formerly Marilyn Nelson Waniek), twice a National Book Award finalist, is the author of five books of poems, *For the Body, Mama's Promises, The Homeplace, Magnificat* and, most recently, *The Fields of Praise: New and Selected Poems*, all from LSU Press. She is a professor of English at the University of Connecticut, Storrs.

Molly Peacock has published four books of poetry, most recently *Original Love* (Norton) and the memoir Paradise Piece by Piece (Norton)." She lives in New York and London, Ontario, and was president of the Poetry Society of America from 1989 to 1994.

Adrienne Rich's most recent books are *What is Found There: Notebooks on Poetry and Politics* (1993), *Dark Fields of the Republic: Poems 1991-1995*, and *Midnight Salvage: Poems 1995-1998*. Her numerous awards for poetry include the Lenore Marshall/*Nation* Award, a MacArthur Fellowship, and the Dorothea Tanning Prize.

Timothy Steele's collections of poems include *The Color Wheel* (Johns Hopkins, 1994) and *Sapphics and Uncertainties: Poems 1970-1986* (Arkansas,

1995). He has also published two books of literary criticism: *Missing Measures: Modern Poetry and the Revolt Against Meter* (Arkansas, 1990) and *How You Say a Thing: An Explanation of Meter and Versification* (Swallow Press/ Ohio University Press, 1999). He is as well the editor of *The Poems of J.V. Cunningham* (Swallow Press/Ohio University Press, 1997).

Anne Stevenson, an American longtime resident in the U.K., has published eleven collections of poetry, including the *Collected Poems* (Oxford, 1996). She is the author of *Bitter Fame*, a biography of Sylvia Plath, as well as a new study of Elizabeth Bishop. Her collected essays *Between the Iceberg and the Ship* appeared in the Michigan Poets on Poetry series.

Frederick Turner, Professor of Arts and Humanities at the University of Texas at Dallas, was educated at Oxford University. His dissertation was entitled *Shakespeare and the Nature of Time*. A poet, former editor of *The Kenyon Review*, and regular contributor to *Harper's*, he has published 17 books. His forthcoming book of poetry, *Hadean Eclogues*, will be published by Story Line Press.

Kathrine Varnes has published essays or poems most recently in the pages of *Connotations*, *The Woman Rebel*, *The American Voice*, and *College English*. She has written on epistolarity, feminism, poetry, and recent literary history. She is the Editor, with Annie Finch of *An Exaltation of Forms: Contemporary Poets Celebrate the Diversity of their Arts*, forthcoming from Michigan.

Kevin Walzer is author of the poetry collection *Living in Cincinnati*, published by the Cincinnati Writers' Project, and editor of a collection of essays on the poet John Haines (Story Line). His critical book, *The Ghost of Tradition: Expansive Poetry and Postmodernism* is just out from Story Line.

Carolyn Beard Whitlow, Associate Professor of English at Guilford College in Greensboro, North Carolina, has published poems in many journals, including *Kenyon Review*, *Callaloo*, *Indiana Review*, *Massachusetts Review*, and *13th Moon*. She was a finalist for the 1991 Barnard New Women Poets Prize, and Lost Roads published her first book of poems, *Wild Meat*, in 1986.

Christian Wiman's first book of poems, *The Long Home*, won the 1998 Nicholas Roerich Prize and was published by Story Line Press. His poems and critical essays appear in *Grand Street*, *The Threepenny Review*, *Poetry*, *The Sewanee Review*, *Triquarterly*, and other places. He lives in San Francisco.